VENABLES
THE ENGLAND ERA

VENABLES

THE ENGLAND ERA

BRIAN WOOLNOUGH

MAINSTREAM
PUBLISHING

EDINBURGH AND LONDON

First published in Great Britain in 1996 by
MAINSTREAM PUBLISHING COMPANY (EDINBURGH) LTD
7 Albany Street
Edinburgh EH1 3UG

ISBN 1 85158 756 X

A catalogue record for this book is available from the British Library

Typeset in Century Schoolbook
Printed and bound in Great Britain by Butler and Tanner Ltd, Frome

Contents

Preface		7
ONE:	Out of Work	11
TWO:	The End at Spurs	14
THREE:	Appointed England Coach	27
FOUR:	Welcome Tel	36
FIVE:	A National Hero	40
SIX:	Norway Frustrate Again	44
SEVEN:	No Lessons Learned	47
EIGHT:	Getting Tougher	51
NINE:	Not Convincing Yet, Terry	55
TEN:	Brainless England	60
ELEVEN:	The Umbro Cup	64
TWELVE:	The First Sign of Strain	71
THIRTEEN:	Another Norway Nightmare	81
FOURTEEN:	Tel Under Pressure	92
FIFTEEN:	From Wembley to the Witness Box	101
SIXTEEN:	Tel Resigns	107
SEVENTEEN:	How Does He Do It?	116
EIGHTEEN:	Countdown To Euro 96	121
NINETEEN:	It Can Only Happen In England – Football's Coming Home	126
TWENTY:	More Confusion	132
TWENTY-ONE:	Hell in Hong Kong	139
TWENTY-TWO:	The New England Era	145
TWENTY-THREE:	The European Championships 1996	151
TWENTY-FOUR:	Gazza the Great	163
TWENTY-FIVE:	Football Comes Home	168
TWENTY-SIX:	Never So Nervous	173
TWENTY-SEVEN:	England's Euro 96 Players	180
TWENTY-EIGHT:	German Penalty Heartbreak Again	186

Preface

Terry Venables and I gave each other a little hug. 'We got there in the end,' I said to him. 'It was a bumpy ride at times but we got there in the end. And it was so close.'

We were standing inside the media centre at England's training HQ at Bisham Abbey. It was the morning after England's dramatic European Championship exit at the hands of Germany following another penalty shoot-out. Venables was drinking black coffee before going into a radio interview. He had already done television, the written press were to come and then a Sunday newspaper conference.

He answered: 'Yes, we got there in the end. I enjoyed it. There were not too many dirty tricks.'

I said, 'At least I was always up front with you, in the front asking questions and telling you how it was going to be. I was never sneaky.'

'No,' he added. 'You were never sneaky.'

For two and a half years Terry Venables and I enjoyed that kind of relationship. There was respect but it was never a close friendship. Along the way we exchanged questions and answers, good humour, a few fierce conversations and solicitors' letters.

I have known him for many years, and even ghosted his column when he first worked with the *Sun* newspaper, but you never really get to know Terry Venables the man. You never really know what he is thinking or what is going on inside his head. However, I certainly felt that I got to know him better during his reign as England coach. The word 'know' perhaps should be swapped for 'appreciate'. For here was a roller-coaster ride through an amazing period in English football history. There is no question that I changed my mind about Venables, over and over again, during that period.

In the end, I found myself wanting him to stay. So many times I had felt that England had to get rid of him for on- and off-the-field reasons, and yet it ended with feelings of sorrow for him. Why did he have to go? He once said that it was the pending court cases but then that changed to the lack of support from the FA, particularly

International Committee member Noel White. There were moves just before and during the European Championships, by people inside Lancaster Gate and close to Venables, to retain him in some advisory capacity. But the FA big-wigs clearly did not want Venables to continue. They were grateful for some glory but their attitude was 'enough is enough'. White told me after the win over Spain, when pressure was beginning to mount: 'There is no chance of Terry staying on in any capacity'. The knowledge Venables has will eventually be lost to a lucky club somewhere, either at home or abroad.

Venables disappeared without bitterness or regret and you have to admire his decision not to sling any mud against White and the FA. 'I am a contented man,' he said. 'Everything I set out to do I fulfilled, without, that is, buying the final ticket. I enjoyed winning. The players and I won together and we go out together.

'Over the years I have had personal pressure and I have dealt with that. I went into the finals knowing the situation with the FA. I put pressure on them for a decision on a longer contract and they made it clear that they did not want me. OK, I am a big boy.

'I do not feel that bad about leaving. There are always new challenges, different targets. I have no idea what I will do next and, contrary to what some people have said or may think, I do not have anything lined up. First there are other things to do [*his court case*] and they will not be so enjoyable. But they have to be faced and dealt with.'

Venables was talking at his last official press conference. It was his goodbye and when he had finished there was a round of applause from the journalists who had followed him through thick and thin for those two and a half years. It was a good moment – a private moment, if you like. Was that a tear I saw well up in the corner of Venables's eye? If it was it would have been a rare public show of emotion.

That was it. Over.

Venables had ended in glory at Wembley. Just as he had started. After the German defeat he left the pitch to a standing ovation from an emotional capacity crowd. They knew that England were back, despite defeat. He gave them a last wave as he disappeared down the tunnel.

In 1994 he had stood in the middle of Wembley. The stands were empty but he was the centre of attraction with flashing camera bulbs welcoming him into the job. He held his arms out in a 'here I am' pose. A few weeks later a big Wembley crowd said hello to him at the start of his first game against Denmark.

From Denmark to Germany. As I said it was a roller-coaster ride of emotions. It was interesting, stimulating, exciting and satisfying to be right in the middle of it. And time-consuming.

I would like to thank my wife, Linda, for being so understanding along the way. She is used to phone calls in the early hours, and me cancelling dinners and engagements because of the demands of the *Sun* and the profession. The Venables era took up different emotions and demands. Many times she would be talking to me and I would be miles away, thinking of another chapter, another question to ask. But, as Venables said, you have to be a good team. Together.

He gave England back a good football team. He restored the pride, and for that we should all be thankful, whatever we think of him.

ONE

Out of Work

The Royal Oak public house, Chingford, Essex, Saturday, 14 August 1993. Around midday.

The Saturday lunchtime trade was just beginning to get busy. There was the hustle and bustle of the staff as they prepared for bar lunches and snacks, locals arrived for their usual tipple and the conversation bounced around from politics to sport, from local events to the state of the beer. It went back quickly to sport and football because this day was the start of the 1993–94 season, a day of anticipation and excitement for everyone connected with the game.

Most of the men and women gathering in the lounge of the Royal Oak that Saturday lunchtime were unaware that one of the most extraordinary stories sport has known was taking shape right under their noses. One man sat away from the others in the lounge bar. He sipped his coffee and read the morning newspapers. He was hardly noticed. He was particularly interested in Spurs because, after all, they were his team. A lot went through his mind as he ordered a second coffee and there was a tinge of sadness about him. He looked a forlorn figure, a man lost in thought.

The man was Terence Frederick Venables. The only man to play at every level for England. The former Chelsea, Spurs, Queens Park Rangers and Crystal Palace player. The man who had managed QPR to promotion and the FA Cup final, who had won the Championship in his first season with Barcelona and who had taken Spurs into Europe and to FA Cup glory in 1991.

But for the first time in 35 years Venables was not involved in the opening day of the English season. It hurt, annoyed and frustrated him. He thought about what his Spurs players were doing as they prepared for their opening match at Newcastle. He reflected on the manager who had taken his place, the Argentinian and Spurs favourite Ossie Ardiles.

He tried not to think long about Alan Sugar, the man who had helped him take over Spurs in a partnership that was supposed to have been the dream ticket for the famous North London club. But

11

Sugar was never far away from Venables's thoughts. Even when he was with his family, as he was this Saturday, sitting in the pub owned by his father, Fred, the thought of Sugar left a nasty taste in Venables's mouth.

A few months earlier Sugar had sacked Venables – kicked him out of Tottenham. No one thought that the ruthless chairman of Amstrad Computers would get away with it. But he did. There had been an outcry and public support for Venables but the sacking had been completed. So here was Venables 'on his own' on the very day when football is so special for so many people, a day from which dreams are born, when players and managers fantasise about the nine months ahead. 'Could this be our season?'

Every time Venables thought of Sugar a great deal of bitterness entered his head. Often hatred. There was a feeling that he had to get even. He had to fight back, to clear his name and win back what was rightly his – money, certainly his pride, perhaps his job. It was a feeling that was to dominate his life completely for the next three years. In the end it took over his love of football and he resigned as the coach of England, a job that had always been his particular dream. It is certainly bitterness and hatred that dominate this book and this story.

On the previous Friday I had spent some time with Venables. He had to cancel a lunchtime appointment but called me a number of times on his car phone. Eventually we met for an afternoon drink. He poured out his heart to me and said that he felt that Sugar was trying to drive him out of the game. He said: 'They sacked me on the final day of last season and now they are trying to discredit me on the first day of the new one. They are trying to drive me out of the game and it seems they will stop at nothing.'

He then talked of a dirty tricks campaign, a vendetta, orchestrated, he believed, by Sugar, and added: 'Their plan is to turn the fans against me and I will leave it up to the supporters to make up their own minds.' Venables was furious over stories that he used Spurs money to provide funding for his Kensington club, Scribes West. He added, 'It is the dirty tricks game and they are using the first day of the season for a platform.'

Then came a comment that was to hold the very key to everything that Venables was to go through as the pages unfolded in the coming years. He said: 'They are after me with everything they can get their hands on. They want to ruin me, but they will not win. I am determined to clear my name and I will go as far as I can go to do it.' And he did. He went all the way. To the very limit. Putting his pride, his off-pitch reputation and his personal life before anything else. Apart from Sugar, not once did he say who 'they' were. Sugar obviously was, in Venables's mind, the instigator, but who were the others to whom he kept referring?

At that stage, in August 1993, as Venables finally got up and wished his dad goodbye, no one dreamed that he was soon to become the coach of England. After all, Graham Taylor was still in charge. The Football Association had no reason to believe they were about to dip their toes into controversy, and Sugar certainly would not have believed that his rival and enemy would soon be the biggest name in English football.

Venables was delighted that Tottenham won their first game of the new season, 1–0 at Newcastle, and that night, as usual, he spent at his club with friends and others who enjoyed the party atmosphere created in Scribes West. When he went to bed in the early hours of Sunday morning he wondered what was going to happen to him. There were a million things to sort out. Football was his life and yet now there were other problems that needed his attention.

This start of the football season was different. Who would employ him? What about compensation from Spurs? Had his reputation been damaged beyond repair? And there was, of course, the biggest problem of all. What was he going to do about Alan Sugar? It was the question he asked himself right up to and through the European Championships.

TWO

The End at Spurs

The bitter dispute between Terry Venables and Alan Sugar started inside White Hart Lane and has spilt across the world. It was the classic boardroom battle – two men brought up the hard way who made good. Venables, the footballer with a difference. Sugar, the businessman with millions. They have one thing in common. Stubbornness.

The stubborn streak remains today. They do not like each other. Indeed, there is hate between them. It will probably last until they both die. That is sad because that kind of feeling is not worth it; a feeling that must eat away inside you day in, day out. If there is a winner – and how do you gauge victory in this conflict? – then I suppose it has to be Sugar. At the time of writing this book, Venables has been sacked by Spurs, lost two court cases, resigned as England coach and was preparing for more long legal battles. I do not know many men who would have put up with that before being acclaimed as England's greatest manager since Sir Alf Ramsey.

That is exactly why this story is so intriguing, so mystifying in parts and, as so often happens with Venables, so open-ended. The story of his exit at Spurs has been well documented in his own autobiography, in every newspaper around the football-loving world, on TV, on radio, in magazines. Since he returned to this country Terry Venables has had more media space than any other person I can think of. Yes, more than Princess Diana.

He has voiced his opinions strongly in his book and dipped into his thoughts many times. They are thoughts that have angered Alan Sugar, and Venables is the subject of a furious court case pending between the two men. He has told us of how their business and personal relationship deteriorated over the two years they worked together, the angry boardroom meetings, Sugar's fierce language, the breakdown of communications between them, the power struggle . . . after all, it is the relationship between these two men which is at the very heart of this Terry Venables story in the England years.

What would have happened to Terry Venables had he never met Alan Sugar? Would the late, disgraced Robert Maxwell have taken over Spurs? What would have happened had he swallowed his pride and just got on with being coach of England? We will never know. Nor, sadly, will he.

Before I examine the end at Spurs through the thoughts of two men who experienced every minute – Sugar and former Spurs director and friend of Venables, Jonathan Crystal – I take two extracts from Venables's autobiography. The first relates to the day Terry was sacked, about three hours into a meeting in the Spurs fourth-floor boardroom on Thursday afternoon, 6 May 1993.

'We were once more discussing the White Hart Lane computer system, when I tabled the report that I had commissioned from Creative Project Management. It contained substantial doubts on whether the link to Amstrad's mainframe was an appropriate system for Tottenham, suggesting that it was not the labour-saving, cost-cutting dream scheme that had been suggested. I put it to Sugar that the costs associated with the link to Amstrad were unjustified and that there was a more cost-efficient way forward.

'Jonathan Crystal, who was pouring himself a cup of coffee at that time, supported me. Sugar immediately lost his senses and, rather than confront me directly, rose to his feet and charged across the room towards Jonathan screaming, "You c**t, you fucking c**t, you arse-licking fucking c**t." I put myself between them, because I was afraid that Sugar was going to hit him.

'Sugar then ran back to his seat, tipped the contents of his briefcase all over the table and stormed out. As he left, he threw a letter at me, saying: "You had better read this." The letter told me I was fired.

'There had been no advance warning of what Sugar was planning, but the letter was obviously premeditated. It was like carrying a knife in your pocket. You do not arm yourself with a knife unless you intend to use it.

'Even when he tossed the letter at me, Sugar still could not meet my eyes. He evidently did not have the guts to take me on head to head and instead displayed his aggression towards Jonathan, attacking me by proxy. The end result was the same, however. In football you can take a broken leg better than you can take spit in the face and what Sugar had done was the equivalent of spitting in my face. There could be no backtracking now; this was war.'

The other extract is the most sinister allegation and revelation made by either man against the other. Prior to the court case following Venables's dismissal he wrote in his book: 'On 1 June 1993, just over a week before the date set for the full hearing of the court case, Jonathan Crystal was telephoned at home by Sugar. Shortly afterwards, Jonathan phoned me in a terrible state.

'When I asked him, "What the hell has happened?" he said, "I have had a threat from Alan Sugar. He told me that if I care about my future and my family, I should meet him today, since he had something to show me which would affect my family and my career."

'Jonathan was particularly concerned by the threat to his family, since, as Sugar knew, his father was in his late seventies and in frail health. Sugar wanted Jonathan to meet him in Brentwood at Amstrad, which Jonathan refused, but he eventually agreed to meet him at White Hart Lane that afternoon.

'After a meeting I went up to my office and was there around ten to five, when Jonathan came in, white-faced and looking like death. When I asked him what had happened he said: "I am not saying anything here." I arranged to meet him up in town later that evening, when he told me what had happened.

'Jonathan had arrived at White Hart Lane at twenty to five and was met on the stairs by Sugar, who led him into the deserted Dave Mackay suite. Sugar said to him, "I've met your mother and father, they're nice people." In normal circumstances that would have been a friendly remark, but in the context of this meeting, Sugar's words had a sinister undertone. "If you go against me," continued Sugar, "if you give evidence against me, I'll make sure I damage your family and your future."

'He then accused Jonathan of being blinded by loyalty to me and said that if Jonathan produced an affidavit for the court case that Sugar did not like, he would swear an affidavit of his own, making serious allegations about Jonathan's professional conduct.'

Of all the stories I have read, watched and listened to over the two years of Venables's England reign, this is the most explosive. Can it be true? Would Crystal make it up? It is a serious allegation, a claim that is hard to believe, and one that Sugar has every right to react to. He certainly denies the story. True or not, the story reflects the lengths that the two men will go to in order to win a war. It indicates the bitterness that can come with a power struggle.

In my taped interview with Crystal he refers to the story like this: 'He did not want me to give evidence against Terry and tried to blackmail me. He threatened my family. Yes, I did take it seriously, perhaps not seriously enough. But the blackmail is part of my life I am not prepared to talk about. There is no question that it happened. There is no question that he [Sugar] accepted that it happened. The judge referred to it and there is a document of record. After the threat I went to my car and wrote down everything that was said. It was communicated to his lawyers in 24 hours. It was such a strange thing to do. The man is utterly ruthless.'

The plot thickens. The story gets better. The intrigue goes on. It is all part of the end for Venables at Spurs. It was the end of one era and the opening of another, and how many times have we said that about this amazing character?

Here is Sugar's story of how it started at Spurs and then went

16

wrong, and it provides a fascinating insight into the chairman of Amstrad and owner of one of the biggest football clubs in the country. He says: 'I had seen and read a lot of publicity about the poor state the club was in. I was a Spurs fan, my family had been for yonks. I am afraid it is the same old cringy story, the lad on the rails being taken to the club his family supported. You know how it is, father holding son to see over the heads, the same old story, the one everyone tells.

'I wanted to rescue the club. I cared for it. That is why I went in, that is the truth. No one asked me; I offered myself. I had watched this famous club from the outside. I watched from afar as Irving Scholar flew to Rome to do the Gascoigne deal and read that it was the transfer that would save them. I thought, "That is good. Ten million or so for Gazza, that will save them." Then he got crocked in the 1991 FA Cup final and I knew that was it. I could sense that without that deal they were in big trouble.

'Terry had supposedly been talking to some Arab about a takeover, Uncle Tom Cobley, then Maxwell had come in at the eleventh hour. Then I came in. Terry and I got together in June 1991 after I had made contact and in two or three weeks we had done a deal by buying out the shares owned by Scholar and his friend Paul Bobroff.

'I had met Terry once or twice before just to say hello but had only really made up my mind about him from things I had read in the newspapers. My concept of Terry was his public image. He was a wealthy man running pubs, clubs and owning properties and what attracted me was that he said he would put some of his own money into the situation.

'In view of the fact I had no experience of running a football club it would be a great partnership. A famous person, whose football skills were renowned, and also someone with good business acumen.

'I know now I should have done more due diligence on him. The long and short of the story is that he had no business acumen at all. When I took one look at the books I knew that Tottenham Hotspur Football Club were in a mess. An absolute mess. The club was a total and absolute disaster.

'I remember asking myself, "Who is answerable for this?" but I am not going to look too far back. It is history. I wanted to improve and that is what we have done since. My understanding was that I would look after the financial side of the club and Terry would look after the football.

'Unfortunately he wanted to take an overall reign on everything. He started to dabble in things beyond his comprehension. Every time this was brought to his attention, rather than accept it, there was conflict. He would say to me, "I can do it" or "My team can do it", but they could not. And that is it. I brought one of my people in called Colin Sandy. Colin, who has now moved into another of my contracts, did a good holding job for me at the club. But the conflicts soon started and they were eventually to break up the partnership . . . after that all hell broke loose . . . end of story . . . it is history.

'It was unsavoury to have to ask him to go. The people he had around him did not help the situation, they helped create the friction. Crystal has got intelligence and he had the opportunity of making sure the relationship between Terry and me was good. But never once did he correct Terry and tell him that he was wrong. Crystal is a barrister but I would never use him.

'Another henchman was a guy called Eddie Ashby. Crystal received no money from Spurs but Ashby, through a company his wife owned, received a salary. He is Terry's right-hand man as far as finance is concerned.'

Sugar, for the first time, admits that initially after Venables's sacking, he was surprised at the uproar it caused. He never expected it to be fierce, or to go on for so long. He says that he does not like confrontation, the bitterness, the aggro and would much rather get on with running Amstrad and Spurs. But, like Venables, he will not let go.

He adds: 'All those lies in his book, it is outrageous. The terrible inaccuracies, the slanders; he questions my integrity and honesty as a businessman. It is outrageous.

'There is the claim that I did not like the publicity he received. That is rubbish; he is entitled to the praise on the football side. When there is a press conference on the football side of things I stand aside, you have seen that. I do not get directly involved unless it is a row with the Football Association, or something like that. I am capable of running the club, nothing else, certainly not the team. I do not interfere with the playing side in any way.'

Sugar initially banned Venables from White Hart Lane, although the ban was lifted halfway through the 1995–6 season after pressure from the FA's mediator. 'The football club is like my home,' said Sugar. 'If people come into the directors' area they come at my invitation. I would certainly not invite Venables to my house. The man has thrown so many stones at me, caused me so much grief, why should I let him in? Yes, the fact that he is England coach does make it a difficult situation.

'The best thing that could happen is for the publicity to stop. I take no pleasure from saying that he is my enemy. I would rather everything, and everyone, shut up and let things go their own way. This whole thing has taken up so much of my business time. It would be easy to walk away from the confrontation . . . why should I have all this aggro? But once in the cesspit, you are in and, when it gets up to your waist and rising you have to paddle like mad and try and get out.

'The first thing I had to do when Terry left the club was ignore the adverse publicity. I had to concentrate on doing the right thing for the club. I had to finalise all the legal stuff so he was formally dismissed through the courts. Then I had to find a new manager [*Ossie Ardiles*] and allow him to buy some new players.

'What I will say now is that time is a great healer. Perhaps people now have got to know me better, the way I tick, what kind of person I am. Venables has gone. He is not coming back. End of story. The fans know I have got the best interests of the club at heart. I am doing the best I possibly can for Spurs, as I always said I would.'

Whenever you talk to Sugar you get the impression you are sitting on a time-bomb. He is a man not to cross. If you do he will blow your head off. It is a volcano waiting to erupt, as so many people have discovered. He demands loyalty and respect and rewards those who work hard for and with him. He knows what he wants and goes for it. He has no time for cheats, cowards and those who do not like the way he runs things. He is an awesome opponent.

There is much that goes on in football that he does not like. If he had the inclination and, indeed, the power, there would be many men who would have to run for cover if ever the time came when Alan Sugar could throw his weight behind a campaign to clean up and clear up the game. Graham Kelly and the FA have already discovered that you take on Alan Sugar at your peril.

There are so many stories about what went on before and after he arrived at White Hart Lane. I doubt if some will ever come out, unless Sugar and Venables meet across a courtroom. Venables quit as England coach because that is what he intended to do. Somehow, though, I doubt if these two rivals will ever come face to face in court. Let me put it this way: deep down I do not believe that either man wants it. There is too much at stake for them both, let alone the outcome of the case. There is too much mud-slinging lined up for any good to come out of such a case.

Sugar dips into Spurs' past with a lot of reluctance these days because, basically, he is fed up with it. He sacked Venables because he thought it was right for the club. End of story. But it will not go away and he will not be silenced when it comes to accusations against him and his club. He adds: 'It was interesting that when the FA decided to punish us for the illegal payments thing our new manager at the time, Ossie Ardiles, said that other people had got away scot-free, while the people in charge – Ossie, the players, me – were being punished.

'OK, let us get this straight. The FA obviously decided that individuals were not the issue. When they punished us they talked about the club and not the person, for obvious reasons. The FA chose to go for the club. They knew that Spurs broke rules, it is there in black and white. They know which people broke those rules. But they chose to go for the club. Why? That is not for me to say. The Premier

League inquiry into Tottenham started in November 1993. There is still no sight of a conclusion. Why? You will have to make your own conclusions.'

Sugar thought long and hard when I asked him if he had been surprised that Venables was made England coach. Was it an embarrassment to them? We were sitting in his office on the top floor of Amstrad's HQ in Brentwood, Essex. He is surrounded by a bank of television screens, phones and computers. He talks to you but still has an eye on the screens, half a mind on his business empire.

Almost a minute went by before he answered: 'In normal circumstances he would have been the logical choice. The FA probably looked at the situation and, quite rightly, took in that he had not been found guilty of anything. He is not a criminal. They had to say to themselves that what was happening in his private life was none of their business. They could not take into account rumours because nothing was proved. So, no, I was not surprised that he was chosen. As far as football is concerned, he was the obvious choice.'

There is no question that Sugar has changed since he took over at Spurs, indeed, changed in many ways as a person. He certainly loves football more now than he did. He understands it better, he cares more about the game and where it is heading. He also worries about his public image. He knows what most people think: here is a gruff, tough Londoner who cares about no one but himself. They would be wrong. There is more to Alan Sugar than that. As I have said, he is ruthless and dare you cross him, you have an enemy for life. But there is definitely a human side, a softer person inside the tough exterior.

Let him try and explain. He says: 'My perception of Terry was created by what I read about him. It was not until I got to know him afterwards that I found out about the real person. I suspect the FA's perception of me came from people with an axe to grind. They did not know me so they thought to themselves, "You do not sling your weight around here with us, you need to be knocked into shape. How dare you shout your mouth off? Do not tell us what to do." I hope people now realise that the image was not fair or a true reflection.

'But ask the man in the street what he thinks of Alan Sugar and the answer will be rough and tough. That is what the FA felt about me. I believe that could have been amplified by Terry. Who knows?

'It is a picture painted by various people and I believe the FA thought it to be true. They were after me and got at me through my football club. They found out that I fight hard when I believe I am wronged. That is not to say I enjoy doing it. Yes, I say what I mean but I do not sling my weight around just for the sake of it. I still say the FA went about dealing with us the wrong way. If they had said that they accepted in the general spirit what we had done since coming on to the scene, the help we had given them, and suspended the sentences until we did it again, then there would have been no altercation. That would have been an elegant and clean way of doing it and then they would not have lost face.

'They did not do that. It is what got my back up. That is why I went after them. I believe they were after me. Yes, I really believe that. Now there is mutual respect. In business you often get that, respect after a battle. Graham Kelly and I understand each other better now. Kelly has got a difficult job at the FA.'

There is no doubt in my mind that Sugar has changed from the first day he walked into White Hart Lane, certainly from the day when he sacked Venables. He has become closer to the game. At the start he felt like a stranger who had come almost unwelcomed into a family gathering. Now he is much more part of the establishment. He feels a great responsibility towards the game. He should, for he is one of the most powerful figures in football.

He gave me this interview slightly reluctantly because Alan Sugar now only wants to go forward. He does not want to harp back but appreciates that the Terry Venables case is part of his life and one that he will be remembered for always. With no dispute between these two tough, stubborn men there would be no Venables story. It would be just another football tale, rather than one of amazing intrigue.

I doubt whether the real truth, the whole truth and nothing but the truth will ever come out. I suspect that when I see this book in hardback and sitting on a bookshelf somewhere, I will still be asking myself questions which will remain unanswered. The biggest will remain, 'Why DID you really quit England, Terry?'

It was interesting to talk to Jonathan Crystal about the Venables era at White Hart Lane and how it ended, of his relationship with his friend and his thoughts about Alan Sugar. Crystal was right in the middle of a bust-up as a Spurs director and he sat in on the board meeting when it all ended. This is his account of the extraordinary story.

He says: 'I have known Terry since the late 1970s. We were introduced by Malcolm Allison and became close friends. We once agreed to meet for breakfast at the Carlton Towers. It became a daily routine, Terry on his way to QPR and me *en route* to the office. We were two different people. I am middle-class, was brought up in Leeds, my father was a doctor and I became a barrister. Terry's background was much tougher. His father was a docker, then a lorry driver. But there was a chemistry between us and a lot of trust and confidence grew.

'We became close friends, shared things. I watched him at QPR and had great admiration for him as a person. He is his own man with no fear. He is eloquent and much more intelligent than people think. To a lot of people he is the Cockney with the gift of delivering one-liners. He is much more than that. He is a deep thinker. He can be a loner and spends a lot of time on his own, plotting and planning his strategy football-wise. Many times I popped in to see him and he would be surrounded by pieces of paper, the victims of his non-stop note-taking and idea planning.

'At that stage in our friendship I cannot say that he ever mentioned to me a desire to manage England. It was not an ambition. He always wanted to own his club and that probably came from his close relationship with Jim Gregory, then the owner of QPR and now at Portsmouth. There is no doubt that Jim believed that one day he would pass Rangers on to Terry. Jim treated Terry like a favourite son. He was one of the family and Jim trusted him so much he would have given Terry the crown jewels to look after.

'It was a hell of a blow for Jim when Terry decided to go to Barcelona. Jim looked at him in amazement and said: "What do you want to go there for?" And he meant it.

'All the years I have known Terry we have never had a disagreement. We have exchanged words, but never rowed. He often used to say, "The only people you can have disagreements with are your friends", and he did not like upsetting people. If Terry needed something doing legally he would ask me for advice. It was never a professional relationship because not once did he pay me a penny. And I received no money from Spurs as a director. I was in there because of one thing: my friendship with Venables.

'He made mistakes, like all people. He got involved once with a guy called Paul Kirby, who was an FA Councillor, and a company called Transatlantic Inns. I never really liked Paul, there was something about him. He was always too quick to buy champagne. I suspect that Terry took him on face value rather than anything else.

'Terry loves champagne and I was grateful for his generosity once when my father was awarded the OBE. Terry and I had not been in touch for a while but a bottle of the best vintage still arrived at my father's home with a congratulations note. That is the kind of bloke he is. Busy, but he has always got time for people he likes and respects.

'Barcelona was a wonderful experience for him. It has been well documented how he pulled the cigar out of his sock and handed it to the Barcelona president Jose Nunez, during their interview. It was the start of a great relationship he had with the Spanish people. I can still see his face the first time he made that long walk from the dressing-room, past the chapel and up into the bowl that is one of the great stadiums in the world. It was a special moment for him.'

What happened next is history. Back to Spurs after the sacking of a disgraced David Pleat. An often uneasy relationship with chairman Irving Scholar. In his autobiography Venables alleges that Scholar interfered from the start, as he had been warned. Venables said that he was excluded from the business discussions and often felt that he was working in a vacuum. Venables says that he was not aware of the strain building up on the club and he admits that had he been aware of the true state of Tottenham's business dealings, then he would probably have walked out there and then. Sugar backed this story up when he took his first glance at the books.

Venables claims that he could no longer sit back and watch the club sinking into liquidation, and that he came up with the idea of forming a consortium to buy out Scholar and his co-director and major shareholder Paul Bobroff. He says that he had a growing ambition to move into the boardroom. Enter Sugar and the start of this epic tale.

Even at that early stage of the story there is conflict. Venables says that Sugar was recommended and introduced by a friend. Sugar says that he contacted Venables himself with an offer of help after reading about the demise of the club his family had supported for generations. Crystal cannot support either story but he relates the end to the two FA Cup semi-finals Spurs played in the space of two years, both against deadly rivals Arsenal. In 1991 Spurs beat Arsenal with Paul Gascoigne driving in one of the greatest free kicks ever seen at Wembley. Crystal says: 'On the Monday afterwards the directors took a much more entrenched view towards the money crisis inside the club. Agent Dennis Roach had been sent off to Italy to find a purchaser for Gazza but a Cup final place raised the question: do we need to sell him? It instigated much discussion but the answer was eventually yes. Five weeks later came the takeover.'

In the final against Nottingham Forest, the infamous final that will go down in history as Gazza's crazy Cup final, England's outstanding footballer severed knee ligaments after an horrendous tackle on Forest full back Gary Charles. There then followed months of speculation about the on-off move to Lazio. Gascoigne eventually went to Italy with Sugar and Venables now working together.

It was the semi-final two years later that Crystal pinpoints as the beginning of the end for Venables. 'We lost this time, 1–0 to Arsenal. Tony Adams got the goal for them from a free kick. Terry was screaming at his players to watch out for Adams coming round the blindside but they could not hear him because of the noise of the crowd.

'A few weeks later came the board meeting when Sugar handed Venables his letter of dismissal. But let me ask these questions. Would Sugar have sacked Terry had Spurs reached the Cup final? Of course not. How can any club sack their manager on the eve of the showpiece of the season?

'Also, Sugar sat through that meeting knowing he had the letter in his briefcase. Why wait until the conversation got around to Tottenham's computer information about Amstrad? There had been amicable discussion and no hint of what was to come. Would he have produced the letter had the meeting gone well throughout? I found it astonishing behaviour. I can only presume that everything else said in that meeting must have been insecure. Why not just walk in and give it to Terry from the start, get it out of the way?

'When people have said to me, "What went wrong between them?" I honestly believe it was triggered by the crowd chanting Terry's name and not Sugar's. When they sang "Terry Venables' blue and white army" Sugar was angry. He could not understand why the crowd, who knew he had put his own money in to help save the club, were not chanting his name too. He felt, with some justification, that he deserved a lot more public credit. But it was the reaction of someone who, at that stage, did not understand football.

'Sugar never got to grips with the fact that Terry was a football man and the crowd loved him. Terry saw their partnership as the creation of a successful football team, while Sugar at that stage saw it as an income and profit operation.

'I did not think the break was inevitable. I was certainly surprised when Sugar produced the letter and threw it down. It involved an element of calculation, something that I dould not understand. I was probably naive – perhaps Terry too – because I certainly had never dealt with anyone like Alan Sugar before.

'I recall him taking me out for dinner right at the start of his relationship with Spurs. At that dinner he showed me bank statements of his, revealing how much money he had. It was an incredible situation for me, an unbelievable one. To see that someone had 60 or 70 million pounds against his name. I now believe that it was a show of power and strength. He was showing me immediately, straightaway at Spurs, exactly how much power he had. It was made clear to me what resources he had in the event of a row or a split between us.

'Everything was related to money. Even at board meetings. It was often associated with crudeness. "I am not going to spunk my money over the wall," he would scream at us. He does have an unfortunate manner and his language can be from the street and very powerful. It is certainly not nice to be the subject of one of his jokes because he is relentless. You cannot run the risk of crossing him without the risk of being flattened. He has huge resources. Alan Sugar is a very powerful man. I admit that I do not really understand him, his motives or how he operates as a person.

'I have never really related money to my own life. It is certainly not a focal point. There are other things more important to me and I am happy and contented with what I have got. Alan thinks that because of his money and power he can bully people.

'At the board meetings he would sit at the head of the table, with Terry on his right and Tony Berry next to him. I would be on Sugar's left and then Colin Sandy. He would never rage at Terry and hold eye contact, it was always me. He would also think nothing of laying into Sandy, who was his man on the board, and Sandy was not in a position to protest.

'It was clear, and certainly is now, that he did not like me, Terry or Eddie Ashby. I think he gave me some credibility as a barrister but could not understand why, when it came to the crunch, I, as a Jew, would not vote for another Jew [*Sugar*] before I voted for Terry. He could not see what Terry had got that he did not.

Crystal then refers to the alleged blackmail and says, 'His attempt to blackmail me was the most offensive thing that has ever happened to me in my life. He apologised in an affidavit but the scars will remain with me. I just do not want to talk about this. I did take it seriously . . . but probably not seriously enough.

'There was never a suggestion either that the Sheringham deal was improper. There was no way that Sugar would have allowed money to go missing, he was running the finances. He and Colin Sandy signed the cheques. There was no question of Terry selling Lineker or buying Sheringham without the club knowing. Frank McLintock would have been paid with Sugar's and Sandy's knowledge. I felt that this tainted all the allegations against Terry that were to emerge after his sacking. Sugar never said that he did not like Terry dealing with Eric Hall. The complaints came afterwards.

'Sugar's strategy was to discredit Terry. He could not beat him in the popularity stakes. So he had to anaesthetise that by trying to discredit him. Sugar made serious allegations under privilege of court and has never repeated them in public. Brian Clough would love him to repeat the bung allegations. Sugar will not do it because he cannot control what would happen next. He knows that once he goes into a witness box he cannot control the situation. I have my doubts whether Alan Sugar will ever go into a witness box against Terry Venables.

'Alan Sugar is a remarkable man, with remarkable abilities to make money. Contracts are important to him. He often hides behind big-time lawyers and his extreme wealth. I will probably never meet anyone like him again. We have not spoken since I finally left the board in November 1993 and I doubt if we ever will again. But I will never forget the experience of being a director under his chairmanship.'

The rows, of course, continued. Long after the sacking of Venables and Crystal. And long into many nights. In September 1994, on the day Venables launched his autobiography, Sugar attacked his rival at a sportswriters' lunch. He called the book 'Grimm's Fairy Tales' and said that without him there would have been no deal at Tottenham. Under question he raged: 'I fought off Maxwell and the merchant bankers. On the night the deal was done he was not there, nor was his money.

25

'I still thought it would be the deal of a lifetime. Here was the man who was God's gift to football and I would put in the money. But my perception of the man was wrong. He thought I would do this and that and then sit in the corner of the directors' box. Not me, I started to ask questions. He treated me like a Sugar-daddy. A mug. Well, I might be a lot of things, but I am certainly not a mug.

'Terry in my opinion is the author of his own misfortunes. The players loved him but he wanted more.'

Venables now regrets going into business partnership with Sugar. 'It was the biggest mistake of my life,' he says. 'It was right at the time but hindsight is a valuable thing. We all make mistakes and sometimes they are too late.'

Venables has had so many opportunities to put the dispute behind him for good but he has chosen to continue the war. He gets credit for following his beliefs but I believe he should have ended it and swallowed his pride. There should be no wrongful dismissal case against his sacking at Spurs. It was certainly a mistake to publish his autobiography at a time when relationships between the two men were at their worst.

He had the greatest job in the world in his hands and he has chosen to throw it away. Had he swallowed his pride and concentrated on football, Terry Venables would have had all the credibility and money he wanted. His name would have been in lights. The English public wanted him. They wanted him as the coach of England, not as a former manager who fought for his name in court. They did not worry about what he did or did not do, or what football laws he broke or did not break.

But he chose the other route. I wonder if eventually he will regret that too. One thing is certain in my mind. Terry Venables should still be in charge of England. It will remain a mystery to me why he chose to go. No one will ever convince me, certainly not Terry himself, that he quit because he did not have one hundred per cent support from the FA's International Committee, or that he quit just to clear his name.

THREE

Appointed England Coach

There was one thing that really impressed the Football Association's International sub-committee when they sat down and offered Terry Venables the job as England coach. Apart from his knowledge of football, his personality and ability to charm the birds off a tree, what impressed the sub-committee was that Venables never once mentioned money, or how much he would get if he was offered the job or, indeed, said yes.

This is a surprising twist in the story, considering that money frequently dominates Venables's England era. Money, for instance, is at the very pulse of his war with Alan Sugar. Furious at being kicked out of his job at Spurs he vowed to get even with Sugar, and that meant going to court to get the money he felt he was due. Indeed, at his first meeting with the FA, he told the men on the sub-committee that he would settle out of court with Sugar if he received a good enough offer. That never came and hence his ongoing war and subsequent resignation.

Money was to dominate on many other occasions during his reign. He sued newspapers and went to court with Spurs director Tony Berry and businessman Jeff Fugler. Those courtroom battles were for small amounts in comparison to the money that he could earn as England coach, if he was to be successful. Yet not once did money come up when he sat and talked with Sir Bert Millichip, Liverpool director Noel White, Graham Kelly and Oldham chairman Ian Stott, the men who made up the sub-committee and who were handed the responsibility of finding the best possible coach following the debacle under Graham Taylor.

Jimmy Armfield, the man the FA employed to go out into the game and come back with recommendations, confirmed: 'Terry did not mention money at all when the negotiations were taking place. That was something that I know impressed the committee. Terry wanted the job to prove himself to the nation. There had been a real down period in his life and here was the greatest job of all being offered to him.'

It was only after he had agreed to the job that Venables met chief executive Kelly, this time with lawyers on both sides, to thrash out his contract. He signed for considerably less than he was earning at Tottenham. His salary as England coach was believed to be around £130,000 a year, though the figures for football managers are always guesses. But it was known that at Tottenham he was picking up a minimum of £250,000 a year as chief executive of the North London club.

There is no question that Venables would have more than doubled his salary with the FA had he decided to stay, especially after a successful European Championships. And the spin-offs from sponsorship and commercial deals would have taken him close to £1 million a year. But he turned his back on all that for courtroom fights, battles that could cost him his wealth and pride. They are fights that could bankrupt him and lose him everything. It was certainly a gamble, the biggest of his career.

When Graham Taylor resigned, under extreme pressure, in November 1993, it also put the Football Association under the spotlight. Not for the first time, they had got it wrong when choosing an England manager. Taylor had never been good enough. The job was too much for him, especially tactically, and he will always be remembered for being called a turnip by the *Sun* newspaper after we had lost 2–1 to Sweden in the 1992 European Championships and gone out of the competition. 'Turnip' Taylor is a catchphrase that will never go away, as Taylor discovered when things started to go wrong for him before he quit at Wolves, his first job since England.

They say that the tabloid newspapers are too powerful for the England job. I cannot go along with that. If you are big enough, indeed good enough, you cope. If you accept the biggest job of all you have to expect to be placed in the spotlight from day one and take all that goes with it. Any man who says that he does not want to be England coach because of the newspapers is either not telling the truth or is simply not good enough in his own mind to say yes.

Taylor was a dream to work with, it was just that on the pitch he let himself down and opened up the criticism. Venables on the other hand was a completely different character for the media to take under their wing. He came with a reputation and that saved him from a lot of stiffer criticism. 'Don't worry, Tel will get it right' was said a million times along the way as we waited for the European Championships. I have to say that covering England was not such good fun under Terry. There was not the family atmosphere created by Robson, or the tales of the unexpected we experienced with Taylor. But fun, games and headlines take second place if you can be a winner.

One decision the FA thought they had got right was the next England coach to follow Taylor. They had made so many previous mistakes. Sir Alf Ramsey had been sacked and kicked out without feeling and not once was his experience and expert knowledge used – scandalous behaviour by the men who run our game. Don Revie disappeared in the middle of an England tour to negotiate a new deal with the Arabs, Bobby Robson was allowed to resign and hold a press conference before we went to Italia 1990 and Taylor had gone in a blaze of turnip headines and controversy.

The poor old FA just could not have known that less than two years later Venables would resign before the European Championships. They had taken him on still looking over their shoulder but had grown to like and respect him. Just when the people at Lancaster Gate who matter, Kelly and Millichip, had made up their minds about him, he quit.

Taylor, of course, will have to live with the Turnip nickname and his failure at international level. It became a rope around his neck at Wolves and you sensed that when he returned to Watford, he had reached his point of no return. This time he was back amongst friends and the public that knew him best, and were warmest to him. But he had to succeed, or disappear for good. You get the impression that there is so much about England he would like to say. It has begun to come out in dribs and drabs and he clearly feels that the England experience is weighing on his shoulders. 'I carry the England baggage with me and people are not prepared to let go,' he says.

'At Wolves I had a three-year contract to gain promotion. After 18 months they chose to break it. There is a minority of people who do not have the patience. It started again in the media, you know the kind of thing. The ex-England manager is under pressure again. I needed people to stand by me. They did not, so it was best to go.

'No one can take away from me that I fulfilled an ambition. I wanted to become the England manager and achieved it. I know it did not go well and that we did not qualify for the World Cup. But I can say that I WAS manager of my country, and that is a lovely thing to take with you for someone who loves football and his nation.'

Before the disappointment of failing to qualify for the World Cup and subsequent exit from Lancaster Gate, Taylor did take England to the European Championships in Sweden. He recalls what happened, and the pressure that 'hems you in' as England manager. 'We qualified for the European Championships in 1992 with only one defeat from 21 games. I had a right to be optimistic.'

But a draw against Denmark, another draw with France, followed by the defeat by Sweden meant that England and Taylor returned home early to the vegetable patch. Also in the game against Sweden he substituted Gary Lineker, England's top scorer, the idol of the nation who was playing in his last international. It was a decision that he was never forgiven for. He says: 'What people had forgotten was that Gary had not been playing well. You have to be strong as the manager because there was a game going on. I could not think about the public turning on me. I wanted to win the game. What would have happened had the substitution worked and we had gone on and won?'

Taylor says that he was not aware of the turnip nickname for a few days afterwards as he stayed in Sweden while his assistant Lawrie McMenemy came home with the squad. Eventually it caught up with him and he says: 'You have to be mentally tough. If I read every newspaper and reacted to every opinion then I would go under. To me, opinions are only worth something if you can back them up with facts or experience. I was far more concerned with a TV crew knocking on the back door of my parents' home, marching into the kitchen and demanding, "What do you think of that defeat, then?" (after the 2–0 defeat by the USA on the American tour in 1993).

'Listen, my head is high. It always will be. When I walk into a pub I can face football supporters. I will tell you something, my image is much better with the public than the press would allow. Professionally I was hurt by what happened with England. We did not qualify and it hurt. I can understand what Don Revie did.'

I certainly cannot accept that comment by Taylor. Revie deserted his country, turned his back on the job for money and greed. In my book he will go down in history as the worst England manager of all. Taylor, I hope, did not mean that. He did let England down. He just was not good enough.

Taylor's comments only emphasise what pressure these men are under. So when he left what would the FA do and how would they handle it? There was now real pressure on them. We had failed to qualify for the 1994 World Cup in America, which FIFA frowned upon because it meant a big loss of revenue for them – and they did not hide their disappointment from FA chairman Sir Bert Millichip. The FA chairman was told at top-level meetings how FIFA wanted England at the American World Cup.

It was chief executive Graham Kelly who came up with the idea which was to save FIFA's face. He approached an old friend in Jimmy Armfield and asked him to become their headhunter, the FA's man out in the field and the person responsible for recommending a new England coach to the sub-committee. Armfield and Kelly were old friends from Blackpool, and Armfield, the former Bolton and Leeds manager who also worked for BBC Radio and the *Daily Express*, happily said yes. And off he went, into the game, covering thousands and thousands of miles, writing endless reports and holding countless meetings, before he came back to Lancaster Gate with the name the professionals wanted.

Armfield spoke to managers, coaches, PFA chief executive Gordon Taylor, even the old England pairing of Graham Taylor and his assistant Lawrie McMenemy. Armfield is a decent, honest man and he took his integrity into his new job. Not once did he reveal the name of any person he spoke to for advice and not once did he reveal the shortlist, headed by Venables, that he gave to the FA. He has often joked with Venables that even in Terry's autobiography he got the names on the shortlist wrong. Venables said the other two were Howard Wilkinson and Gerry Francis. But Trevor Francis, then with Sheffield Wednesday, was shortlisted. He recalls: 'I was interviewed and told that I was on the shortlist of three. I was never told who the others were.'

Armfield even spoke to some old friends in the media and that was the first time that journalists had played an official part in the selecting of a new England coach. Armfield said: 'I never travelled so fast and so far. I gathered all the information I could because I knew it was such an important decision.' Armfield gave his BBC Radio producer a couple of interviews from a game that he was covering for *Five Live* on a Saturday afternoon, without giving anything away, but not once did he appear on television. 'I wanted to keep a low profile and just get on with the business,' Armfield insisted. 'When the FA first asked me I thought it was a good idea. It was the first time that the professionals had been asked. I did not want the most popular name, I wanted the best man for the job.'

Armfield's own choice before he was approached by the FA had been Kevin Keegan at Newcastle. He had made that clear in a strong BBC Radio interview. Armfield then spoke to Keegan in his travels but discovered that the former captain of England was reluctant to quit St James's Park. He was not the only person Armfield spoke to with a reluctance to take on the biggest job of all. Armfield found these stumbling blocks in his search:

1. One or two managers simply did not want to know. Keegan was among those.

2. Others could not afford to leave their huge club salaries. Armfield discovered that at least three Premiership managers were earning more than double what was on offer for them at Lancaster Gate.

3. There were a lot put off by the media criticism that had followed Bobby Robson and Graham Taylor around. They told Armfield that it was bad enough getting stick in one city, let alone all over the country. People were in secure jobs and they did not want to leave them for the hassle of becoming the England coach. It disappointed Armfield but it did not put him off. He went on searching.

What Armfield realised was that he needed someone with backbone. Someone big enough to take everything on his shoulders and do the job his way. Someone who could handle the media and the pressure as well as have respect. That was crucial to Armfield because he knew that in some quarters there was not enough respect

31

for the people inside Lancaster Gate. It was a big decision and there was pressure on him, as well as the big-wigs rubber-stamping his choice.

Armfield's first choice, ironically, was not Venables. There was one man that he went back to twice to interview and try and persuade but he would not change his mind. Armfield has told no one his name and we must respect that, although I can only presume that it was Keegan. He adds: 'People were not clamouring for the job.'

The longer Armfield searched the more the clamour was for Venables. Don Howe, Bobby Robson's number two for years who had dropped out of the limelight under Taylor, said: 'Terry is the best coach in the game, he is young and available. For me he is not only the ideal choice, but the obvious one.' Everywhere Armfield went people in the game said the same thing. Give it to Terry. No one in football paid any attention to the off-field controversy. So Armfield went back for his first meeting with the FA, with a fat dossier and a shortlist, topped by Venables. When he told the committee he was met with the first obstacle. Millichip said: 'Terry Venables? Over my dead body!'

Millichip was the man who had to be persuaded. An old-established member of the FA, Millichip is fiercely proud of his position as chairman and his reputation around the world with the men who run the game at the highest level. He is respected and he was damned if he was going to be bullied into getting it wrong again, especially as he would retire after the European Championships. Venables had been through the mill for months with stories of his war with Sugar, BBC *Panorama* programmes about his business dealings and every controversy that could happen. No, Venables was not for him.

Venables had still to be approached officially although his name was now in newspaper headlines at least four times a week. At the start he certainly could not believe that he was in the running, especially as he had taken a huge swipe at the FA in his father Fred's book, distancing himself from them with this kind of comment: 'I now believe that only a certain sort of person gets to be manager of England and unfortunately I am not their kind of guy. I am no longer interested in managing England . . . sod them . . . forget it . . . I will do something else.' Those comments were made in 1991 and I wonder if the sub-committee went looking for them when they were making their decision. Venables must have been embarrassed, but that is football. It is a sport that forgives and forgets so quickly.

Had the FA not broken with tradition then there is no way that Terry would have got the job. Had they not employed Armfield then it would have been down to a committee again and Venables would not have been in the frame. His name would not even have been discussed.

Millichip knew this, despite his early protests. So Millichip relented and the FA instructed Armfield to meet Venables and open discussions. They were held in private and the first time that the two men came together was a week before Christmas at the Royal Lancaster Hotel in London. The meeting lasted three hours and the men then spoke again on Christmas Eve. Armfield told Venables that things were moving forward, and in his favour. Armfield discussed the possibility of Venables becoming a 'caretaker manager' but Venables dismissed this out of hand.

Armfield quizzed him about the court cases with Sugar and asked if there were any more skeletons in the cupboard. This amused Venables because in the previous few months he had seen the police, the Fraud Squad, the Inland Revenue, the Customs and Excise people, the DTI, and none of them had pinned anything on him. When Armfield left that meeting Venables felt that the job was his. Agonisingly, he had to wait another month before meeting the full sub-committee. Then he was called to the Football League Commercial Department's offices in Old Marylebone Road where, in the inner chamber on the seventh floor, he met the men with destiny in their hands.

The men – Millichip, White, Stott, Kelly and Armfield – sat around a large mahogany table. Questions started to fly about the game itself, the future and the England set-up and Venables found himself relaxing and enjoying himself. Not once during the interview did the sub-committee mention Graham Taylor. They only referred to him as the old regime. They asked him about Sugar, Eddie Ashby and his business affairs. It was no surprise that a decision was not made at that meeting and Venables was kept waiting for some time.

Venables turned down Wales and dismissed reports linking him with the Nigeria job before he finally got the call he had been waiting for. It was 25 January 1994 when Terence Frederick Venables was invited to become England coach. Venables shook hands with Graham Kelly and accepted. It had been a long road.

But Millichip had done his homework and in the time that it took the FA to decide what to do he sought proof about all the allegations made against Venables. Not once could anyone give Millichip any information to back up any of the allegations. Millichip was slightly surprised because of the amount of stories that had appeared but deep down he was delighted. He had grown to like Venables as a person. He found his personality infectious.

There was a clause written into the contract with Venables and the FA agreeing that the job be terminated immediately if something arose in the future that was proved one hundred per cent against Venables. Terry was happy with the clause because he was confident. He knew that all the skeletons had come out and had been chased away.

The new England coach made his entrance at Wembley on Friday,

29 January 1994. He stood on the famous turf, his arms spread wide and then held a press conference sitting alongside Millichip and Kelly. In the background was Armfield. He had got his man, the coach the game wanted, the professionals' choice, and Armfield was proud.

'At the interview he was forthright. He came over as I knew he would – confident, strong and his love of football was apparent. And despite what other people think, football is his life. He would dearly have loved to have got the job earlier than this.' Millichip was also impressed: 'The moment I met him I knew it had to be him. For his charm, charisma and knowledge. This time we have turned to the professionals and they got it right. I certainly do not want to go through again what we have been through before.' Poor old Sir Bert. How could he have known that before the European Championships, and before he retired as chairman, he would have to go through appointing an England manager all over again?

Apart from coming home with the name, the biggest part Armfield played in the appointment of Venables was changing the title from England manager to England coach. 'I thought that was important,' he said. 'The title of coach allows you to get on with just that, looking after the players at senior and B level. Manager means so many other things. I told him to leave that to people inside the FA.'

Venables quickly appointed Bryan Robson as his right-hand man. Robson, the Middlesbrough manager, was only involved on match situations but Venables said that he was the obvious choice to be groomed as the next England coach. Don Howe was brought back and Dave Sexton put in charge of the Under-21 side, with Ray Wilkins as his assistant.

Venables was stunned to discover that there were no dossiers left for him at Lancaster Gate. There was not one bit of information from the England managers before him, not even Ramsey. No videos, no details about foreign opposition, no thoughts on record of the men who had sat in his chair before. Venables quickly went about putting that right.

Everything was in place for the start of the new England era with Venables saying: 'More than anything I want to put the pride back into our football.' Would he? Could he? He got an ovation like no one had received before at the start of his first game with Denmark and the rest of the countdown to the European Championships is plotted in this book.

Armfield certainly did not believe that in just over two years he would be faced with again finding the FA an England coach. He is now an established member of the FA's hierarchy and defends them strongly. He adds: 'I get comments about men in grey suits as if I am now one of them. It also annoys me that Graham Kelly takes so much criticism. Graham is a nice man, who treats the tea lady just as importantly as a committee man, and he is good at his job. He can be firm and there is a lot more about him than people realise. The easiest thing to do is bash the FA because, generally, no one will fight back.'

I felt really sorry for the FA over Venables's resignation. They had been brave enough to back Armfield and give Venables the job. They defended him when the skeletons appeared again, and then, having come through the first two years, which everyone says is the toughest, he quit before England had even played a competitive game under his control.

The England job certainly does funny things to you. Just ask Taylor. It turns you grey, it makes you get wired up for sound and do television documentaries when some of your players do not even know they are on film. It provokes you into producing comments like 'Do I not like that' or 'Tell your mate he has just lost me my job' (after the controversial World Cup defeat in Holland), but for Taylor there is still no job like it. He adds: 'If I could do any job it would be the manager of England again. If the FA asked me tomorrow I would go back. Any man, woman, football manager with ambition should want to do it. I do not believe any of the men who have said they do not want it.

'You have to take it. Your country needs you. You have to have a go. Even if it does not work out – and it did not work out for me – it is still the greatest job in the world.' Bobby Robson's attitude is the same. When his name was being linked with a return I rang him at a hotel where he was preparing for a cup match with his successful Porto side that night. He wanted to know what was happening and asked if there was any chance of Terry staying. Then when he realised his name was being mentioned he said he would come back tomorrow. 'You have to,' he said. 'It is YOUR country calling.'

But Terry Venables, deep down, did not want it that badly – certainly not, it appears, with the passion of Taylor or Robson. When a close friend asked Terry whether if the FA trebled his money, apologised for the lack of support from some International Committee members and gave him a four-year contract, he would change his mind, he did not think twice. 'No,' he said. 'Definitely not.' Noel White and he came face to face in the Liverpool boardroom after his resignation and the Anfield man got him a glass of white wine and said he was sorry that Venables had resigned.

It is ironic that on the eve of the European Championships Venables had a meeting with Kelly and White to discuss the controversial flight home from Hong Kong when £5,000 worth of damage was done to Cathay Pacific Airline property. He told them the players were accepting joint responsibility and that there was a bond of loyalty in the squad. The players were particularly impressed with Venables's loyalty towards them. I wonder if White squirmed when Venables spoke of loyalty.

There was never any softening of views from him. No change of mind. His decision, he said, was final and that attitude left the poor old FA having to get it right all over again. To whom would they turn this time?

FOUR

Welcome Tel

England v Denmark. Wembley, 9 March 1994.
England 1, Denmark 0. Scorer: Platt. Attendance: 71,970.

England Squad: Seaman, Flowers, Parker, Jones, Pearce, Le Saux, Adams, Pallister, Walker, Anderton, Gascoigne, Ince, Batty, Platt, Le Tissier, Shearer, Ferdinand, Beardsley. Ferdinand dropped out. Wright called up.
England Team: Seaman, Parker, Adams, Pallister, Le Saux, Ince (Batty), Gascoigne (Le Tissier), Platt, Anderton, Shearer, Beardsley.

He emerged at 7.55 p.m., a small, chunky man with an infectious grin and swamped in a big overcoat. He was the kind of man that if you passed him in the street you would not look twice in his direction. But this was no ordinary man. This was the first public appearance of the saviour of English football. Nothing quite like it had happened to Terry Venables before.

Six months before he had been out of work and fearing that football had kicked him in the teeth. He believed that his enemy and arch rival Alan Sugar, the man who had sacked him from his beloved Spurs, wanted him out of the game for good. But as the clock ticked towards eight o'clock on that night, 9 March 1994, it was a moment and a match he would remember for the rest of his life, whatever happened to him in the future as England coach – on and off the pitch. The moment he appeared the roar went up, the camera bulbs flashed, the music played and Terry Venables was the hero, the saviour of the English game and the people's choice rolled into one.

In his extraordinary career there had never been a moment like it. He had been chaired high by jubilant Barcelona fans after winning the Spanish Championship, he had celebrated at Wembley with Spurs and he had been supported by grown men when his fight with Alan Sugar was at its peak. That was with clubs. This was the country acclaiming him. It was special and he knew it.

Venables recalls the ten minutes before his first England game with a great deal of pride, and surprise. He says: 'Nothing had been on my mind except the match and the players. I had felt comfortable with the players from day one. We had responded to each other. When we got to the ground there had been a good reception from the supporters as the coach drew up outside Wembley.

'I decided to keep it simple and loose in the dressing-room. No last-minute tactics. All the preparation work had been done on the training ground. When the players left the dressing-room I wished them luck and they were gone.' Venables had experienced that moment many times in his career, the time when his players go out to warm up and he is left alone with his staff in the loneliness of the dressing-room. The Wembley dressing-rooms are not like many Premiership grounds. They are certainly not modern, spanking new, tiled areas. But they do go with the stadium and you can smell the history, recall the great players, the great managers who had stood in the middle of the home dressing-room and given their last-minute instructions. Just as Venables had done on that night to remember.

'I mentioned one or two things to Don Howe and Bryan Robson and then followed the team out,' added Venables. He could hear the noise rumbling around up the slope that takes the players on to the lush turf of Wembley, but not even Venables could have expected what was in store for him. As he walked around Wembley's perimeter he was chased by cameras, radio and TV monitors, security guards – they all wanted a piece of Venables. The fans stood to him, welcomed him as one of theirs. They could identify with Tel Boy, the Cockney kid who had played at every level for his country. Now he was in charge and the message that sang out at Wembley that night was plain and simple: 'Tel is here, we will be OK now.'

England's supporters had suffered at the hands of Graham Taylor. They had seen us huff and puff and then fail to qualify for the 1994 World Cup. The caviare and champagne was on the table now. The expert, the master coach, the man who could turn an ordinary side into European Champions. If there were questions to answer, that first night was not the time to ask them. It did not even matter how England played. A win was essential but it was not a day for inquests.

Venables said: 'The reception was wonderful. A warm greeting that I did not expect. I had known the public were on my side, that is half the reason I got the job, and the way they reacted that night only confirmed it. It made me proud, excited and humble all in one. I felt the feeling from the professionals in the game had worked its way through to the public. It was a lovely feeling. One that made me desperately want to deliver for them. I felt responsible.'

Venables had already delighted the country by recalling Peter Beardsley, the little forward Taylor refused to pick, and here was Beardsley in the side to face the Danes for his 50th cap. Venables also gave first caps to Graeme Le Saux of Blackburn and Spurs' Darren

Anderton, the winger he signed from Portsmouth, who were both to go on and form an important part of the Venables era. Matthew Le Tissier, another people's favourite, was in the squad and came on as a second-half substitute to replace Paul Gascoigne.

There were 11 changes from Graham Taylor's last squad with the heaviest casualty being Arsenal's Ian Wright. Poor Wright. He must be the only player in English football history to score four goals (against San Marino in Taylor's last match) and then be dropped.

Every England move, every attack, every touch by Paul Gascoigne, David Platt's winning goal, the final whistle was greeted with ecstasy. 'There, I told you,' the crowd were saying. 'The bloke is a genius.' There was movement and new ideas from England and no one worried that we only won 1–0.

Back he went in front of the reporters, first TV and then radio and on to the after-match press conference. 'It was lovely,' he said. 'I did not think about how the fans would react to me. All I did was plan for the game and hope for the win because I knew that is what the fans wanted most. I also wanted to win for the confidence of the players and the atmosphere we created together with the public has to stand us in good stead for the future.

'I believe it was an improvement from what we had seen from England before. We got the ball down and played and it was a stunning goal from David Platt to win the match. We gave Denmark problems. Had Gazza not picked up an injury I am sure he would have scored a couple of goals. They were opportunities that he usually accepts easily.

'The European Championships are a long way off but we can win them. We are at home. Yes, we can win. Why not?' Why not, indeed?

There was not one person at Wembley who would have dared say anything different. This was the start of Venables's honeymoon period and the nation was in love with him. In fact it was love at first sight.

One rule Venables had made was no Thursday morning press conferences. Bobby Robson used to meet us the morning after at Lancaster Gate with coffee and bacon rolls to chew over what had gone on at Wembley. Graham Taylor was more organised, sitting behind a table at a top London hotel, usually with a huge photograph of the previous night's action. Venables said that he did not want to get into an immediate heavy inquest. 'You must deliver your own verdict rather than ask me about it,' he said.

Venables did hold a short sharp press conference at around 11 p.m. on the night of a game before he went to the bar for a pint with his friends and associates. I cannot really see the point of those late-night press conferences. Most reporters are emotionally drained after working flat out for more than three hours, delivering hundreds of words and quotes to their national newspapers. Venables too had not had enough time to gather his thoughts for an in-depth inquest.

After the first victory over Denmark, however, he was happy to talk, even if there remained a reluctance to go overboard. 'It is fair to say that I never thought this would happen to me,' he admitted. 'How could I have dreamt this six months ago? It was impossible, wasn't it? The most pleasing thing about the night for me was the crowd, their warmth and the good atmosphere they spread.'

Venables had been called a lot of things in the previous months, but never a hero. On this night there was a special place in the nation's heart for him. They had taken to El Tel just as the English take to other sporting heroes like Henry Cooper, Frank Bruno, Gary Lineker and Nigel Mansell. Venables had more than 71,000 people eating out of his hand.

The day after England's victory I wrote that it was remarkable how being sacked by Sugar, dragged through controversy and kept waiting by the FA had not affected Venables. On the outside he was a man without a care in the world. I added that I did not believe that he would drop his guard completely until after the European finals. He has a lot to say but wants the platform of the finals behind him before he opens his heart.

It was way past midnight when he finally left the building. His dad, Fred, was there, so was Eric Hall, his close friend and sometimes business agent, a lot of well-wishers, many back-slappers and those who just wanted to be around his company. Sir Bert Millichip, FA chairman and the man who had voiced the biggest doubts about employing him, walked by with his wife. 'I think we may have made the right choice,' he said. 'I have never seen such a reaction to an England manager. Let us hope that we have not made a mistake this time and that Venables can lead England to victory in the European Championships. It was not a decision we took lightly. We thought long and hard but judging by tonight it was the best one we could have made.'

Millichip was later to admit to me that he should have appointed Venables earlier, probably before Taylor and certainly after the previous European Championships in Sweden when we failed to win any of our group matches and came home in disgrace and disarray. This gives something of an insight into the non-positive thinking inside Lancaster Gate. The whole country could have told the stuffed shirts at the FA that Venables was a better bet than Taylor but the International Committee, in their wisdom, could not see it.

Millichip added: 'His peers wanted him in and I am glad we took notice. I was concerned initially. But he persuaded me and then convinced me. It would take something sensational, something to creep out of the woodwork, for there to be a change now.'

So after one game Venables had the country, the players, the media and the men who employed him on his side. One hundred per cent. How long would it last? It is the question that dominates this extraordinary story.

FIVE

A National Hero

England v Greece, Wembley, 17 May 1994.
England 5, Greece 0. Scorers: Platt (2), Shearer, Beardsley, Anderton. Attendance: 23,659.

England Squad: Seaman, Flowers, Jones, Pearce, Adams, Bould, Pallister, Parker, Le Saux, Anderton, Wise, Richardson, Platt, Ince, Merson, Le Tissier, Beardsley, Shearer, Wright, Ferdinand. Parker withdrew. Barton called in.
England Team: Flowers, Jones (Pearce), Adams, Bould, Le Saux, Anderton (Le Tissier), Platt, Richardson, Merson, Beardsley (Wright), Shearer.

If they loved him before, the English public were ready to immortalise Venables after this. It did not matter that Greece went on to become one of the worst teams at the World Cup in America, here were England winning 5–0 at Wembley. It was unheard of.

There were surprises in his second squad, particularly Kevin Richardson of Aston Villa, a player who had done the rounds in English football but had been given a new lease of life by the then Villa manager Ron Atkinson. Steve Bould of Arsenal, too, came from nowhere to take his place in the party. Both players were at the twilight of their careers. It was an even bigger surprise when both players were given their debuts against the Greeks. Venables explained: 'Age does not matter to me. Richardson is outstanding in what he does, in that role he plays just in front of the back four. Bould has been consistent for seasons at centre half in one of the best defences in football. It is also a bonus that he plays alongside Tony Adams.

'Both players can stay in this squad right the way through to the European Championships. That is my thinking. I have not just brought them in as one-cap wonders.' Richardson was dropped next game, never to return, Bould played once more, then got chosen for a further squad before being discarded. That was no surprise. No one in their right mind believed that Richardson and Bould would be around in June 1996. They were to become just two of some strange selections by Venables – Barry Venison in and out, the non-selection of Le Tissier, John Salako in and out . . . I suppose we must allow the England manager his thoughts and ideas, even if it does mess players around.

Every move he makes is public and when you talk to the players they are happy to be around, even if it is only for a few days. Quite rightly. Playing for England is the highlight of their professional lives. Venables made it clear from very early on that he was going to do the job his way. He said: 'The England squad is not easy to select. Everyone has an opinion. I was no different when I was on the outside looking in. I have to bring players in when I can and take a look because I must make up my mind about them. Because there are so few matches my time is limited. I do not like giving caps away but if you do not look you do not know. I can also make up my mind about a player during training.

'In my mind I am trying to find out who the number twos are in every position. That makes it easier to establish who the number ones are. I want to swell the squad with quality and that will help everyone. I want competition for every place. I do not want anyone to feel he is an automatic choice.

'This is my pressure now. The game belongs to everyone but it is my choice that matters. What team goes out there and how they play, I take the responsibility and will continue to do it my way. I accept that the press will have their say sooner or later and anticipate that there are some tough days ahead.

'But in the forthcoming months if I try and please too many people this is not going to work. There are times when I am not going to be able to win. For instance if I pick Spurs players people will say I am favouring my old club. If I do not select them I will be accused of holding a grudge because of what went on.

'I can tell you now that I do not have favourites, nor do I intend to harm people's reputations. If I think he is good enough he goes in. If not he does not get selected. That is plain and simple to me and will be the policy I carry through. It has been the same throughout my career. I will stand or fall by the sides I select and how they play. But if I try and please thousands then it is not going to work.'

Venables had clearly enjoyed himself in the two months since the Denmark victory. It was certainly different for him. He had been used to working at a million miles an hour ever since he was a player at Chelsea, Spurs, QPR and Crystal Palace. He was never one to relax and have a lot of rest time. He was inquisitive of managers, asking them a series of questions about coaching, managing and running the club. Tommy Docherty, his manager at Chelsea, once said of Venables: 'He was a bloody nuisance. He never stopped asking questions.' It was all part of the Venables future plan, of course, and a career which took him to writing books while he played and then on to a series of business adventures.

He had to keep busy. But now this, the most important job in English football, was different. He explains: 'If I am honest I miss the day-by-day running of a football club. Being with the players day in and day out. For more than 20 years I have been churning out results without the time to think. Now I am standing back and it is going to take some getting used to.

'I am sure I will enjoy it more six games down the line, and even more when we start to approach the European Championships. I would have liked more matches. But I inherited the schedule and, with other nations trying to qualify for the Euros, it is difficult to get real quality opposition just when I need it most. But we knew about the tournament for a long time and the commitments. Something should have been done to make sure we had more and better games.

'It has left us scratching around for opponents to play, especially in 1995. I am pleased that we are going to arrange a summer tournament next year. That will give me a great opportunity to form some kind of platform. I hope by that time, when I come out of that tournament, we know where we are going.

'All my energies are with England now. Since the game against Denmark I have thought about things a lot, watched so many videos, seen the Denmark game over and over again. I am reaching a pattern of my life as the England coach. It is frustrating at times but, yes, I am loving it.'

Venables certainly loved the match against Greece, even though it was easy. The Greeks arrived with a World Cup reputation but left with every Englishman asking himself the same question: 'How come they can qualify and we cannot?' On the face value of that night it made a mockery of the fact that we were not going to be playing in the world finals. But that was the reality. This was a new era and although England were repairing the damage left behind by the Taylor regime the fact is that we, as a nation, were light years behind the rest of the world when it came to being good enough to qualify for finals. In 1990 we reached the semi-final under Robson, yet here we were trying to work up to that again. Four wasted years and Venables was aware of that fact. He had nothing to lose. England surely could not get any worse than the Taylor years. Could we? Please, no.

Greece came and went in a flurry of goals – two more from David Platt, and one each from Alan Shearer, Peter Beardsley and Darren Anderton. It was easy, too easy, and that worried Venables. He said: 'I trust that the fact that people thought it was easy will not camouflage the fact that Greece had qualified for the World Cup. It is too easy to dismiss them. You have to praise us and say that this was a good performance, a particularly good performance.

'There was nothing to suggest, going into the game, that they were not a strong side. Had we struggled people would have said, "How come England cannot beat Greece convincingly at home?" So we beat then 5–0 and everyone says that Greece were poor. Sometimes you cannot win.'

But the public wanted Venables to win. They felt after two matches that here was a winner. If some pressmen and other media critics were still to be convinced – and at this stage I was included – it was not reflected in public opinion.

There had been talk of a Christmas tree formation from Venables with Alan Shearer playing alone up front, supported quickly by other players, although as soon as he said it he realised that it could lead to public ridicule. What happens if the lights go out, Tel? . . . etc, etc. But at the moment the lights were flashing. Everyone hoped they would never go out, all the way to the Euro finals. We wanted English football to sparkle again. After two matches, six goals scored and none conceded, Venables was in control.

SIX

Norway Frustrate Again

England v Norway. Wembley, 22 May 1994.
England 0, Norway 0. Attendance: 64,327.

England Squad: Seaman, Flowers, Jones, Pearce, Adams, Bould, Pallister, Parker, Le Saux, Anderton, Wise, Richardson, Platt, Ince, Merson, Le Tissier, Beardsley, Shearer, Wright, Ferdinand. Stand-by players: Pressman, Barton, Scales, Sherwood, Wilcox, Lee. Parker withdrew. Barton called in.
England Team: Seaman, Jones, Adams, Bould, Le Saux, Anderton (Wright), Ince (Le Tissier), Platt, Beardsley, Wise, Shearer.

This was Venables's third match and the last game of the 1993–94 season. Norway came to Wembley as the team who had destroyed our World Cup dream. Forget Holland and that disputed penalty and non-sending off of Ronald Koeman, it was the Norwegians whom we loused up against.

A 1–1 draw at Wembley was bad enough, the defeat in Oslo in June 1993 was the pits. Taylor got it so hopelessly wrong the players did not know what was going on and Norway beat us 2–0. Revenge at Wembley on a bright Sunday afternoon would have been sweet. It was not to be and did I hear Taylor laughing his head off as England trooped away after a frustrating, disappointing goalless draw? You could not have blamed him.

The squad was the same which had gathered for the match against Greece. On this day Paul Ince returned to his anchor midfield role and the little Chelsea captain Dennis Wise was preferred in midfield to Paul Merson of Arsenal. But it was Venables's turn to feel let down at the hands of the Norwegians. The game was a flat, end-of-season anti-climax. Venables had called Norway a sore which had become inflamed, an amusing reference to the World Cup disaster. On this Sunday afternoon they were a pain in the backside, a tough, tall, powerful side who refused to be unlocked. They are not an attractive, adventurous side and the reality was that England did not have the ideas to penetrate them.

There was one controversial incident when an Alan Shearer free kick was tipped on to the post by Eric Thorstvedt and Platt – who else? – tapped in the rebound. But Danish official Kim Nielsen ruled out the goal, saying that Shearer had taken the kick too quickly. Venables complained bitterly: 'The advantage should always be with the attacking side, I thought the referee got it wrong.'

Victory would have been nice, defeat was unthinkable for the England coach. Especially at the hands of this lot, especially at the end of the season. He wanted to remain unbeaten and that is just about the only thing that England took out of the game: an unbeaten record under the new coach.

It was back to reality for Venables after the mauling of Greece. It was obvious that there was a long, long road to be negotiated before England had a side good enough to challenge for the European Championship crown. To be fair to Venables he had never entered into the hysteria surrounding his appointment, or got carried away after the victories over Denmark and Greece. He was either hiding his true feelings or being ultra-sensible. But England could not break down Norway and there were bigger and better sides to combat, especially in matches that mattered.

Venables went to the World Cup, along with the rest of us, to see what the best of the world could offer. He left behind an England side in the process of repair. The bonuses in those first three matches were undoubtedly Blackburn full back Graeme Le Saux and Spurs winger Darren Anderton. He had used 21 players in three games and Le Saux and Anderton could definitely be pencilled in as certainties for the European Championships squad.

The coach praised Richardson for his contribution against Greece, but at 31 these, surely, were hollow words and Richardson had no chance of maintaining his place in the squad, let alone the team. The fans wanted Matt Le Tissier, Andy Cole and Chris Sutton but Venables refused to be pushed in any direction. There had been a training get-together, a match in April in Germany called off because it clashed with Hitler's birthday and a B international against Northern Ireland at Hillsborough in May. England won 4–2 with Arsenal's Paul Merson outstanding.

The clamour for places and the bid to impress Venables was on. He insisted: 'No one will be eliminated until I have had a chance to see them work, work with them,' he said. 'I would rather look at players now and next season than not be sure when I get to the European finals.

'Next season I will experiment at the risk of results. I have to be pleased with what we have achieved together so quickly. Considering the mood of the country when I took over there is now one of great expectancy. That is healthy although it brings a certain degree of pressure.

'We have played three different types of opposition and emerged unbeaten. I could not have asked for more than that. I am satisfied and happy about the future.

'I have already learned a lot. Take the Norway game for instance. This team knocked us out of the World Cup. I wanted to see if we could put pressure on their defence without conceding goals. Yes, we could have played better. But at this stage it is not all about winning for me, it is about learning. About the players, how we play and, yes, about me. I would say that a team is forming in my mind but the finals are a long way ahead and so much can and will happen.

'There are questions at this stage to answer, like how long will Peter Beardsley last? At the moment he is remarkable, he just seems to go on and on. Will Paul Gascoigne be back to fitness when we want him?' Ah, waiting for Gazza. Here is a question that was to dominate England's build-up to the finals. Gazza, clown or genius? One of THE great players or a misunderstood immature guy who could never live up to the billing he gave himself in 1990? At this stage he was a living nightmare, to Venables, English football and himself.

There is no doubt in my mind that Venables at this stage was planning out England's destiny in his own mind. He is in love with football and everything about it, and here he was in control of the biggest situation of his life – the England coach with the whole country expecting him to deliver. Believing he would. He went to the World Cup as a spectator, determined to prove them right and give the nation what they wanted. But deep down he knew that he had the biggest job of his life on his hands.

There had not been the same pressure on Taylor because he had been ridiculed from the start by some. With Venables every man, boy and dog thought he had more chance than Taylor of succeeding. There were some who thought that he should never have been allowed near Lancaster Gate but that was for non-football reasons. As a coach this was it. The best we had.

Venables had been to a national coaches seminar in Lisbon where he discovered to his horror other delegates laughing at our demise. He recalled: 'Some countries talked to me as if, as a nation, we were naive at football. They take digs at us because we have not qualified for the World Cup. One guy told me that England were once feared by the rest of the world, but not any more.

'That hurt me. I found myself holding my head high. I am proud to be English and proud to be the English coach. I have been appointed to put the record straight, to restore some pride. That is what I intend to do. I know how difficult this job is. I did not come into this with my head in the sand. I feel for Graham Taylor. I know what he went through.'

SEVEN

No Lessons Learned

England v USA. Wembley, 14 September 1994.
England 2, USA 0. Scorer: Shearer (2). Attendance: 38,629.

England Squad: Seaman, Flowers, Adams, Pallister, Bould, Le Saux, Pearce, Anderton, Lee, Platt, Le Tissier, Ince, Ferdinand, Wright, Shearer, Barnes. Ince and Bould withdrew. Venison, Ruddock and Wise called up.
England Team: Seaman, Jones, Adams, Pallister, Le Saux, Anderton, Platt, Venison, Barnes, Shearer (Wright), Sheringham (Ferdinand).

A new season and a season that was to become known as the year of the sleaze. There had never been, nor will there be again, a season like the 1994–95 winter of English football. It reeled from one disaster to another: the Bruce Grobbelaar affair when he was accused of throwing matches, Paul Merson's drugs and drink problem, George Graham sacked as Arsenal manager for accepting a 'bung', Eric Cantona's kung-fu attack on a spectator, the return of hooliganism . . . the ugly list went on and on.

It was great for newspapers, sad for the grand old game. If you loved football and you were a journalist in the middle of it all, you had mixed feelings. The excitement of the story coupled with the horror of the damage that such things would do to the image of the sport. Graham, a close friend of Venables and someone who has moulded his style and outlook on the England coach, in my opinion gave football the biggest body blow of all when he was sacked for taking an illegal payment from Norwegian agent Rene Hauge. I will never forgive him for it and do not believe he should ever have been allowed back into the game again. How the BBC had the audacity to employ him as an expert for their Radio Five football coverage at the start of the following season is beyond me. Graham was eventually dropped three months later for admitting in a *Sun* newspaper book serialisation how and why he took the money.

Venables was not spared controversy. Before a ball was kicked his old club Spurs were hit by the Football Association over claims of illegal payments made to players while Venables was in control of the club. At an FA hearing Spurs were kicked out of the FA Cup, deducted 12 Premiership points and fined £600,000, plus ordered to pay £100,000 costs. It was a verdict that turned new owner Alan Sugar into a man obsessed with getting even with the FA and he vowed immediately to fight it all the way.

Manager Ossie Ardiles said after hearing the shocking verdict: 'The people who have put us in this mess walked away scot-free. Nothing has happened to them. That, surely, cannot be right?' Sugar fought and won, turning it into a legal wrangle, and wiping the floor with the FA. Spurs were reinstated to the FA Cup and had their points reduction reduced to six and the fine wiped clean. It was a comprehensive victory and one that was acutely embarrassing to the FA. They had left a legal loophole open and Sugar barged his way through. It proved one thing: Sugar was a street-fighter when he believed he was in the right. Anyone in his way would get trampled on.

It was an insight into the determination of Sugar. He was clearly not a man to be crossed. Venables too was a stubborn, proud man and there the problems were for all to see. When the going got tough, each refused to budge an inch. It was a stubbornness and a pride that was to cost Venables his job. Sugar felt so strongly that he banned Venables from going back to White Hart Lane, a ban that ran for the entire season. It was an incredible situation, the England coach unable to return to the club he once helped save from ruin – and he never returned to the day he resigned as English coach.

For the first game of the season, Spurs at home to Manchester United, England scout Ted Buxton, a former Spurs employee, was even barred from the directors' box, forced to sit in the stand and to talk to potential England players in the car-park. It was war. Even though the ban was lifted, reluctantly after pressure from FA chairman Sir Bert Millichip, you knew that Sugar and Venables would never, ever, be 'together' again.

The new season was a vital one for Venables. After three matches and two wins and a draw he knew that he had to sustain the momentum. He had the players and the fans on his side and it was important to keep them there. He was clearly still going to treat the new campaign as an experiment and admitted before the start: 'I may have to lose a game or two to get what I want.' That was fine, just so long as we could all see something taking shape, something positive, something refreshing, something good.

Venables had persuaded the FA to employ England's first full-time scout and his close friend Buxton, sacked by Spurs in the bloodshed of White Hart Lane, was welcomed into Lancaster Gate. One of the things that I discovered in writing this book is Venables's fierce loyalty to those who stay in his network of friends and companions. Buxton was 'looked after' by his friend and loyalty is a great quality to have. I admire Venables for it.

Before the USA game Venables also predicted that Bryan Robson would eventually be his successor. He said that he felt that it was important for a new England manager to be groomed rather than the FA be surprised and left looking for a new man when the manager in place was either sacked or decided to quit. Venables felt that Robson was the obvious candidate, especially as he was to work alongside him all the way through to the European finals. Robson's own loyalty to Venables was indicated much later when he went public with a fierce show of support after the grim, goalless draw in Oslo. As I have said many times, the Venables clan is strong, inside and outside the game. There are a few journalists inside the framework of club Tel and their duty to him is never to criticise, through thick and thin.

There was a big surprise in the squad for the game against USA, colourful opponents who had surprised many people with the quality of their football at the 1994 World Cup where they journeyed into the quarter-finals. Venables recalled John Barnes, a player who had flattered to deceive for so long in an England shirt. Barnes must have been fed up with the number of times he had been accused of failing to turn his Liverpool form into England class. Yet, here he was again in an England squad. Venables defended the selection, knowing that the English public had probably had enough of Barnes. Even the player said: 'I just could not believe it.' Venables retort was: 'I will not be put off just because a player has been criticised in the past. It is my head on the block and I will choose who I want and for reasons that I know.' When he selected him in the team Venables urged the England crowd to get behind Barnes rather than criticise him, as they had done in the past. 'If there is to be criticism, let it be after the game, not during it,' he said. Barnes, at 30, was also considered to be too old by some, a criticism that Venables strongly defended. 'Rubbish,' he said. 'All of these players I have selected can be around for the European Championships.'

Barnes did not need defending, it was a poor game. USA, I am convinced, only accepted the game because they had never before played at Wembley. It was a bit of football history for them and they did not seem to try a leg in a game that England won unconvincingly with Alan Shearer's double.

USA coach Bora Milutinovic, a Serb who is now coach of the national Mexican team, got in a terrible mess in the after-match press conference trying to defend his team's performance, first talking in his native tongue and then insisting in English that it was a good game. I was probably a bit hard on him but he still refused to answer the question: 'Did you really want to win the match?'

For Venables there was little for him to take home. At least we saw an end to the Christmas tree formation with Shearer and Teddy Sheringham used up front as a twin spearhead. The Christmas tree had clearly begun to weigh on the coach's shoulders and he was happy to point out that two out-and-out strikers were in the team. But Venables said, and he had a point, that when it was Gary Lineker and Peter Beardsley people were happy and yet Beardsley never played as a straightforward striker.

After his fourth game he said that he could see a team forming in his mind. Of the side which beat the USA certainly David Seaman, Tony Adams, Gary Pallister, Graeme Le Saux, Darren Anderton, David Platt and Alan Shearer looked certainties for the first game of the European Championships – injuries and form permitting. Barry Venison had been a sound and admirable replacement for Paul Ince but you'll not see him around in 1996, despite Venables's vote of confidence for all the over-thirties.

Everyone knew there was a long way to go and that we were still only sparring, with the opposition as well as players' attitudes. They knew, we knew, certainly Terry knew, that games like this one were hardly the real thing. USA were a waste of time and space. I hope they are never invited back.

Venables tried to impress upon his players that he would not tolerate anything less than one hundred per cent and that playing for England should mean everything to any player he selects. 'When I got my first cap I heard the news on my car radio and drove straight round to see my mum. That cap meant everything to me. Take Bobby Moore, his 99th cap meant as much to him as his first,' said Venables.

'If I ever felt that playing for England was secondary to some players then those players will become secondary to me. All the players I choose in my squad should not need praise from me. I have shown them what I feel about them.'

Two weeks after the fourth game for Venables, Sugar issued a writ against him, claiming damages over allegations made in Venables's official autobiography. It was part of the war between the two men and Venables was to have to live with allegations, rumours, writs, TV character assassinations and lots more throughout his England career. You wondered how he managed to concentrate on the job, yet he seemed to do so with a smile on his face. It was a remarkable performance. At that stage I felt that if he managed a similar one as England coach we surely must win the Championships. For Venables appeared to have everything under control.

EIGHT

Getting Tougher

England v Romania. Wembley, 12 November 1994.
England 1, Romania 1. Scorer: Lee. Attendance: 48,754.

England Squad: Seaman, Flowers, Jones, Adams, Pallister, Ruddock,
Le Saux, Pearce, Anderton, Lee, Le Tissier, Ince, Wise, Barnes,
Beardsley, Ferdinand, Wright, Shearer, Sheringham, Anderton.
Beardsley and Anderton withdrew. McManaman called up.
England Team: Seaman, Jones (Pearce), Adams, Pallister, Le Saux,
Le Tissier, Ince, Lee (Wise), Barnes, Shearer, Wright (Sheringham).

Game five and there is no question in my mind that at this stage of
his England career Terry Venables was missing club management. He
found it difficult to come to terms with not being with the players
day to day and did not like the huge gaps between matches. It went
against the grain for him because never before had he lost control of
'his' players.

It was also at this stage that he admitted to me that he could
always go back to club management if the England job was not a
success, and probably would when it was all over. He also said that
had he stayed at Spurs, and not been kicked out of White Hart Lane
by Alan Sugar, he would not have even thought about becoming the
coach of England.

He was proud to be in control of England but, clearly, it had not
been a priority for him, certainly not when he was chief executive at
White Hart Lane. He had always wanted to own his own club and
that is where his heart was until Sugar got out the knives and
sharpened them. There is no question that Terry Venables did not
even want to be England manager when he and Sugar were together.
Once he was sacked and the England job became available, only then
did he see it as the next, convenient, stage of his career.

He had wanted it at one time but believed England had passed him
by. In his father Fred's autobiography he even heavily criticised the
FA for their handling of the situation. He had said that he did not
believe that he was the kind of person that the FA would employ. He
had washed his hands of the idea and gone off in a different direction,

looking for new challenges. Now things were different. He was in control of the most important job in English football. Deep down he was not entirely happy and certainly trying desperately to come to terms with the biggest and most important job he had ever taken on.

We chatted for about an hour after one training session and Venables, clearly happy and relaxed to be doing what he enjoys most, coaching, spoke about how his life had changed. 'Do you know something. I love this game more than ever. As a youngster I liked all sports. Football has taken over and I just do not have time to get involved in anything else. Football as a sport has grown so much it is amazing the changes we have seen.

'I have always been interested in new things, new challenges, how someone works, why is he good at what he does, how things work. I suppose this job comes under that category. A fantastic new challenge and one that I am proud to take.

'I have already enjoyed the craft of the job. Looking inside a performance and finding out why a team does things, as a unit and as individuals. As a kid I was a real busy bloke, a nuisance. It would be me who asked all the questions and I used to drive the teachers mad. It was the same with my early football managers.

'Later I would tell people what to do and drive them mad too. But if you do not ask you do not learn and I am still learning today. I am just glad to be in a position now to help others. To make players better, to bring the best out of them. That is what I am good at. I know that. I feel it.

'Whatever people may say about me, now or in the future, I want to win the European Championships for the country. That would make me very proud.

'The crazy thing is that there are a lot of people who do not want you to be a success. There are people out there who do not want me to win the Championships. They are waiting for me to fail. That is because, deep down, they want to do what I do.

'It is a strange jealousy. People cannot understand why I go home in the evening at 8.30 to my restaurant and mix and talk with customers, friends and other people I have never met before. That is my relaxation. I am learning from them all the time. What are those people who collapse in front of the television learning? That is not me. I like to communicate.

'In all walks of life, in all businesses, there is jealousy. People want to do what you are doing. And if they cannot have it, they try and ruin it for you. It is true. Sad, but true. Not enough people say, "He is the England coach, let's really get behind him." In other walks of life it is the same. Someone is good at their job, but someone else, perhaps in authority, wants to change it. Why? Jealousy? Spite? Who knows? But it goes on.

'We beat Greece 5–0 and yet people say, "But Greece are not a good side." Why is there always a down side? You do it well and there is no credit. International sides do not win 5–0 these days and yet when England get a result like that it is still not good enough.

'Everything I am doing in my professional life is geared to June 1996. That is all that matters to me and my target is those finals. I have never been more focused in my life. Of course I miss being a day-to-day manager. For 20 years I was right in the thick of things, churning out results with no thinking time. It was my life.

'I would still like to do it again, either in England or abroad. In the future. Whatever happens with England will not put me off being a club manager again. I know I could go back to being a club coach or a manager, quite easily. I think about it but first things first.

'I was happy at Spurs. Being chief executive and part owning a club was an ambition and one that gave me great pleasure. I would still be there had things not happened. Had I stayed at Spurs I would have preferred to do that, more than England, I think. That was my reaction at the time and it still nags inside me.

'But then England would never quite have happened for me and who knows . . . who knows . . . that is exactly the point. What is next? What do I do after England? That is what is so good about life, no one knows.'

What Venables knew at that stage is that England were scratching around for opponents. 'There should have been more games organised, quality opponents,' he said.

Romania came to Wembley with a reputation built around their indifferent performances in the World Cup and the fact that they had two stars playing at Spurs, Ille Dumitrescu and Petrescu. To emphasise that he could do no right, Venables was criticised over his non-selection of Andy Cole. It was not helped when Cole fumed: 'What more do I have to do?' Venables insisted that he had nothing against Cole and was not snubbing him. 'But I must pick who I want and when I want. If I start trying to please everyone then I might as well pack it in.' David Platt was unavailable and Tony Adams of Arsenal skippered the side for the first time. There were two surprise selections: Matt Le Tissier started for the first time under Venables and there was a recall for Ian Wright of Arsenal.

It was not a special game, more of an interesting one with Robert Lee, playing in place of Platt, equalising for England. Venables was not disappointed: 'Romania are technically gifted footballers yet they did not outplay us. That is encouraging. They kept the ball and at times we could not take it from them, you expect that from continental teams. We had to be solid and we were. I was encouraged by a number of things.

'After half an hour I thought we would win the game. When Alan Shearer was going through and was blocked by Petrescu I thought it was a clear offence and that Petrescu should have been sent off. Had

Shearer been allowed to go on he would have scored and we would have won.'

Le Tissier, not given the free role he enjoys at Southampton and stuck more out on the wing, was disappointing. He never stamped his authority on the game. Ian Wright struggled too, not for the first time at this level, and you felt that they would both be fortunate to be around when Venables settled on his Euro 96 squad.

It was the second draw out of five. No alarm bells yet and the coach remained super confident. 'I am enjoying the job, more than I thought I would.' As Venables says, we will just have to wait and see what happens, what is around the corner. Because you can never tell.

NINE

Not Convinving Yet, Terry

England v Nigeria. Wembley, 16 November 1994.
England 1, Nigeria 0. Scorer: Platt. Attendance: 37,196.

England Squad: Seaman, Flowers, Jones, Barton, Adams, Pallister, Ruddock, Le Saux, Pearce, Beardsley, McManaman, Lee, Platt, Ince, Wise, Barnes, Le Tissier, Sheringham, Ferdinand, Shearer. Pallister, Ince and Adams withdrew. Howey and Ehiogu called up.
England Team: Flowers, Jones, Howey, Ruddock, Le Saux, Wise, Platt, Lee (McManaman), Barnes, Beardsley (Le Tissier), Shearer (Sheringham).

'I want players who can win, who know how to win,' said the England coach as we moved towards an easy-looking fixture against Nigeria. England won thanks to another goal from David Platt, but we were far from convincing.

It was an interesting selection this time. Matthew Le Tissier was axed to substitute, there was a new defensive pairing of Neil Ruddock and Steve Howey and Dennis Wise, the little Chelsea captain, was included. The Wise call-up was interesting because in the early hours of the previous Sunday morning he had been arrested for beating up a taxi-driver outside Scribes West, the London nightclub owned by Venables.

The incident involved the police and received a great deal of publicity on the Monday morning but, incredibly, Venables did not mention it or what he felt of Wise in his press conference that day. Was he asked? I was amazed that nothing had been said when I contacted my office from Kapsenberg, Austria, where I was with Kevin Keegan, who had been handed temporary control of the Under-21 side because of domestic problems for Dave Sexton. It was, firstly, strange that Venables should not mention Wise and, second, incredible that he should select him. He would have earned far more respect if he had pulled Wise aside before training that Monday morning and told him to slip away quietly and sort out his problem. Then he should have explained the situation to the media.

But that is not Terry's style. It seems there always has to be intrigue, questions unanswered. The fact remained that Wise had been wining and dining in the club owned by the England manager in the early hours of the day before he reported for England duty, and was then arrested for beating up a taxi-driver. The police were involved and there was a good chance that Wise would face criminal charges. Terry, I felt, lost the opportunity to show some steel and, once again, his loyalty to some players went overboard.

Just to prove the point the moment Wise reported back to Chelsea he was called in by manager Glenn Hoddle and stripped of the captaincy. Hoddle, in a few minutes, had done what Venables should have carried out days earlier. Hoddle showed some courage. Venables did not. Hoddle got it right, Venables hid behind the fact that he wanted Wise to play against Nigeria. It only added weight to the argument that Venables favours certain players.

Nigeria, so colourful, exciting and potent in the World Cup, offered no such threat at Wembley. Perhaps it was too cold for them? We saw the same thing happen when Cameroon visited us after the 1990 World Cup. They promised a lot but failed to deliver.

But we must not take away from England that they won and ended the year on a positive note. Venables was rightly happy, if not with the performance, then with the way the team and his own planning was going. He said: 'I believe I have got the nation on my side and the rest is up to me. I have said this many times, and I have said it to myself every day. I aim to give the nation a team to be proud of again. I want the opposition to be frightened of us. To want not to play England.'

However, he did make a Graham Taylor-type clanger in the build-up to the game. He said that it was not important for England to beat Nigeria. I knew what he meant but it was the wrong choice of words. Venables's credibility would have dropped alarmingly had we lost to Nigeria. 'I disagree,' he said. 'What is important at this stage is the development of the team. Results come second.'

Platt was the match-winner and at this stage under Venables where would England be without him? It was his 24th goal on his 50th appearance and Venables paid this tribute to him: 'Platt is remarkable. He can do anything you ask of him. This time he had to play in a holding role. You do not like to tie him down but his timing is so good you can play him anywhere. You are never surprised when he pops up with a goal. To get 24 in 50 caps is a great record. He reminds me so much of Bryan Robson, who also had this knack of arriving at the vital time to score important goals.' Praise indeed about how important Platt is to England. What would we do without him? It was a question England would have to answer at a later date. Platt himself, forever the diplomat, said afterwards that he would love to achieve the double of 100 caps and 50 goals for his country. It was a tough prediction, tougher than Platt could ever have expected.

It was Wise who provided the cross for Platt's header and there was praise from the coach for the little Chelsea midfield star. He said: 'I would compare him to Alan Ball. Wise is a winner, he is a good passer, he keeps the ball, is hard to knock off it and is a great crosser. Some people say he is unfashionable. To whom? You can temper your behaviour as you get older but if you have not got ability you cannot gain that. He has got it. Passing is not an easy skill at the top level. You will be surprised how many people do not have anywhere near Wise's ratio. That is not my opinion, that is fact.' Impressive credentials. Strange that they should have come after a game in which Wise should not have taken part. Also, impressive credentials for a player who did not eventually make the Euro squad.

Ruddock too made a significant contribution, especially alongside young Howey. It was a partnership that had never played together before and Ruddock, a Venables signing for Spurs, and Wise were quick to dispel the growing feeling of favouritism towards them. Wise said: 'Maybe people do think we are Terry's favourites but if we play as we did against Nigeria they cannot complain.' Ruddock added: 'Even if Terry was not the manager, with the form I am in now, I would be very upset if I was not in the England set-up. I know I can hold my own at international level.'

Venables then had to suffer the longest wait of his England career so far. It was February 1995 before England played again and the England coach was left alone with his thoughts, his planning, videos of all the players and sides in Europe and the dream of being a success. He hated the waiting, not being used to it, although he admitted that he was coming to terms with it. 'It is the hardest part of the job,' he said. 'Just when you get something going you have to stop.'

Republic of Ireland were next, in February 1995, in Dublin, Terry's first away fixture. Big Jack Charlton did not want to lose to his old rival and so the pressure was on Venables.

Shortly before he announced his squad Dennis Wise was found guilty of assault and criminal damage. This time Venables had to react and he did by leaving the Chelsea star out of his squad of players to make the short journey to Dublin. 'It was my decision,' he said. 'And I was under no pressure from anyone at Lancaster Gate. I have spoken to Dennis and decided that it is best for everyone if he takes a break from playing for England while he sorts out his other problems. I think it is the right decision.'

Wise's absence allowed Matthew Le Tissier to return. It was a huge game for the Southampton star and people's choice. Would he be given a free role, like with his club, the position he wants? No, this time he was asked to play up front and when the game kicked off you sensed that Le Tissier had reached the point of no return with his career under Venables.

What happened next has been well documented and I have no

intention of dwelling on the return of hooliganism in this book. Scum, morons, bastards, call them what you like. They ripped the Republic of Ireland's Lansdowne Road stadium to bits and caused abandonment of the game after 27 minutes. The scenes were horrendous and shocked a lot of people, especially those younger reporters who were new to travelling with England and certainly new to the horrors of this kind of hooliganism. Some said they were ashamed to be English. Sadly, I and others had seen it all before.

When you have seen a 40-year-old man, his face painted in the colours of the Union Jack, urinating over a frightened local child in Germany, when you have seen a Luxembourg girl thrown through a shop window, when you have seen so-called supporters with Rottweiler dogs, when you have seen old-age pensioners scattered by a wild rampaging mob, you are no longer shocked. Saddened, yes. I am never ashamed to be English, though. It just makes me want to fight back and try and make sure this kind of thing never happens again. But that is something we have been saying for years and, inevitably, it does happen again. And will.

Venables called it organised crime, yob rule. FA chief executive Graham Kelly called for a full inquiry and there were questions raised over the future of the European Championships being staged in England. That was never in doubt and we must all pray that hooliganism does not return. But the police, FA and others in authority know that it could.

There are many discussions and theories as to why it does. I happen to agree with Brian Clough, the former manager who said a lot, often controversially, though it was always compelling listening. He said that discipline and standards begin at home, with the parents. Find me a hooligan and I will give you a parent who does not care or is at fault, he said. It cannot be the only reason but it was an answer, especially in the early days of hooliganism when football fought a battle every week. Hooliganism in football is currently under control with the massive work made by clubs, police and local authorities, but in society today there is too much lack of respect for other people and their property. Too many young people are not afraid of discipline, punishment or being caught doing wrong.

I had first-hand experience of it in the winter of 1995–96 when, on a train going to Grimsby, Nigel Clarke of the *Daily Mirror* and I were spotted by some Chelsea fans. I call them fans but they told me that some of them had been banned from Stamford Bridge for five years, and seemed quite proud of it. One of them, his face an ugly mass of hatred, suddenly took a lunge at me, catching me in both eyes with pointed fingers as he snorted something about hating all reporters, especially me and the *Sun*.

It was an attack that caught me by surprise and left me depressed, as well as with a black eye. So what do you do when it happens to you? Hit him and run the risk of ten of his mates joining in? That, probably, is what they want. It was a packed link-line train, full of mothers and children. These yobs showed complete disregard for people. They had been drinking, of course, but it was more sinister than just the effects of drink. It was the contempt that depressed me, and the behaviour of grown men, some in their thirties with children of their own. It is impossible to reason with them. One did say that he used to be a thug who fought all the time, but now he had settled down. You could have fooled me.

Hooliganism always smoulders under the surface. It raised its rotten head in Dublin and it would not take much to trigger it off again. I will never forget the agony on the face of Jack Charlton, when he attended the after-match press conference in Dublin. It was the face of a confused, upset and angry man. He was close to tears as he said: 'Why? This kind of thing has never happened to us before. Never.'

Venables wanted to continue the match but it was probably best, for football reasons, that it was abandoned. England, when it was called off, were getting murdered. We were 1–0 down and the defence was cut to shreds every time Ireland attacked. Hooliganism, ironically, could just have saved Venables from his most embarrassing moment so far.

As for Le Tissier, he was lost in the controversy, and for 27 minutes lost in an attacking, main striker role foreign to him. We waited to see if he would ever be given another chance. I wondered if Venables, under pressure from media and fans, had included him in a tough away match for the Saints star to hang himself. We will never know. But I had my doubts whether we would see Le Tissier again in an England shirt.

TEN

Brainless England

England v Uruguay. Wembley, 29 March 1995.
England 0, Uruguay 0. Attendance: 34,839.

England Squad: Flowers, Walker, Jones, Barton, Adams, Howey, Pallister, Ruddock, Le Saux, Pearce, Anderton, Lee, Venison, Platt, Sherwood, Redknapp, Barnes, McManaman, Barmby, Beardsley, Shearer, Sheringham. Shearer dropped out. Cole drafted in.
England Team: Flowers, Jones, Adams, Pallister, Le Saux (McManaman), Anderton, Platt, Venison, Barnes, Sheringham (Cole), Beardsley (Barmby).

Terry Venables has been called a lot of things in his career, most of them complimentary – until he became England coach, that is. But never brainless. Yet that is what Uruguay coach Hector Nunez labelled Venables's team after a tedious, poor, goalless draw at Wembley. Nunez said that we lacked creativity, leadership, fantasy and brains. It was the most damning verdict yet on the Venables era. Venables quickly denied the criticism and the comments no doubt trapped a nerve with him. 'I did not exactly see fantasy football from them,' he snapped. 'What I will concede is this was my most frustrating night at Wembley.'

It was a performance, however, that triggered off a series of icy situations between myself and the England coach. On the Friday morning in the *Sun* newspaper after England's disappointing display I wrote that I hoped Terry was not going to become a turnip like his predecessor, Graham Taylor. I said that after eight games and 14 months Venables had yet to show us a new improved England. The way England were playing we did not seem any further forward than we were when Taylor was sacked. It was an article written with tongue in cheek but with genuine concern and it ended with the comment: 'Let us hope Tel gets it right. The whole country is behind him, willing him to win the European Championships. Otherwise he will go the same way as his predecessors.' It was not an article Venables appreciated.

The following week I received a curt letter from him in which he announced that he wanted nothing to do with this book. He said that he withdrew all co-operation 'for obvious reasons'. It was a strange comment to make considering this is not a book that ever sought co-operation or first-hand information from Venables. It is a book about him, not by him, a book of insight into his ideas, squads, players and him as a person. The only time I asked for a small interview was to go over a few of his early matches, explaining situations, tactics and thoughts. He gave me it at Bisham one Saturday lunchtime after a get-together, and that was all.

I wrote back and said what a pity that after all these years he should write and not contact me by telephone with his thoughts. Ironically, at the same time he had written to Joe Lovejoy, the *Sunday Times* football correspondent and one of the reporters known to be firmly in the Venables camp. Terry had not liked something Joe had written and complained. The letters, I believe, give an interesting insight into Venables the man. Here is someone who clearly cannot take criticism, however small. It is known in the game that Venables reacts to people when he does not like something they have done, and certainly favours those who only write good things about him. But I believe an England coach has to be bigger than that, much bigger.

A few days after my letter had reached his office at Lancaster Gate we spoke on the telephone and he accused me of siding with Alan Sugar and criticising him only because that is what Sugar wanted. I was not having that and told him it was rubbish. Anyone who knows me well knows that I am my own man, especially when it comes to journalism and asking questions. If I believe that someone should be criticised I do it, regardless of friendship or relationship. The bottom line is that England were playing poorly with no sign of coming together, so why not say it? You have to be brave in journalism. I cannot stand reporters who sit on the fence or who refuse to ask questions because they are frightened of falling out with the person in front of them, or refuse to write something because they are too close to the situation.

As for siding with Sugar, that is ridiculous. I know Alan Sugar no better than I know Terry Venables. As I have told Terry many times before, I hope that he wins the European Championship and I will be the first to shake his hand and write about him in glowing terms. If we fail I will be the first person to ask him where he got it wrong. He knows that and, deep down, there is respect. It goes both ways.

But what an intriguing character he is. Here is an England coach who always leaves you with a question unanswered. He is someone who seems to be looking over his shoulder, someone who opens his front door and then closes it again before anyone is let inside. Who knows Terry Venables and what makes him really tick? Not many people, I bet. You can probably count them on one hand. In a way I have sympathy with that side of him.

I just wish Terry would not be so touchy when it comes to the press. He has this bee in his bonnet about us and I am afraid it will always be there, buzzing away. These are some of his thoughts on the media, especially the written press. He says: 'I do not want nice things written about me or the team but I do want fair things. Facts, let us deal in facts.

'The press like a fight just as long as they are the only ones who can punch. Linford Christie had a go back and they did not like it. They accused him of whingeing. Well, I am going to have a go back when I feel it is necessary. What I would like to know is how they become qualified to criticise me and England? What credentials do they have to become experts? I would say 50 per cent of reporters in this country are not qualified to criticise me or England.

'Most managers and players take the hammer given out to them. Yet I have never come across a group so sensitive as the reporters themselves. I enjoy working with the professionals behind the scenes, we are getting on well and making progress. The problem comes when the media are around. I often see good come out of a game, even a defeat, and yet they say, "Impossible, it was rubbish." Who are they to judge?

'I have told them many times that if they do not like me or what I stand for, OK. If I get stick I will take it but I will also have a go back because that is my nature. I do not read one paper during England games, they are a distraction.' Funny, that, when he later accused me of writing rubbish for saying that David Platt's knee injury was worse than first feared.

'I have got to the stage where I do not care any more. They can say what they like, throw away what they like. Terry Vegetables! Listen, that catchphrase has been used against my family for years. The honeymoon was over for me after three weeks. But I believe all sportsmen under attack should have a go back. Why shouldn't we? At the end of the day I will do this job my way and to the best of my ability. I will walk away eventually saying that England played the Terry Venables way.'

There are reporters known to be in the Venables camp. There is nothing wrong with that as long as their friendship, loyalty, fear, call it what you like, does not interfere with the truth. If England are poor, do not say they were good. Because you cannot fool the public. Venables adds: 'There are some I follow and I will go with, Powell [Daily Mail], Ken Jones [Independent] and Lacey [David, of the Guardian].'

There are others like Joe Lovejoy of the Sunday Times, Rob Shepherd, once of Today and now with the Mail, and Martin Samuel of the Sun, who are staunch supporters. Of all the national reporters I believe that only Powell and Jones can be termed as true friends of the England coach.

Lacey is a different kettle of fish. He gains his accolades through respect from his articles and comments in the *Guardian*. But David can be as cutting as the tabloid men, it is just that it is hidden away in his piece rather than smashed over the back page in bold type. His cutting comments did produce one memorable rebuke from the then England manager, Ron Greenwood, during the Spanish World Cup in 1982. England were going through a tricky time. Keegan had gone missing for treatment. (He drove himself back to Germany for treatment during the night. What would that story produce now? Four, five pages, including the front?) Brooking had not kicked a ball and the build-up to the first game was pressurised. Greenwood on that particular day was grumpy and said that he refused to hold a press conference because he had been let down by one man and one paper. The tabloids looked at themselves and my colleague on the *Sun*, John Sadler, thought he was the guilty man. Hugh McIlvanney then growled from the top of the concrete banking on which we sat in front of Greenwood, 'Come on, Ron, you might as well name him. Otherwise we will be sitting here for ages and will all get tarred with the same brush.' 'OK,' said Ron, 'it is that . . .' and there was a long pause while he plucked up courage to name names, '. . . it is that bloody David Lacey.' Everyone fell about laughing and we got on with the training.

So it is not only Terry who is touchy. But I fear some more bumpy rides for us all before the European Championships are over.

As I expected against Uruguay, Matthew Le Tissier was left out of the squad. His world had come crashing down. The Southampton player had been given just three hours and 14 minutes in Venables's seven matches in control and it looked as though, already, Le Tissier's last chance had come and gone. He was the latest casualty of the debacle in Dublin. 'I can make no promises to any player,' said Venables.

Out too went Paul Ince. He was given compassionate leave because he had to appear with Eric Cantona in front of Croydon Magistrates Court to answer charges that they attacked fans during Manchester United's infamous game at Selhurst Park against Crystal Palace. Venables had contacted United manager Alex Ferguson and both men agreed that it was best for Ince to have some time off to resolve his off-pitch problems.

There were five Liverpool players in the squad, helping Venables to build his club spirit, and one of them looked to have a good future. Jamie Redknapp, son of West Ham manager Harry, was a popular choice. Many people believed that he could play a significant role in the European Championship squad.

It was not an inspiring performance. The nearest England came to breaking the deadlock was when Andy Cole, who came on as substitute for Alan Shearer, hit the bar with a header. It was just left for this Venables team to be called brainless.

Brainless? Only time will tell what is going on inside that head of Venables.

ELEVEN

The Umbro Cup

England Squad: Flowers, Walker, Barton, Neville, Adams, Pallister, Scales, Le Saux, Pearce, Anderton, Batty, Platt, Ince, Gascoigne, Barnes, McManaman, Barmby, Beardsley, Shearer, Collymore, Cole, Sheringham. Adams, Ince and Cole dropped out. Unsworth, Cooper and Redknapp called in.

England v Japan. Wembley, Saturday, 3 June 1995.
England 2, Japan 1. Scorers: Anderton, Platt. Attendance: 21,142.

England Team: Flowers, Neville, Pearce, Batty (McManaman), Scales, Unsworth, Platt, Beardsley (Gascoigne), Collymore (Sheringham), Shearer, Anderton.

England v Sweden. Elland Road, Thursday, 8 June 1995.
England 3, Sweden 3. Scorers: Sheringham, Platt, Anderton. Attendance: 32,008.

England Team: Flowers, Barton, Cooper, Pallister (Scales), Le Saux, Barnes (Gascoigne), Platt, Anderton, Beardsley (Barmby), Shearer, Sheringham.

England v Brazil. Wembley, Sunday, 11 June 1995.
England 1, Brazil 3. Scorer: Le Saux. Attendance: 67,318.

England Team: Flowers, Neville, Scales (Barton), Cooper, Pearce, Anderton, Platt, Le Saux, Batty (Gascoigne), Shearer, Sheringham (Collymore).

It was during England's first Umbro Cup match against Japan that I began to worry. Sitting in the press box on a June afternoon, I realised that this England team were poor, a team without passion, pride, ideas and the basic skills to beat the Japanese on their first visit to Wembley. I found it embarrassing and very annoying.

Then I looked at Terry Venables, at first making notes while sitting high in the main stand just below the press box, and then down on the bench surrounded by his men and the other members of the England squad. I wondered what was going through his mind. I wondered what was going through the minds of the people who employed him, Sir Bert Millichip, Graham Kelly and the others. If they were honest they would have been thinking the same as me. This is awful, terrible. What the hell is Venables playing at? This was the ninth game under his control and the reality was that England under Venables were no better off than when Graham Taylor was sacked. There was an argument that it was getting worse.

For the remainder of the game I looked hard. Very hard. But I could not see the work of the master tactician that the FA had employed or that the game had so desperately wanted. I had seen some embarrassing England performances over the years – a draw in Saudi Arabia, the shame of losing to the USA in Boston. But to be outplayed, outfought and then baited by the Japan players was too much. Their goalscorer Masami Ihara actually said: 'It was easy to play against England. In the European Championships other nations will find England easy if they play like this.'

Venables after the match was his usual self – on the outside strong, noncommital, evasive, unconvincing. But who knows what was going on behind the barrier, on the inside? It was something that remained a mystery. Through good and bad the attitude from him was the same.

I thought a lot about him as I drove home that Saturday night. I wondered if he got up on the stage at his West London nightclub and sang a solo at his beloved karaoke night. 'My Way', perhaps? I wondered if he really cared about the England job, what it meant to him. He had shown no remorse after the game. The fans were crying, the opposition were laughing, the critics (some) were beginning to question him, but Terry remained just the same 'Good old Terry'.

What will his reaction be if we win the European Championship? Or are humiliated? After a game when David Unsworth of Everton, Liverpool's John Scales and Stan Collymore, then of Forest and now Liverpool, made their debuts, I suggested that Venables should walk away from the job if he felt that England were going nowhere. After all, we had relied on a deflected goal from Spurs' Darren Anderton and a penalty from David Platt to save our embarrassment. It was not the result so much as the performance.

We had to wait until Tuesday in Leeds for the reaction. Surely, after reading some reports, particularly mine, he would at least get angry. The squad trained at a local sports complex and the players had their hands printed in cement for a local ceremony before Venables faced the press. One journalist produced the quote of the day when he watched the palms being pushed into cement and said: 'They should be used to having their fingerprints taken by now!'

Venables's reaction to the first 'heavy' press conference under his control was superb. It was the first time he had been questioned about his ability as a coach and here we were, sat in front of him and David Davies, the press executive, who always sits alongside the English coach at conferences. When Graham Taylor first took over it was always him and Lawrie McMenemy together facing the media and the music. Taylor changed that and went solo for the second half of his reign. I can never understand why Davies has to be there, other than to call a halt.

This time Venables was ready for a grilling but once again got off lightly with the first question. 'Any injuries?' Any injuries! Who cared, who bloody cared? I felt like weeping. Why do some journalists think so negatively? Here was a situation that called out for a rounded attack on the England coach. We reflect the fans, the man in the street who pays good money to see England play and all they had been talking about over the weekend was England's grim performance. Yet the press conference kicks off with 'Any injuries?'!

When we eventually got round to talking about the important subject of the day only two journalists seemed interested, Nigel Clarke of the *Daily Mirror* and myself. Nigel is a Venables fan but at least his news sense is intact. The others, on that day, were either intimidated by Venables, not bothered or just incapable of realising that they were sitting on a good interview. How the trade of covering England has changed over the years. National newspapers are going through a different era when deep experience or the ability to pull exclusive stories does not seem to mean everything to sports editors any more. Today we have young men, in their twenties and thirties, some who have never covered a World Cup, some who got the job without covering an England international, others who would not know what a 'big story' was, right in the front line. Some of those are intimidated by Venables's stature, others are too close to be able to criticise. One correspondent actually said to me: 'England are awful but I cannot be too critical because I cannot afford to fall out with Terry.' Why not? Why not ask what you are really thinking? Why not do the job properly? In the end you gain more respect.

Graham Taylor had more respect for those journalists who were up front and said what they felt rather than those who spent their time trying to keep in with the then England manager. In the end, of course, Taylor was an easy target as the entire nation turned against him.

I wonder what that correspondent's sports editor would say to the attitude that it is impossible to upset Venables? The results are often feeble, pathetic press conferences with Venables as he, and others for that matter, are let off the hook.

On this particular Tuesday lunchtime session Venables handled everything that Nigel and I threw at him so well. You had to admire his style as he refused to be bullied or beaten. It was a masterful display. Did you expect the criticism to start? I asked. 'Are you sure?' was the answer. 'Look back in the files and see what happened to other England managers.' Why can't we play? 'Wait until the European Championships.'

What happened to other managers was that they were bashed when things went wrong, praised when it was good (the same rules apply to Venables) and respected when it was all over. Yes, even Taylor. Robson was someone the nation and the media grew to admire and love. He was honest and open, his heart was on his sleeve and he took you inside his feelings. He never ducked one question that I can remember. Taylor went, with us shaking our heads in disbelief at some of the antics that he got up to. Like singing the line from the Buddy Holly hit 'Oh misery, misery, what's gonna become of me' the morning after England had surrendered a 2–0 World Cup qualifying lead to the Dutch at Wembley. Or the time he brought a huge alarm clock into a Saturday morning press conference because he had been criticised the previous Monday for only giving the media 25 minutes. Under Venables you are lucky to get ten. I can still see Taylor's face the morning after the defeat in Oslo by Norway which virtually ended our World Cup dream. He looked drawn, tired and shattered. A broken man. Yet he sat there giving his answers and not ducking the questions. He said he had failed. Whatever happens to Venables before he quits, I just do not see him allowing those kind of reactions to be made public.

The stories about Robson are famous and I take no shame in relaying now some of my favourites at this stage of the Venables story. It seems appropriate because under Robson and Taylor there were always light moments. England's media relationship under Venables is too often delivered with a scowl.

Robson took us to the semi-finals of the World Cup in 1990 and in the quarter-finals we met Cameroon in Naples. Cameroon were the surprise side of the tournament with their physical approach and exciting attacking football. England were first out of the dressing-room and were waiting at the top of the tunnel when Cameroon appeared. Out they came, huge men with bulging muscles, staring eyes, holding hands and making loud chanting, jungle noises. It was intimidating, even scary.

The noise made Robson appear from the England dressing-room and he walked slowly down the area between the teams. He stopped a few times, looking the Cameroon players in the eyes, shaking his head, putting his hand to his mouth and walking on. At the top he went to walk past, turned and in a booming voice shouted at his England team: 'Hey, fellas, that lot can't fucking play, look at them.' Brilliant! For 15 minutes Cameroon kicked lumps out of England.

A few days later as England prepared to meet Germany in the

semi-finals Robson sat down beside his skipper, Terry Butcher, at the side of the swimming pool at the team's hotel. He said: 'Butch, have you got a minute? I have been thinking about the Germans. It is the biggest game of all our lives. The country expects. Do you know how many people will be watching us back home on the box? Millions and millions and millions. What are your thoughts? How do you think we should approach it? What about the team?'

Butcher was honoured and began to tell the England manager who he thought should play and how. After a couple of minutes he turned to look at Robson for a reaction. He found the England boss fast asleep, eyes closed, mouth open and away with the fairies. Robson had not listened to a word. Butcher was so angry he took a running leap into the pool from 20 yards and soaked the unsuspecting England manager.

Before England played their first game Bryan Robson picked up an injury and was eventually to go home and take no part in the finals. His condition was not helped when the players, wanting a night out, bribed the security guards on duty with a few quid and went off into the town for some beers. They slipped back in the early hours and, as often happens, incidents occurred. One of the pranks found Bryan Robson tipping Paul Gascoigne out of bed and damaging his own toe in the process! As usual, manager Robson slept on. He did, however, get to hear about the boys' night out and wanted to know how the skipper came to be injured. He called a team meeting and demanded an explanation. The first hand up was that of Gascoigne. 'This should be interesting coming from you,' said Robson. 'Robbo did it on the bidet,' volunteered Gazza and the room fell about laughing. Meeting over and Bobby Robson, to this day, does not know how Bryan Robson's injury jinx struck again.

I could fill the chapter with more Robson stories. Like the time he organised a golf tournament for the players in America and boasted, 'I know this course like the back of my hand, I will win it,' only to be disqualified for playing on the wrong course. But they were completely as one, Robson and the players. After the 1990 semi-final defeat the German players could not believe it when they saw the England coach outside the dressing-rooms rocking to and fro with the sound of laughter and singing. The song as the team went off into the night was 'Blaydon Races' and leading the singing was Gazza and his manager. Great moments. Great, great memories.

Venables, of course, is close to his England players. They respect him as a coach and a man. Only time will tell if a true fondness will develop and that can only happen at a big tournament, a World Cup or European Championships.

They certainly did not look with him when we played Sweden in the second Umbro Cup tournament match at Elland Road. Before the game both Teddy Sheringham of Spurs and Venables had said that

England, under his control, were capable of becoming as good as Brazil. It was a bold statement and a difficult one to live up to.

He kept Colin Cooper at centre half and gave Warren Barton his debut at right back. Both players looked like novices while Sweden swept through England's defence as if it did not exist. We were 2–0 down after 36 minutes and left for dead within 23 seconds of the interval. Once again it was a shambles and Venables, the master coach, did not seem to know what to do. Also worrying for England was the form of goalkeeper, Tim Flowers of Blackburn. Playing because of injury to David Seaman of Arsenal, Flowers looked a bag of nerves and made vital mistakes. It was form he was to take into the 1995–96 season.

They say you have to be either 'lucky' or a 'winner' and the gods were on Venables's side that night. England scored two goals in the last minutes, Darren Anderton's lifesaver hitting both posts before going in with the final kick of the match. Relief? You could have cut it with a knife. Every picture tells a story and Venables's face said it all. He raised his arms as Anderton's shot crossed the line. Then he quickly disappeared down the tunnel.

Paul Gascoigne had come on as substitute for the second match running, this time after 63 minutes. He was not yet match fit and this Umbro tournament was a slow stepping-stone for Gazza before the real thing. Next season was going to be the biggest and most important of his life.

The one plus for England was the crowd and their reaction to being able to see an international on their doorstep. The Leeds public responded and it was an eye-opener for the FA who have considered taking England games out to the provinces for some time. There was more atmosphere inside one corner of Elland Road that day than in the whole of Wembley for the Japan game. I can never understand why the FA do not allow schoolkids or under-tens in for £1 when they know the crowd is going to be tiny. I said so after Japan and it was interesting that for the first match of the 1995–96 season, against Colombia, there were reductions for school parties.

The Umbro Cup went back to Wembley and Brazil on the Sunday afternoon. More humiliation. At least this time we were beaten by the world champions and that was no real surprise. Venables pushed Graeme Le Saux into midfield and he produced a stunning first goal for his country that put us ahead at half-time. Reality, though, soon reasserted itself. Brazil, inspired by their new Pele, midfield star Juninho, upped the pace and we were left for dead. Brazil scored three times in the second half to inflict England's worst result at home since 1972. It was also Venables's first defeat as England coach.

That tournament left us all heading for holidays and much-needed breaks with more questions than answers. The biggest, as always, is why can't we pass the ball, control it, be aware, see things, organise ourselves and be as skilful as the continentals? It is a question that has been raised since I first covered football at this level in the early 1970s. Let us go back to the grass-roots and teach the kids properly, they keep telling us. Well, two generations of kids have grown up and retired and still we are light years behind the best in the world. Perhaps Venables will give us the answers before he goes.

The Umbro Cup, however, left us with not one plus point. Not one. We ended still waiting for Gazza, while Cooper, Barton and Scales did not look like England internationals, Unsworth deserved another chance, Stuart Pearce looked past his sell-by date, Gary Neville showed he'd got a chance at this level, Alan Shearer had stopped scoring for his country and thank goodness for Mr Reliable, David Platt, and the exciting Anderton.

All gloom and doom? Not so if you listened to Venables at the end of the season. He said: 'I feel pleased. That is my opinion. I know a lot of people will not share it. We are on the right track. I never said that we would win the European Championships but I expect to do well. We were good for an hour against Brazil and I am optimistic. I have to make it right on the night and I am optimistic that it will be. I am confident.'

It is not a confidence shared by the masses. At the end of the season Venables's record, from ten meaningless friendlies, reads won five, drawn four, lost one, for 16, against eight. It was not a great record but Venables has the finals to hide behind. 'Judge me next June, in a year's time,' he said. We had to wait. We had to believe him. He has achieved miracles before and if he could turn this lot into European Champions then it would represent his greatest achievement. Much bigger than winning the Spanish Championship with Barcelona. Much bigger than winning the FA Cup with Spurs. Much bigger than taking on Alan Sugar.

And through it all Venables did not give away one secret. At the end of the season no one had a clue as to his best team, how he wanted to play or, more significantly, what was going on inside his head. Was he enjoying it, what was his best team, did he know? We had to wait and hope.

TWELVE

The First Sign of Strain

England v Colombia. Wembley, 6 September 1995.
England 0, Colombia 0. Attendance: 20,038.

England Squad: Seaman, Flowers, Jones, G. Neville, Adams, Howey, Pallister, Le Saux, Pearce, Barnes, McManaman, Redknapp, Platt, Lee, Batty, Gascoigne, Wise, Sheringham, Beardsley, Collymore, Salako, Shearer. Platt, Collymore and Pallister dropped out. Ruddock called up.
England Team: Seaman, Neville, Adams, Howey, Le Saux, McManaman, Redknapp (Barnes), Gascoigne (Lee), Wise, Shearer (Sheringham), Barnes.

Terry Venables looked straight at me and this time those famous eyebrows were not dancing. He snapped: 'I am not going to answer that question.' 'Why not?' I said. His answer was just as short and cutting. 'Why don't you make it up like you normally do?'

It was a pathetic attempt to avoid the issue of Matthew Le Tissier, and the first time in 21 months as England coach that he had dropped his guard. We had seen Venables avoid questions and play them back with a straight bat that Geoff Boycott would have been proud of. But never had he lost his cool. Certainly not in public.

It had been such a simple subject, such an obvious question. Bobby Gould had recently been appointed manager of Wales and expressed interest in Southampton's Le Tissier, the people's champion but a talent and a player Venables had yet to identify with. He had selected him seemingly reluctantly, and then discarded him and now was the opportunity for him to say, one way or the other, if he wanted him. It was a question the whole country was asking and I thought a perfectly reasonable one to confront Venables with, especially at an official England press conference. His reaction indicated to me that, for all the humour and confident outgoings, Venables was feeling the pressure of taking his country towards a major championship.

He then brought up three stories I had done the previous week and said that 'we' were not happy with them. Who is we? The FA? Terry and his mates? The players? 'I am not concerned about answering your questions,' he added. 'You can ask what you want and I will answer how I like.' He then went back to the original question about Le Tissier and said: 'I will not be talking to Le Tissier and neither I nor the FA will be trying to block him playing for another country. It is up to the player, he must decide what he wants to do.'

Venables, of course, still left the whole situation of Le Tissier up in the air. He could have left the door open, even slightly, by asking Le Tissier to wait and see how things progressed on the road to the European finals. Instead he kicked him out of his plans without actually being honest enough to say what he really felt about the player. Le Tissier, at this stage, had become Venables's Achilles' heel. All he had to admit was that he did not really fancy him as a player, wanted something different from the players in his side, and the matter would have been over and done with.

Poor Le Tissier's father rang a colleague of mine the next day in despair at what had happened. He admitted that they had given up on Matt ever playing again for his country. After flirting with playing football at the highest level, England was probably over – certainly under Venables – for a player most managers in the country would die for. Chelsea manager Glenn Hoddle, for instance, would have happily written out a cheque for £10 million for the player he wanted to build his side around. It will be interesting to see what he does when he names his first England squad after the European Championships as Venables's successor.

All this took place on the Monday lunchtime before the match against Colombia. The next morning Venables was faced with tabloid headlines such as 'Tiss Off to Wales' when they so easily could have read 'Tel Keeps Matt Waiting'. It was a poor piece of public relations and one that could have been avoided. It materialised later in the week that Venables had contacted Southampton chief executive Lawrie McMenemy to talk about Le Tissier. Would he have done it had there not been such a storm surrounding this particular situation? We will never know, although I doubt it. Venables was forced into a corner and had to get out of it.

Le Tissier too was forced into a corner. After his next game for Southampton, at home to Newcastle, he confirmed that he would not play for anyone else except England. He even said, not for the first time, 'I have nothing to prove to anyone. I believe I am one of the best players in the Premiership. I was shell-shocked when I was dropped after the game against the Republic of Ireland. When the England coach rang me I was too stunned to ask him, why? I just stood there open-mouthed with the telephone in my hand.' Le Tissier also said that he was worried about being known eventually as just another talented player who did not win the caps his skill deserved, like Alan Hudson, Tony Currie . . . the list is long. Isn't it strange how England managers have fought shy of some pure talent over the years?

At that stage Le Tissier could have had no idea exactly how the Venables snub would affect him. Towards the end of the season, however, he had lost the Southampton captaincy, being criticised by many for his lacklustre performances and had a string of 'Where do I go from here?' meetings with his manager Dave Merrington. I have to say that in the second half of the 1995–96 season I was disappointed with Le Tissier. He could and should have done more to prove Venables wrong. Instead he retreated into his shell and there was a lack of character about him. All he did was prove Venables right. Another challenge fell to Le Tissier at the start of 1996 season when Southampton employed the tough, no-nonsense Graeme Souness as their manager.

The first squad of a new season, especially one at the start of a European Championship season, is rather like the first squad named by a new England manager. There is expectancy in the air. It was no different when the media were called to the Park Court Hotel in Lancaster Gate on Tuesday, 29 August, for Venables's first offerings of the season.

Apart from the absence of Le Tissier there was no Paul Ince, who had been transferred from Manchester United to Inter Milan during the summer. Venables admitted that he had been disappointed with Ince dropping out of the Umbro Cup tournament at the end of the previous season. Ince withdrew after facing the ordeal of a three-day court case over allegations that he had struck a spectator during the infamous Eric Cantona karate kick brawl at Crystal Palace. I was in court for the last day when Ince was found not guilty and the relief, particularly for his wife Claire, was evident. It was understandable that he wanted a few days away after that rather than play football but it was probably more advisable to have reported first and then allowed Venables to release him. I just hoped that the England coach was not going to leave Ince out for too long because of a grudge.

Ince, for me, is our outstanding and most consistent midfield player. He has grown in stature, certainly on the pitch, over recent seasons. There is, however, a problem with his role in the side. Paul wants to be noticed all the time. It is no coincidence that his nickname is 'the Guv'nor' and that is how he likes to play, as the boss of the team. He does not like to be restricted and enjoys charging forward to attack as well as using his considerable talents and determination in midfield as a ball-winner. The problem arose because Venables wanted him to be the anchorman just in front of the back four and that was too restricting for Ince. It was certainly hard to imagine, and sad to see, an England squad at that stage with no Ince and Le Tissier. A European Championship squad without Ince just would not make sense.

There was also no Les Ferdinand of Newcastle, who had started the season so well with his new club, or Andy Cole, Manchester United's

£7 million man who was back in Premiership action following a shin splints operation. Ferdinand's exclusion caused a few raised eyebrows but it was only a few matches ago when most critics were saying that big Les may not have the heart for international football. He had dropped out of matches, particularly under Graham Taylor, when his country needed him most. I was not disappointed that Cole had not made it. I do not believe that he is international class.

Venables showed again how loyal he is to players he knows and likes by retaining Teddy Sheringham of Spurs. Is he blinkered in some area? Only time will tell. With only seven games planned before the Championships time is not on his side. The coach insisted, however, that he is perfectly placed in his own plans for June 1996. 'I am exactly where I want to be in my preparation,' he said, and there was not a flicker of doubt in his delivery.

There was one surprise in the 23-man squad and that was the recall of John Salako, the former Crystal Palace winger who had signed for Ron Atkinson at Coventry during the summer. It was Salako's first appearance since the days of Taylor and a serious Gazza-type knee operation. Venables explained that he had been interested in Salako throughout the previous season and been impressed with his start at Coventry. Salako himself admitted that he was surprised but revealed that for the first time since his operation he felt completely back to normal. That was encouraging and good news for Gascoigne, as he and Salako had had their first knee operation in the same year, 1991.

I just hoped that Salako was not to go the way of other one-cap wonders we had seen under Venables. Kevin Richardson, Barry Venison and Steve Bould had all played and been praised by the coach. When Bould arrived on the scene to play alongside his Arsenal team-mate Tony Adams, Venables had said: 'Age does not matter to me. Players like Bould and Richardson, who are around the 30-year mark, can easily be with me for the European Championships.' Oh no they can't, Terry. And oh no they weren't.

There was another strange happening in the squad although no one picked it up immediately. Venables had named 23 players when he usually goes for 20 or 22. Why 23? We were soon to discover. Skipper David Platt had apparently contacted Venables to explain that he needed an operation and asked Venables to name him in the squad rather than be left out and chased by the media before Arsenal played Nottingham Forest that same night. Venables agreed. But why did he not just say to Platt that the best thing to do was for Arsenal to issue a statement and leave him out? Players have been injured before. They have missed games before. Why did Platt think he was so different that it needed a guessing game? Later that night Platt scored a superb goal for Arsenal before his club manager Bruce Rioch announced that he was going into hospital on Thursday for an operation. It was a strange way of handling a simple situation.

So to Bisham again. This time the media had been issued with new passes, an accreditation badge on a label to be worn around the neck. They were to be worn at all times but, typically, half of the journalists forgot them on match night and had to reapply. Show me a bunch of journalists and I will show you disorganisation.

All eyes were on Gazza in training: his hair, his weight, his antics, his tricks and, oh yes, was it time for him to start a game for the first time since Venables's first game against Denmark back in March 1994? Hell, that seems such a long time ago. Gascoigne, not for the first time, holds the key for an England manager. With Gascoigne at his best England have a chance of glory. Without him, or with a half-fit Gazza, we become just another ordinary team. I had seen him play for 25 minutes in Cyprus for Glasgow Rangers in Europe and he did not look match fit. He needed games but it was not worth delaying his comeback any longer.

After the first day's training on Friday Venables said: 'Paul looks much fitter and better than when he arrived for the Umbro Cup. Over the next few days I will assess if he is ready to start an international.' Gascoigne's fitness is going to be the big question of the European Championship season. Will we ever see the player that dominated the 1990 World Cup and then a year later swept Spurs to the FA Cup final? It is one of the tragic stories for football and the next few months are going to make or break his career. On and off the pitch.

Once again the Premiership matches were postponed to help Venables in his build-up and to prepare the players expertly for the friendly international. I cannot see the point, however, in the players reporting on Thursday night, training Friday and Saturday and then being allowed home on Saturday afternoon. They then report back on Sunday night. Why not keep them for the entire six days, which is what the FA requested from the Premier League?

The system for the media at Bisham is for the journalists to request to speak to players and then sit down with the England coach to discuss injuries and other subjects. There are two problems here. One is that some players do not want to speak to the press, the other is that David Davies and his FA team often dictate whom THEY want us to speak to, and when. A classic example was on the Monday before the games when the request went in for Dennis Wise. 'No, you can have him tomorrow,' said Davies. Everyone presumed quite rightly that Wise was in the team and that he would be used as a pre-match interview. What threw everyone was that Gascoigne was paraded before the media on this particular day. Did that mean that he was not in the team?

There then followed an amusing conversation between Venables and Mike Parry, Davies's former number two, who was operating at his last international before returning to journalism with the Press Association. Parry told Venables that it would be better for Gascoigne to talk to the press on his own rather than sitting next to the coach. 'If that happens all he will say again is that you saved his career,' explained Parry. 'And what is wrong with that?' snapped Venables. The coach insisted on being in on the Gazza interview to 'inject some humour into the meeting'. Gascoigne is the only player who is treated with kid gloves by the FA and the only one that Venables sits 'in' with. Anyway, the humour soon disappeared when the conversation switched to Le Tissier.

I like Gascoigne. He is the best British player I have seen since George Best and beneath the surface he is a passionate man who just wants to play football for his country. I just wish people close to him would leave him alone to stand on his own two feet. Why do we treat him like a baby who cannot handle himself in public? He is 28 years old, for heaven's sake. If he goes on again about people hating him and giving him hell, or news reporters following his every move, I will scream. How does he think pop stars or movie giants cope? It is about time Gazza grew up. We are on his side and there is not one newspaperman in the country who does not admire him as a footballer. We are willing him to be successful again. We are desperate for him to be dancing around Wembley with the European Championship trophy in his hands. Can he live with the pressure that surrounds him?

Gascoigne admits that the outside pressure he lives with will only stop when he quits playing. 'I know that now,' he says. 'I have come to terms with it. While I am playing the Gazza thing will never end. Never. To me I have always been just a footballer, it is you lot who write all the other stuff. I thought my blond hair suited me, I liked myself in pink suits, it was only other people who drew attention to it. Man, I cannot go for a shit without someone wanting to know what colour it is.

'My ambition is to play as well as I did before. I know I can. The magic is coming back although it will take a couple of more months.' Gascoigne on this day wanted to talk and he would have opened up completely had Venables not been sitting on his arm. Gazza always gives the impression of someone who wants to be loved. If he could just relax a bit, accept that criticism is part and parcel of a footballer's life, he would enjoy himself much more. He should realise that the praise he has had outweighs the criticism by a long, long way.

There are times when it seems that Venables would rather the press were not in attendance. He has a chosen few journalists whom he likes; the rest of us are an irritation. David Davies does not always help. There are times when he is not strong enough to handle the England coach and make it known that the media have a huge part to play in football in this country.

On the Saturday before Colombia, Davies interrupted an interview with Tony Adams for no other reason than that Venables was in a hurry to get away. Then when Parry told Davies that the morning papers wanted to speak with the coach, Venables raised his eyebrows in an 'Oh no, not them as well?' statement. It was extraordinary behaviour and only kept the 'them and us' argument alive. How different it all is under Venables than the open house days of Bobby Robson and Graham Taylor. How Venables needs to be successful.

The two previous England managers were different people altogether, warmer, more open characters who put their hearts on their sleeve instead of hiding behind a cold mask. Terry tells you nothing; the other men sat and talked for hours about football, life and anything else that took their fancy. OK, they did not win anything. Robson took England to the World Cup semi-finals in 1990 and Taylor was a disaster, and that is the bottom line. Venables says that we must judge him only in June 1996 and, of course, he is right. That is what matters. If England are crowned European Champions then all will be forgotten and Venables will go down in history as only the second England manager to win something. The other, of course, is Sir Alf Ramsey.

There are interesting comparisons to be drawn between Venables and Ramsey. He talks about Sir Alf a lot and has modelled himself, it seems, on the 1966 World Cup winner. Ramsey did not like the press and only talked to them when he was forced to. There is the famous story of that day at Wembley in 1966 when three journalists approached Sir Alf after the victory over West Germany. Friends and supporters of Alf, they were elated and shouted, 'Alf, we won, we won.' Alf looked at them coldly and answered: 'What do you mean, *we* won?'

Then there was the time he stepped off a plane on a foreign visit and was greeted by flashing cameras and a TV crew. 'Sir Alf,' the interviewer said, 'welcome, welcome, we are going to take you straight to the studios where you can talk to the nation. We are going to treat you like royalty.' 'Oh no you fuckin' ain't,' came the clipped reply in Alf's best controlled English and then he got on the team coach with his players, leaving the media man stranded, open-mouthed and unhappy.

Ramsey's players, however, would not hear a word said against him. The late great Bobby Moore once told me: 'Alf was a players' manager, no one else's. He loved our company and we respected him as a bloke and manager.' Sir Bobby Charlton tells a lovely story about Ramsey. At the finish of a long end-of-season tour, involving three countries and five matches, Bobby sat down next to Alf at a banquet. 'How are you, Bobby?' Alf asked. 'I will be pleased to get home,' replied Charlton. 'Oh, I wish I hadn't brought you, then,' snarled Ramsey. But it did not stop Charlton respecting and liking his national manager. There was an aura about Sir Alf, a respect, an expectancy of success.

The same applies to Venables. Ask any England player or any player he has worked with and they will say that he is the best coach they have experienced. They feel confident in his company. They believe he is a winner and that, after all, is what matters to everyone.

I just wish more people in football would recognise the job the media have to do, or do for the sport. Take George Graham, a close friend of Venables and someone who has been influenced by the England coach. Before Graham was sacked as Arsenal manager for taking an illegal payment he treated the press with contempt. He was not co-operative in any way. At the start of the season he worked for BBC Radio Five as a match analyst and co-commentator and had the audacity before the first game he covered, Chelsea v Everton, to say on air that he now appreciated more the media's role in football and how much they contribute to football. What hypocrisy! Would he have said that had he still been a manager? No way. He only said it because he was then a media man. Radio Five were wrong to give him the job. He had been banned for a year world-wide for dragging football into the gutter and should have been kept on the outside until he had served his sentence. The BBC eventually admitted the error of their ways and dropped Graham.

Venables always names his team on a Tuesday for a Wednesday international and the one against Colombia brought a refreshing change and a breath of fresh air. With Rob Jones, Peter Beardsley, Gary Pallister and Darren Anderton, who would all have played, out with illness or injury, Venables turned to the kids. In came Jamie Redknapp for his first cap, and Nick Barmby of Middlesbrough and Steve McManaman of Liverpool started for the first time, with Newcastle's Steve Howey named in defence. Gazza too was back and thank heavens for that. There was also a place for Dennis Wise, the Chelsea player who had been recalled for the first time since being found guilty of assaulting a London taxi-driver outside Venables's club.

Venables said that it was a good time to throw in the kids and on Gazza he admitted that it was a great time to be able to select him again. This was, after all, the start of the most important season of Venables's career. He admitted that when I asked him if, after all he had achieved in the game as a manager and player, this was the biggest season for him. 'Yes, absolutely. There was just as much pressure on me in Barcelona but this has to be my most important season because the country is involved and it means so much to so many people.'

This was potentially the start of a rare interview from Venables. He was talking now like a person rather than a football manager.

Here was a pressure-cooker situation for him and he was ready to reveal what it meant to him as a person. He was relaxed and in the mood, a reporter's dream when the subject could be difficult and hard to prise open. He was just about to go on when he was interrupted by one of 'those' questions at a press conference that make you want to scream with frustration . . . 'Is Stuart Pearce fit?' . . . and the moment was lost, gone. Rob Shepherd, then of *Today,* tried to coax Venables back a few minutes later but the chance of a rare interesting message from the heart was over.

I still believe that most of the football writers in the country are scared of the England coach or, more significantly, scared of their relationship with him. It was interesting to note Venables's reaction to a story written by Joe Lovejoy of the *Sunday Times,* who had revealed that the coach had lost two stone on a champagne diet to fight off the risk of a possible heart problem. Tel thought it was a funny story and said: 'Blimey, do not put the mockers on me already.' I just wonder what Venables's and the FA's reaction would have been had a tabloid done the story with a back-page headline along the lines of 'Venables in heart scare'. They would have gone berserk with apologies demanded and the threat of legal action. As they say, funny old game, football.

Gascoigne's selection put 3,000 on the gate and saved the FA and Venables the embarrassment of playing in front of an all-time low Wembley crowd. If Gazza and a new black hairdo excited the crowd, it was a crazy Colombian goalkeeper who brought the house down. In the 22nd minute Rene Higuita saved a Jamie Redknapp cross-cum-shot with a forward flip when he jumped on to his hands and booted the ball away with his feet above his head. It was an astonishing piece of showmanship that even Gazza appreciated. 'I have never seen anything like it in my life,' he said.

There were those who said that the crazy Colombian and Gazza's new hairstyle took up more interest than the game itself. That was unfair because there were some encouraging things about this first game of the 1995–96 season. For a goalless draw it was entertaining and interesting. Alan Shearer, Gazza and Dennis Wise hit the woodwork and England so easily could have had the winning start to the season which means so much. At last there were really encouraging signs that the team and Venables knew what they were doing.

Redknapp and Gascoigne were my two outstanding players. Redknapp took to international football superbly. He did everything simply and kept his shape alongside Gascoigne. It was a debut that suddenly put pressure on the missing David Platt. Gascoigne does not yet have his old sharpness, but his passing, awareness and pure infectious enthusiasm make him a must now for every England team. Please God, let him stay clear of injury because he means everything to this England team. Please God, don't let him make a fool of himself off the field.

There were boos at the end but they were not warranted because, compared to the Umbro Cup performances against Japan, Sweden and Brazil, this was a display to build on rather than take apart. The one concern for Venables was our lack of goal power. This was our third 0–0 draw and under his 11-match reign we have scored only 17 goals. Significantly Alan Shearer has now not scored for seven matches. Venables said: 'The lack of goals does not worry me, nor does Shearer's blank run.'

It is hard to understand what worries the England coach. He remains the mystery man of English football. No one really knows what is going on inside his head. He says he knows what he is doing and that England are right up to schedule on the road to the Europeans. We have to believe him and hope that he is right.

Venables's record after 11 matches (not counting the abandoned game in Dublin) reads: won five, drawn five, lost one, goals for 16, against eight.

THIRTEEN

Another Norway Nightmare

Norway v England. Oslo, 10 November 1995.
Norway 0, England 0. Attendance: 20,006.

England Squad: Seaman, Walker, Neville, Jones, Adams, Howey,
Pallister, Pearce, Beresford, Redknapp, Gascoigne, Lee, Southgate,
McManaman, Stone, Wise, Barmby, Ferdinand, Sheringham, Shearer.
Gascoigne and Howey dropped out. Bould called in.
England Team: Seaman, Neville, Pearce, Pallister, Adams, Wise
(Stone), Redknapp, Lee, Shearer, Barmby (Sheringham),
McManaman.

A funny thing happened on the way to Oslo, Terry Venables's first
England match on foreign soil – or rather several 'funny things'.
There was a lively court issue, criticism from Norway manager Egil
Olsen and our own Kevin Keegan, a job offer from Inter Milan and
a denial from the Italians, then an offer of a new contract from
England, and condemnation from the FA for the treatment the
tabloids gave their coach after yet another boring draw.

Poor old Terry. Life is never dull when he is around. There is
always something going on, whether it is good or bad, clear-cut or
cloak and dagger. The Football Association knew what and who they
were taking on and the build-up and follow-up to Oslo emphasised all
that is good and bad about Venables – and certainly how mysterious
he can be.

It was the reaction to the dismal display from the heavy Sunday
newspapers that really staggered me. They spent three days in Oslo,
had Thursday to gather their thoughts, had a press conference with
Venables on the Friday morning and yet could only come up with an
attack on the tabloid treatment of the England coach. Not an original
thought in their heads, not a story either. Didn't they realise that
this was just the reaction Venables wanted? It deflected from the
truth.

The truth at this stage was that after 12 matches there are no
signs, yet, that he is getting it right. OK, I repeat, I want England
to win the European Championships and that is with Venables in

control. I have nothing against him, find his cheeky approach to the job often endearing but believe that behind the mask he knows that there are problems. If he was more honest with himself and the public then it would be easier to feel closer to him. But the players like him, respect him and believe that together they are on the right lines. That to them is all that matters. With eight months to go before England's first match in the European Championship finals we must hope they are right.

It is not often an England coach goes from the Park Court to the High Court on the day he announces his latest squad. But that is what happened to Venables on Monday, 2 October. The day of drama began at the Park Court Hotel, a middle-of-the-road establishment just down from the FA offices in Lancaster Gate. It was a noon kick-off with Venables in smiling, relaxed and confident mood. How does he do it? No one would have realised that in two hours a libel case called by Spurs vice-chairman Tony Berry was due to start. Yet here was Venables without a care in the world. He was later to say in Oslo: 'I find these outside distractions easy to brush off and handle.' Mind you, he has been coping with them all of his England career.

The squad brought in two more new names. Steve Stone, the Nottingham Forest midfield player, has been outstandingly consistent for two seasons. He was switched to a wide right player by Forest manager Frank Clark and has responded superbly. A bigger surprise was the promotion of Aston Villa's Gareth Southgate from nowhere into the senior squad. Southgate, an intelligent, mature footballer on and off the field, can play in defence or midfield. There was no John Salako of Coventry, discarded after one squad appearance, and Venables still kept Paul Ince waiting in Italy. Once again there were injuries to cope with – no Tim Flowers, Steve Howey, Graeme Le Saux, Darren Anderton, Peter Beardsley, David Platt and John Barnes.

Worse was to follow with the withdrawal of Paul Gascoigne after he suffered a thigh strain playing for Rangers. It was the cruellest blow of all to Venables. Gazza had been returning to his best form and was outstanding against Borussia Dortmund in the Champions League the previous week. Not another injury scare? We held our breath because Gascoigne is so important to England. But Venables and Rangers manager Walter Smith assured everyone that it was only a strain . . . it may be a strain to you but it is life and death to other people.

Venables surprised everyone by not calling a player in to replace Gazza. It was seen as the final insult to Matt Le Tissier at Southampton, especially when Venables said: 'Le Tissier could not do the job Gascoigne does for the team. Gazza gets from box to box.' It was a snub that angered Le Tissier's manager, Dave Merrington, who reacted with this comment: 'If Le Tissier is not in the best 19 players in the country then I know nothing about football. Of course he could fit into Gascoigne's role. Just ask him and he could do any role you wanted.'

So to the High Court in the Strand. The case was for allegations made by Venables in his autobiography against Berry and involved papers stolen from a former employee of Venables and used against him during the Spurs takeover. They were serious allegations and a two-week court case would have been damning and dangerous for the England coach. The last thing the Football Association needed was for their coach to stand in the witness box for two, perhaps three, days and have every detail of the Spurs war turned over in public. For a start it would almost certainly have meant Venables not being able to go to Oslo and that would have been a direct breach of his contract.

Two o'clock arrived with no start. There was a hubbub of activity in the corridor outside the court with both sides sending messages and requests for more time to Mr Justice Tucker. As the packed public gallery in court 14 and seven press box members waited, lawyers and barristers started to carry cardboard boxes full of information, papers and other relevant details into the court. The lawyers acting for Berry, including solicitor David Natali, dumped no less than 14 boxes of info at their feet. It was their ammunition and as one reporter mentioned: 'They would make interesting bedtime reading.'

Venables appeared in the corridor with his wife, Yvette, and was locked in deep conversation with his lawyers and those acting for Michael Joseph, the publishers of the book, and Associated Newspapers and the *Mail on Sunday,* who serialised the book and repeated the alleged libel.

Ted Buxton popped his head into the court to see what was happening. No doubt he reported back to his master that the only three football reporters in the press box were Neil Harman of the *Daily Mail*, the *Daily Mirror*'s Harry Harris and myself. I was staggered that no other newspapers were represented by a staff football reporter. After all, this was the biggest story since Venables took over. Oh well, more ammunition to my argument that tough, hard news reporting with England has never been so poor.

The 'off-pitch' wrangling went on for more than an hour before we were told that something was happening. There would be a trial with the jury being sworn in. Then that changed with information that the case would be over that day. Dramatic stuff and it was almost unreal to see the England coach, hands in pockets, talking to his men outside the court. How the Football Association let it get this far heaven only knows. Surely they could have done something to get it settled out of court?

Why Terry found himself in this situation is also questionable. I bumped into Berry in the gents toilet and he had just been told that it was all over and that he had won. Naturally, he was delighted. 'The last thing that I wanted was to go to court,' he said. 'An apology would have done a year ago.'

The Berry team got more than an apology. They got damages and full costs which came to around £500,000, a huge amount to pay for one paragraph in a book, and Berry, who got just £20,000 as his part of the settlement, said afterwards: 'It was not the money, it was the principle and the truth.

'The book made me out to be a crook and I was not having that. When I realised that Terry was not going to back down I thought to myself, "Sod it", and went for it. I never thought it would come to this. I am disappointed with Terry, disappointed that he did not end it a year ago with an apology and disappointed that he and I, who worked together at Spurs, should come to this. I also think he should have been in court when the apology was read out.

'The last thing he would have wanted was an eight-day or two-week court case. It could have damaged his job as England coach. Why the FA did not step in I will never know. Not once did they contact me and ask what it was all about. Not once. This has been going on for a year and yet we only heard late last Friday night that "they" were ready to do an out-of-court settlement. The only people who really benefit from these things are the lawyers. They are the fat cats from these kinds of cases.'

By the time that Berry had held a small press conference and left the High Court, Venables was long gone. He later made a statement saying that he was delighted that he had not been ordered to pay any money. I thought it was a strange comment considering that it was his book and, OK, Michael Joseph and Associated Newspapers, who had both paid him, footed the bill.

Later, in Oslo, Venables corrected me when I asked him about all the distractions along the way to the game. I mentioned there had been a court case and he quickly jumped in and said there had been no court case. He was right, of course, but it was splitting hairs because it had gone to the wire, both parties were either at or inside the court and a jury was sworn in. It was just yet another day in the life of this amazing character and another chapter of this incredible story.

It was certainly not the best preparation for a match that represented Venables's toughest test. Defeat in Oslo was unthinkable because it would throw up all the old comparisons with Graham Taylor's reign and the nightmare loss in Oslo he suffered in June 1993 when he got it hopelessly wrong.

There was no mention of the court case and Venables was in confident mood as he surveyed the media faces from the desk he sits at for all press conferences at Bisham Abbey. 'I already know my team,' he said. 'And how we are going to play.' He would not be drawn on whether it was time to look at someone else up front, especially as Alan Shearer had gone seven England matches without a goal. 'I am certainly not influenced because Shearer has not scored. I have said many times before that he is more than a goalscorer.'

Les Ferdinand was the centre of attraction. The Newcastle striker had started the season on fire, scoring goals at will. He made the right noises as he sat across the room from Alan Shearer, saying that he wanted to be the number one and insisting that he was not afraid of the big time, something that had been levelled at him when he dropped out of some important matches under Graham Taylor. 'I was injured,' said Ferdinand. 'I have never felt that playing for England was too big for me.' We should have realised, however, that Venables's earlier comments meant that Shearer would be retained and I have to say I agreed with him. Shearer is the best and there was no point in leaving him out.

The way Venables wanted to play was interesting. He is clearly fed up with continued reference to the Christmas tree formation, something he mentioned before his first game. It has followed him now to Norway, the very game that Taylor got wrong. God knows what we would have called Taylor's system in 1993 with two wing backs, Gary Pallister ordered to follow the towering Jostein Flo everywhere and the rest of the players not sure of their instructions. It was not a Christmas tree, more like a Christmas pudding.

It did not bother me what system Venables used just as long as we saw something taking shape and an England team to be proud of. Tactics, however, are his game and there is no question that at press conferences he would rather talk tactics and forget about the outside distractions. But sorry, Tel, life is not like that. The system, however, is bugging him. He said: 'At the beginning I said that I started with a formation and stuck with it for three matches. I can make minor changes and it looks different. I do not know what all the fuss is about. If a team attacks with three up and defends with five at the back, what is that?'

One thing that Venables was adamant about was the reaction of the nation as a whole and the media in particular if he tried to play like Jack Charlton's Republic of Ireland or Norway for that matter. He explained: 'They unashamedly hit 40-yard balls. There is nothing wrong with that. But if I did it, you would not tolerate it. It makes it an extra pressure to win with style. There is a slight arrogance in there somewhere. Maybe we should win first and decorate it later.' We all thought we knew what he meant.

It is easy to contradict yourself when you are England manager. Graham Taylor did from day to day, and dear old Bobby Robson was an expert. It is not surprising considering the number of words the England manager has to say during the course of one international.

I have to admit, though, that I thought Terry Venables would be too smart. On the road to Norway, however, there were two beauties that Robson would have been delighted with.

Before he flew out to Norway, Venables commented on FIFA's world-ranking list which saw England placed lower than they have ever been before. Venables dismissed it as a nonsense and said that it was misleading because England had not been playing competitive games and that was the reason. 'I take no notice of them,' he said. But then after the draw he kept going on about Norway being the sixth best team in the world. 'We should be proud that we have got a draw here and they are the sixth best team in the world, so I am informed.' Wrong, they were fourth best at the time. And it was still a strange comparison to make having described the list as unreliable.

He also demanded that his players be made aware that we could no longer think of the European Championships as the future. 'They are here and on us, we have to be able to deal with teams and get results. My head says experiment until Christmas but my heart says we want to win.' Yet, again after the game, he went back to the fact that it was just another step down the road to the finals in June 1996.

I also found Venables's handling of Neil Ruddock interesting. The big Liverpool defender was called up as a replacement for the injured Steve Howey. But after meeting up with him at the team's Bisham HQ Venables decided that Ruddock's personal problems would not allow him to keep his mind on the job. It had been well documented that Ruddock had left his wife (they are now back together) and was living with another lady. 'I told him to sort out his problems first and then get on with the game,' said Venables. 'When I got to the hotel Neil was on the phone and leaving him out was the conclusion we came to after discussing his situation.' You would think that a 'big boy' like Ruddock would be the first to be able to play for his country despite off-field problems. There have been hundreds of footballers who have carried on despite enormous personal, financial or professional pressures. The England coach, for heaven's sake, goes into every game looking over his shoulder.

Another big distraction came around the corner on the Sunday when Colin Malam, football correspondent of the *Sunday Telegraph,* who is writing a book with Venables, revealed that Terry had turned down a firm offer from Inter Milan three weeks before. Venables said of the approach, made while he was on holiday with his wife, 'I was approached and what the person said to me was for any money, would I be able to leave now and take over Milan?'.

'It was very flattering to be approached by such a big club, I have to admit, but I made it clear to Inter that I was under contract to the FA until the end of the European Championships next year and intended to see the job through. I happen to believe in loyalty and honouring contracts. The FA showed a lot of faith and courage when they appointed me as England coach at the start of 1994 and they have stuck by me through thick and thin ever since. So there was never any chance I would break my contract to take the Inter job.'

The approach, made by a representative of Massimo Moratti, the club's wealthy and pro-English new president, was said to have been made with the offer of a £1.5 million contract over three years, after tax. That was far, far more than Venables was earning at the FA, reported to be around £130,000 a year.

It was an issue that was to follow him to Oslo and back. Not once did he choose to reveal who the person was who made the offer, despite strong denials from Inter that they had offered Venables the job. The FA's reaction was typical. 'We know nothing about it so cannot comment,' said chief executive Graham Kelly just before the squad flew out to Oslo. The FA would not comment but it was to stir up three days of intense pressure on Venables. Was there an offer? Had he manufactured a tentative approach to take the heat off himself before a big game? Were the Italians playing games? Was there another motive behind Venables's revelations?

At a press conference just before the flight to Oslo he denied that he was to be interviewed for the job as the new technical director of English football or that his contract as England coach was to be discussed over the next few days. He did say, however, that he would like a meeting with Kelly before the European Championships to know where he stood on his future. 'It is no good coming out of the Championships with just a week left on my contract and not knowing,' he said. 'I would have thought that it made sense for me, and the FA, to know where we stood. I will say to you that I would like it discussed and sorted before the Europeans.'

I found it amazing that in the space of 24 hours Venables, who was still on trial as England coach as far as the media and public were concerned, had revealed a job offer and then spoken about a possible new contract. The bloke is either clever or lucky. England had still not played a competitive game under him and yet there were thoughts of a new deal. What happens if the FA give him a new contract and he mucks up during the European finals? What happens if he is offered the director of coaching job and then wins the finals? Do the FA reverse the decision and keep him as coach?

Suddenly it all looked messy, with the FA's David Davies trying to leave the path smooth for Oslo. He explained: 'A shortlist is being drawn up for the job as director of coaching, and also the exact job description. We are not naming names and cannot say whether Terry Venables is on that list. The decisions will be made by very senior members of the FA and there is unlikely to be a decision until early next year.'

You could not say the mood of the England camp was one of

confidence when the chartered plane left Luton Airport for Oslo. After all, the manager was the subject of a great deal of speculation and there were a lot of questions unanswered. They were to come to a head again on the Tuesday lunchtime at Venables's team selection press conference. When I asked him if now was the time to clear up the Milan situation he said no. When I said that the situation intrigued me he answered, 'I am sure it does.' He added: 'I must concentrate on the job in hand and that is what you would like me to do, yes, good. I am not in the slightest embarrassed by the fact that Milan have denied offering me the job. You always get two sides of the story. I can confirm that I was offered the job.'

It was here that *Sun* newspaper colleague John Sadler joined me in trying to push what was the biggest story of the week. Again I found it amazing that not one other newspaperman questioned Venables about the predicament he was in. Coming on the eve of the most important game of his career it was potentially a massive story, but they did not say a word. They were happy to write their back-page leads, as they had done the previous day when again saying nothing. I can only put it down to the fact that they do not know, or care. Sadler mentioned integrity and honesty and Venables said: 'You must draw your own conclusions, it normally does not stop you. Whether it is Brian or yourself trying to take me down a different road, I must concentrate on the job in hand. At the end of the day it is my decisions that are going to count and, as always, I am prepared to take criticism.' Not once did Venables lose his cool or drop his guard. Yet had he named the man who approached him in Spain three weeks earlier nothing would have flared, and there would certainly not have been another question mark over him at the start of his most significant game.

The team was as expected. Shearer was retained with Nick Barmby in the Peter Beardsley role. There was no Les Ferdinand and Venables had already come under pressure from Newcastle manager Kevin Keegan to chop down the Christmas tree and give more support to Shearer. Keegan's comments were strange because Newcastle play with a lone striker in Ferdinand, support him quickly, and if any club formation is like the Christmas tree then it is Newcastle's. Venables said that he would deal with Keegan's comments his way but did add that he found some of the comments in the build-up to the game amusing.

What a contrast to England's organised press conferences was the Norway open day held across Oslo at the Unileve Stadium. With England two players are allocated, not always the choice of the media but often controlled by David Davies and his assistants. A classic example was on the Monday when the press were told that the two players being made available were Robert Lee and Jamie Redknapp. That made sense. Lee was playing because of Gascoigne's injury and

Redknapp is a rising star and popular with all the press boys. Like his dad, Harry, at West Ham, Jamie has an East London approach to life, relaxed, witty and open. I wish there were more like him. Consequently offices were alerted that there would be a piece on Lee being written for Tuesday morning's papers.

When we arrived at Luton we were told that the choices were changed and that Bryan Robson, the Middlesbrough manager who had just signed Brazilian star Juninho, and his player Nick Barmby, would be holding a press conference instead. That was fine but why can't Lee and Redknapp be available as well? The FA had got it wrong again and a number of reporters had to insist on Lee's availability and then had to chase from a nearby hotel where Venables and Robson went to the airport lounge to grab a few words with Lee. It was an unnecessary cock-up.

It is still beyond me why players cannot be made available every day. Not all of them, but a few in a room with soft drinks, coffee and biscuits. The way the FA handle it brings out a definite 'them and us' situation. Please do not talk to me about players not wanting to talk. Those days are surely gone. Players today get so much good publicity, more exposure than at any time in their careers and it helps bring them rich rewards. Any player who then moans about a report that was unkind to him, I only have contempt for.

The Norway press conference was far more relaxed. Manager Egil Olsen held court in one corner and his players either stood or sat around chatting away to everyone and anyone. No blanks, no whispers, no 'you had better speak to the manager first', it was the way all press conferences should be stage-managed. Please take note, Davies of the FA. There was no platform with a little table on it where Davies and Venables sat together glowering down at the media men sitting before them.

One Norwegian player, Lars Bohenin, actually called a press conference himself because he wanted to react to comments made by Nottingham Forest manager Frank Clark following Bohenin's move to champions Blackburn. Can you imagine an England player holding his own press conference? What a panic there would be. Davies running around, the FA trying to find a room, some reporters not even invited – it would have to be cloak and dagger because that is the way it is with England. Sad but true. Doors are not always opened, there is secrecy, even though the FA should know by now that there is always a door and always someone willing to talk.

Olsen spoke of the English wanting revenge for the defeat two years ago when Venables warned his players about getting sucked into the Norway way of playing. 'They will want to suck us in and then hit us on the break,' he said. The England coach also threw down a challenge to his defenders. Show me that you enjoy defending under pressure, show me you can cope, he asked them.

The outcome was one of the most tedious and boring internationals I have ever seen and I have been watching England play for more than 25 years and seen over 250 England games. This was desperate stuff.

We have to give credit to the defence. Tony Adams was his usual domineering self, Stuart Pearce, on what everyone thought was borrowed time, fought to inspire but does not get forward enough at this level now, goalkeeper David Seaman made two outstanding saves and Gary Neville fought hard after a terrible first half. The midfield played so deep it was as if England were scared to cross the halfway line. Jamie Redknapp, usually so expressive with Liverpool, did not produce one telling pass all night, Robert Lee huffed and puffed without delivering, Dennis Wise was played out of position on the right and Steve McManaman never went past people as he does with his club. Oh, Gazza, where are you?

Up front Alan Shearer was alone again, naturally. He had just two chances all night and looked like a player who was getting fed up with the system he was being asked to spearhead. Shearer is class. The best centre forward in Europe. England are turning him into just another striker. Where is the Shearer who strikes fear into defences? Wrapped in shiny paper and stuck on top of the Christmas tree, that is where. I do agree with Venables that Shearer should not be left out, but give him back his identity, and his partner, Nick Barmby, a player Venables signed for Spurs, is clearly going all the way to the European finals and there can be no complaints about that. But Barmby too needs support and the right players around him.

After the game the mood was one of complete depression. OK, we had battled for a draw against a side we can no longer beat, but where was the entertainment, passion, fire in the belly and the signs that England under Venables are coming together? Venables had the audacity to say that it was a good performance and that he was pleased. Pleased! How could you be pleased? But he is the manager and we have to respect his judgement, views and the way England are heading towards Euro 96.

Newspapermen in the after-match press conference shook their heads and expressed the view of 'what a load of rubbish' or words to that effect. It goes without saying that none of them challenged Terry. He and I had an exchange of views about entertainment but once again the England coach had got off lightly.

On television they for once did not duck the issue. The BBC's Jimmy Hill said: 'Viewers at home must have been as bored as we were.' Alan Hansen was more analytical. 'Performance poor, balance not right, style alien to most of the players.' That summed up the country-wide feeling and what the punters back home said in the pubs and in their own living-rooms. Absolute rubbish. That is why I cannot understand the Sunday newspaper specialists who simply turned on the tabloids without an opinion of their own. It is an old and simple trick and Venables and David Davies must have been delighted.

Joe Lovejoy of the *Sunday Times* actually said that tabloids now had two reporters on England trips, one a Rottweiler, the other a lap-dog. I wonder where Joe puts himself? A Venables roadie, perhaps? On this trip he certainly had no opinion about England and instead hid behind what other newspapers had done. He also said that some journalists should know better in their handling of Venables and then fell into the same trap himself.

So it was not home sweet home when England returned in the early hours of Thursday morning to Luton Aiport. There was still one twist to come, however, with the news that Venables, FA chief executive Graham Kelly and chairman Sir Bert Millichip had met for a secret meeting in Oslo to discuss the coach's future. It was exactly what Venables had wanted although the meeting must have been called sooner than even he could have expected. The outcome was that the FA would be happy to have Venables on board as coach until after the World Cup in France in 1998. Millichip said: 'I have spoken to Terry Venables and we have discussed the Inter Milan situation. I now understand that there was some kind of offer made and that is now cleared up. We are happy with that and want Terry Venables to stay with us until after the 1988 World Cup.' It was a statement that shocked many people. Did Venables deserve an extension of his contract without playing a competitive game? I certainly do not think he did. Did he deserve a new contract after the way England had played and were progressing after 12 matches under his control? No he did not, in my opinion. But that was the situation as Venables disappeared into the night with his thoughts. He knew he had the FA on his side. He always had the players. Now he had to win over the public and the media – well, some of us, anyway.

The prospect was Switzerland at home next and then a run-in of Wembley matches all the way to the finals. I spoke with Venables the following Tuesday and he could not have been happier or friendlier. We discussed the England get-together that he had hoped to stage in European week but a number of players' unavailability had forced him to cancel. Then he said: 'Looking back on Oslo the outside distractions do not bother me. I have always been able to blank out the things that go on around me when I am involved with my football team. It has always been the same throughout my career. It is no good me being grumpy and bad-tempered because that would only rub off on the players. Anyway, I leave that for you lot.'

As I have said before, Terence Frederick Venables is an amazing bloke, and this is an amazing story. At this junction no one had an idea about the outcome. Perhaps not even Venables himself.

But, as he says, he has never worried about anything. It was Oslo, however, which proved to be the turning point of his England career. He discovered at a secret meeting that Millichip and Kelly wanted him long-term. But he was soon to learn that White and Scott did not agree.

FOURTEEN

Tel Under Pressure

England v Switzerland. Wembley, 15 May 1995.
England 3, Switzerland 1. Scorers: Pearce, Sheringham,
Stone. Attendance: 29,874.

England Squad: Seaman, Flowers, Neville, Jones, Pearce, Le Saux,
Adams, Pallister, Howey, Southgate, Platt, Gascoigne, Lee,
McManaman, Redknapp, Stone, Sinclair, Wise, Beardsley, Shearer,
Sheringham, Ferdinand. Jones withdrew. Walker called in.
England Team: Seaman, Neville, Adams, Pallister, Pearce, Lee,
Gascoigne, Redknapp (Stone), McManaman, Sheringham, Shearer.

It is 11.20 p.m., more than one and a half hours after England's
impressive performance, and there is a lot of activity down by the
banqueting area of Wembley. David Davies, the Football Association's
press executive, and his new assistant, Steve Double, are in deep
conversation with Nigel Clarke, chief sports writer of the *Daily
Mirror*. A few yards away, in another huddle, are Terry Venables and
Martin Samuel, my colleague on the *Sun* and one of the journalists
inside Venables's 'inner circle'.

What is the subject they are all talking about as the members of
the International Committee say their goodbyes to each other and
disappear into the night? No, not England's performance. No, not the
fact that England, at last, seem to have found something to be proud
of. No, not Steve Stone's superb performance, or Teddy Sheringham's
magnificent second goal. The subject that dominated their
conversation and the subject on most journalists' minds that night
was the latest revelations by the *Mirror* against Venables. The word
was out that there was more to come and the FA and its coach were
more worried about that than relaxing and enjoying an important
victory.

The man behind the stories – Venables insists there is a witchhunt
against him – is Harry Harris, the *Mirror*'s chief football writer.
Harris by now had finished his match report and had joined the
throng of people who accumulate in the corridor that runs behind the
banqueting hall. He was soon confronted by Ted Buxton. 'What the

fuck are you playing at, what's your game?' Buxton spat into Harris's face. There followed a fierce nose-to-nose exchange between Venables's closest friend and the 'enemy'. Not many people were aware of the confrontation going on as friends of the players, the players themselves and other hangers-on passed the angry couple on their way home.

That little series of events, I am afraid, sums up life with Venables on the way to the European finals. Intrigue, controversy, cloak and dagger, bad publicity and worry. Oh yes, and a few games of football. We used to write about the internationals, not any more. Politics, power struggles and sleaze are the names of the game.

The build-up to this Swiss game was full of more off-field distractions than any other game. It is amazing how Venables survives, how he keeps his cool, his public image, his sense of humour, the confidence of the FA, but he does. This time it began with another court case and more incredible accusations against him, then one national newspaper (the *Daily Mail*) reported that the International Committee were at last getting jumpy. The FA then gave their coach a massive vote of confidence and revealed how a year ago Venables called in the police because of the alleged witchhunt and conspiracy against him. He gave the police, I understand, seven names – people he believed were doing everything they could to dethrone him.

Venables believes that the court cases, the stories, the separate controversial issues, are all carefully planned to rubbish him in public. He believes it will carry on right until the European Championships. 'Isn't it an astonishing coincidence that these stories happen just before we play?' he said. 'I am glad you have noticed and if you can search for the truth and expose it, go ahead, Brian.' It was said with a huge smile on his face because here was Venables sitting in front of a press conference having once again to talk about other things than football. How many times has that happened? He said: 'Anyone with half a brain knows what is going on. There is a lot I want to say, a lot I will say but at the moment I have been advised that is not possible.

'I know what is going on. I know that certain people are artists at producing things that have nothing to do with court cases. And they always crop up just as England are playing. I have already said that it is a witchhunt.'

Behind Venables's anger and deep frustration this time were court allegations that he appeared to be behind bogus invoices to cover a £50,000 cash payment concerning the transfer to Spurs of England centre forward Teddy Sheringham from Nottingham Forest. There were also claims that Venables, then manager of Spurs, tried to rip off the club by asking an advertising company to overcharge his own club in return for reducing the bill to his nightclub. Venables, it was said, asked the company, Fugler and Fugler, to reduce the bill to Scribes, his London nightspot, and make up the difference by inflating Tottenham's bills.

It was also alleged that Venables's business partner, Eddie Ashby, demanded £50,000 in cash during the transfer of Sheringham. Jeffrey Fugler sued Scribes West for £20,000 which he claimed was owed to him from a marketing deal he arranged. In a witness statement produced as part of the evidence for the trial at Central London Court, Fugler alleged that Venables encouraged him to overcharge Spurs. He said that the meeting took place at Tottenham in August 1992, when Ashby asked him to overcharge the football club. 'I was shocked at this suggestion. I said that I would not even begin to consider this. I repeated my request for payment as promised by Venables.' Fugler also alleged that he heard Ashby demanding £50,000 in cash in connection with the £2.1 million transfer of Sheringham. He said: 'I remember this meeting for two other events. First, Ashby was asking for, and receiving, £50,000 in cash in connection with the transfer and purchase of Sheringham.

'Ashby showed me a number of invoices addressed to him so as to support his claim for £50,000. These were from different companies and yet covered the same transaction. There was no doubt in my mind from what Ashby was saying that these were all bogus.'

Fugler also alleged that former Chelsea star David Webb set up a marketing consultancy as a front for the transfer of two players. He said, 'The second event which upset me was that Ashby took a call from Venables who insisted that a Mr David Webb be paid that day his fee (in excess of £20,000) for marketing services. I was given to understand by Ashby that Mr Webb's marketing consultancy was actually something to do with the earlier sale of two players by Southend United Football Club to Tottenham.'

Fugler said that he was offered extra work with Tottenham to encourage him not to pursue the outstanding £20,000 from Scribes. 'The promise of extra work was the carrot on the stick but that work was never forthcoming,' he added. He said that he never saw any paperwork from Scribes West. 'They were very studious in avoiding that,' he added. These allegations were made in a witness statement filed with the court which the judge, Recorder Williams, certified for release to the press after David Sherborne, counsel for the *Daily Telegraph*, made a successful application initially opposed by Mr Venables's counsel.

Venables added bitterly: 'The *Daily Telegraph* got the statements before I had a chance to read them. No, I am not surprised they did.' The case was adjourned because of the judge's commitments and England's match with Switzerland. 'I will go in the witness box,' said Venables. 'I have no doubt that it will fall right on the day we play Portugal in December.' He was wrong, it was the day after.

Fugler's evidence and the consequent reaction from the *Daily Mail*, who devoted the back three pages of their Saturday edition to the crisis, prompted an extraordinary response from the FA. Davies, who earlier in the week had admitted that Venables was one of his few friends in football, was behind a statement that attacked the 'unproven, wild and anonymous' allegations. Davies revealed that the police were one year into investigating claims by Venables that he was the target of a smear campaign. A Scotland Yard spokesman confirmed the story. 'We can confirm that an allegation of conspiracy to pervert the course of justice was made to Chelsea police on 11 November 1994, against a number of individuals. The matter is being investigated. There have been no arrests and inquiries are continuing.'

Venables also demanded that the anonymous International Committee member, who had been quoted in the *Mail*, should 'speak up or shut up'. He said in the middle of training: 'If there is a guy talking he should come out and say something. No one has said anything to me about being unhappy. This is not helpful. I believe we are at the beginning of something good.'

Strong stuff. Amazing stuff. The FA could easily have chosen to ignore events but instead chose to hand Venables a vote of confidence. Davies was behind that and it is clear that his stature and responsibility has grown inside Lancaster Gate. At this stage I would say that he had become one of the most powerful voices on matters concerning England and football. I believe that Davies was helping to influence decisions. It has been an incredible climb in a short space of time for the former BBC news and sports man.

Inevitably, there was more to come. David Webb, now managing Brentford, was dismayed at having his name mentioned in court. It led to him writing to Graham Kelly, the FA's chief executive, demanding a full inquiry, and it developed into an astonishing situation involving the possibility of bugged phones, including mine!

On Monday, 13 November, two days before the game against Switzerland, I called Webb at his office at Brentford Football Club from my home. It was about 10.15 a.m. I had known Webb for many years and it was a discussion about the stories in the *Mirror* and his own thoughts about his name being mentioned in court. Webb was dismayed and distraught. He was furious that he was involved and we talked about the transfer deals he had done at Southend with Spurs when Venables was at White Hart Lane and about his friendship with the England coach and his relationship with Alan Sugar. Among the things he discussed was his wish that he could bring Venables and Sugar together and end the feud between them. 'I would like to be the man who brought peace,' he said. 'It would be good to handcuff them together and lock them in a room and tell them not to come out until all differences had been resolved.'

It was an interesting situation and I asked Webb if I could use the story. 'No problem,' he said. 'I would be happy for it to come out because this thing between them has gone on long enough.' About an hour and a half later I was watching the England players train at their Bisham Abbey HQ when my mobile phone rang. It was Alan Sugar. He was concerned about the story that I was going to run that day. He told me to be careful because it was a delicate situation. He knew exactly what I had discussed with Webb, even the handcuffs quote! It was unnerving and mysterious, but not the first time I had received such a phone call.

The previous season I had worked for a week on a story concerning John Fashanu and his involvement in an England international against Nigeria. In the end the *Sun* decided not to run the story and the text, although written, was killed. The decision not to use it was taken on a Thursday. That night Fashanu rang me at home out of the blue and asked me what I was doing running such a story. 'You do not know all the facts,' he said. I told him that the story had been killed and he went away happy. But how did Fashanu know what I was writing? How did Sugar know about my exact conversation with Webb only an hour after the conversation had taken place? You tell me. My sports editor, Paul Ridley, thought my phone at home might have been bugged. But I had it tested and there was no bug.

I like Alan Sugar. I have a lot of time for him. He is a ruthless businessman but someone who grows on you and you have to admire his determination to succeed. I have become friendly with him despite not really knowing him. He is not a man you get close to. It is still unnerving when one of the heavyweights of the football world rings you up and tells you he knows exactly what you are planning to do.

It led to more cloak and dagger situations. Webb's letter of complaint to Graham Kelly was passed on to David Dent of the Football League. Dent immediately contacted Webb at Brentford Football Club but failed with two phone calls to make contact. Webb eventually rang Dent back from his car phone, stopping in a bus lane to hold the conversation. Two days later that conversation was offered up to the highest bidder by someone who had taped the phone call. It was offered to the *Sun* and eventually bought by the *Mirror* for an alleged £1,000. One of the things Webb said in the conversation was that at one stage when Venables offered Webb a job with Spurs and then let him down he felt 'like chinning Venables'. That headline was splattered all over the *Mirror*.

Webb by now was looking over his shoulder every time he made a call or left his home. He contacted the police to complain that someone had bugged his car phone. He said: 'I have always been an open, honest bloke. Someone with nothing to hide. If I do not like you I will tell you, face to face, man to man.

'Now I am in the situation where I do not trust anyone. How can

Terry Venables at the High Court after his sacking by Spurs.

A rare picture of Terry Venables and Alan Sugar together after the sacking. They are in the West Ham directors' box. Tony Berry, who later won a court case against Venables, is on the right.

'Welcome Terry.' Venables' first press conference on the day he was appointed England coach. He is sitting next to FA chief executive Graham Kelly.

The first day in charge. Venables spreads his arms wide at Wembley.

'Hello Gazza.' Venables flew to Rome soon after his appointment to meet Paul Gascoigne.

Another legal case. Venables arrives at London County Court.

RIGHT:
Happiness is a win. England have just beaten Spain and it certainly shows on the faces of Terry Venables and Mike Kelly.

TOP:

Venables, Don Howe.

ABOVE:

The Wembley crowd: simply magnificent. They created the best atmosphere that Wembley has ever known.

RIGHT:

Alan Shearer, top scorer in the European Championships, turns away in delight after this third-minute header against Germany.

The moment England went out. Gareth Southgate's sudden-death penalty that was saved.

The last picture of Venables as England coach. He drives away from Bisham the morning after the defeat by Germany.

I? How would you feel if you had a private conversation and the next thing you know, three days later, it is splashed all over the back of the *Daily Mirror*? I have told the police that something is up. When I get up in the morning I look under the bed now, it has got that bad.

'I was even surprised that Kelly had handed my letter over to the Football League. I thought the clean-up committee was the Premier League and FA combined. I did not realise that it was the League too. I feel I am caught right in the middle of a situation that is very, very big. I have spoken to Terry and Alan Sugar since and tried to make some sense of it.

'It is affecting my life. I am trying to train and prepare a football team. But on the training pitch I keep seeing Harry Harris's face on the ball and I kick it as hard as I can. I'd like to kick it out of my life.'

All this, of course, happened in the build-up to an important England international. It was day four in Venables's preparation and we had had a court case, Venables revealing he had called in the police to investigate a witchhunt, an anonymous International Committee member saying that the FA were beginning to worry, a vote of confidence from the FA, bugged phones, Venables's business life dragged across the *Mirror*'s ongoing campaign and the manager himself asking questions of friends in corners of England's training camp.

The days of Graham Taylor seemed a million years away – the days of the turnip, press conference rows about football, his selections and performances. Terry once wrote a book called *They Used to Play on Grass*. Well, before he arrived we used to talk about football.

How ironic that in the middle of the build-up Taylor was sacked by, or parted company with, Wolves, the club he took control of after a long absence from the game following his exit from the England job. His reputation is damaged beyond repair now and there is no doubt in my mind that it was the England experience that was the undoing of Graham Taylor. He desperately wanted the job but was not up to it. But he is a smashing bloke who never once took the bitter personal criticism aimed at him to the stage where it damaged his relationship with the media. The *Sun* was perhaps harder on Taylor than anyone else but at the end when it was all over he wrote to me and his letter began: 'What am I doing writing to a *Sun* journalist?' A sense of humour to the end.

Taylor could have sued a number of papers throughout his career for things said and claimed against him. Not once did he write a letter in anger. How different the relationship is with Venables. He reacts to everything, no matter how big or small. I think he is wrong. The England job is bigger than anything else and criticism, personal and professional, is all part of the game. If every journalist reacted every time his boss screamed abuse at him then there would be no newspapers at all.

Somehow, in between all the aggravation off the pitch and the many things going on inside his head, Venables had to prepare a team for an important international. How he does it is beyond me.

There was still no Paul Ince, despite a flying visit by Venables to Milan to watch Ince and speak with the former United midfield star. A refreshing new name in the squad was Trevor Sinclair, Queens Park Rangers flying winger. David Platt, out for almost nine weeks with a cartilage operation returned, but the England coach would give him no guarantees on the Friday that he would play. 'If he does play he will be captain,' he said.

Sure enough there was no Platt when Venables eventually named his side. It was not a difficult decision because Platt was nowhere near his best at this stage. Venables also defended the poor international scoring run of Alan Shearer and said that he was not worried that the Blackburn striker had now gone eight games without a goal. 'You cannot compare his international record with his Premiership one,' he said. 'You must compare like with like and I am happy with him.'

There was an amusing incident on the Friday at Bisham when Venables revealed that he had given Paul Gascoigne permission to play for Glasgow Rangers against Aberdeen on the Saturday, and that Gazza would fly up to Glasgow on the Saturday lunchtime after training in the morning with England. Then a whispered conversation with some FA staff revealed that Gazza had misunderstood and was in fact on his way back to Scotland as Venables gave his Friday press briefing. The England coach had to quickly make a call on someone's mobile phone to make sure that Gascoigne stayed behind to complete England's Saturday preparation before leaving the party.

It was an extraordinary decision, anyway. What is the point in cancelling the Premiership programme if you let your most valuable player rush off to play for his club on Saturday afternoon? It backfired completely. Gazza got into on-pitch disciplinary trouble after a series of nasty incidents in the game and there were repercussions for Rangers and the player. It led to Gascoigne apologising to Venables on the Sunday night when he returned to England duty and holding his own press conference on the Monday morning. He explained the provocation he is under every time he plays for Rangers. 'They spit at me, do everything to provoke me,' he said. Gascoigne, of course, should be used to everything and anything at this stage of his career.

There were no surprises in Venables's side, apart from his continued loyalty to Teddy Sheringham. 'Loyalty does not come into it,' he insisted. 'I happen to believe that Teddy is one of the most intelligent footballers in the country. He can do both jobs for me up front, play as a main striker or in the withdrawn role. And he scores goals with either foot and his head.' It was a tribute that was to be proved one hundred per cent right in Sheringham's best game for England in an emphatic 3–1 victory. He scored a superb second goal with his head.

Venables was delighted and said, 'I know the country wants us to throw people forward and be exciting, beating sides 5–0. That does not happen any more. Everyone needs to be patient and yes, perhaps the crowd do need educating. One thing is sure. We try to be entertaining. We try.

'We certainly do not want to get everyone behind the ball like Norway. They are boring and you will never be able to throw that at us. You have to play for England with your head, not your heart. We still want to "go for it" but the secret is deciding when that time is right.

Tony Adams added: 'Good players can adapt. I played for years at Arsenal under George Graham and he liked a pressing game. Now Bruce Rioch does not like that so much, and so we adapt. Our main objective is to win but I would rather win the European Championships than any individual international.'

Adams spoke like the captain he is, a great leader of men and an inspiration from the moment he gets into the dressing-room. Venables chose Platt as his first captain but I wonder if deep down he reallly wanted Adams. The two players say that they do not care who it is who wears the armband at the start of the finals. 'As long as we are both there and he gets the winner in the final I do not care,' says Adams.

There was a rallying call from Venables on the eve of the game and you had to sympathise with his sentiments. 'I still believe the public are behind me,' he said. 'The fans do not take notice of all the other things going on, that is the message I get from the man in the street. He wants a winning England team. You cannot pull the wool over his eyes. He is saying to himself when he reads the other stuff, "Oh, for God's sake, let us get back to football"'.

'I believe they realise that all I want from this is a great England team and a triumph in the European Championships. Surely that is simple to understand. I get letters from the public who are disgusted at what is happening to me from the outside.

'I am enjoying this job as much as I did on the first day, despite what has happened. Despite what other people are trying to do behind my back. I am strong, I can cope. My job is to make sure that the players are not affected in any way.'

Adams and Platt both confirmed that the squad was right behind Venables. 'There is no question about that,' Adams said. 'All the players know what we are about and what is expected of us.'

Still, if any England manager needed a victory it was Venables against Switzerland on an autumn evening at Wembley. Thankfully, for him, he got it. England played well and came from behind with goals from Stuart Pearce, Teddy Sheringham and Steve Stone. Sheringham's contribution was significant in so far as it guaranteed his place in the finals squad, if it was not guaranteed before in the eyes of the coach, and Stone was not far behind him in the man-of-the-match display.

Stone, the little balding Geordie, is a bonus for Venables. He impressed in his brief appearance as substitute in Oslo and after replacing Jamie Redknapp in the opening minutes at Wembley produced a non-stop display that caught the imagination of the public. There are no thrills about Stone. He does not have the ability of Gascoigne, the vision of Redknapp or the pace of Darren Anderton, but he has a heart as big as a bucket and will work all day for his team-mates. It is just what England need.

The crowd was small and yet you sensed they were as relieved as the coach. They created a good atmosphere, and for the first time in a while Venables could smile and really enjoy the moment. He could go home and not look over his shoulder, though not for long.

Soon the headlines and the hysteria turned away from football once more. The *Daily Telegraph* revealed that the police inquiry into the alleged witchhunt was over and Venables immediately demanded that they continue their investigation. The *Sunday Express* ran a back-page story from Venables insisting that a vital document in the controversial Sheringham transfer had a forged signature on it. The *Daily Mirror* responded by giving three pages for two days to prove that Venables had signed the document and they even called in a handwriting expert to confirm it.

Are the public interested? Do they care? What would they rather read - more Venables baiting or a newspaper getting behind the England coach? It was an interesting situation for tabloid sports editors. My own view at this stage, with four matches plus a two-match tour left before the Championships began, was to let Venables get on with it. Nothing has been proved against him, the FA are still behind him, and he could well be forming a successful football team. When Venables was appointed the FA knew all about his controversial background. They knew that there would be embarrassing stories, conflict with Alan Sugar, doors opening that led to dark corners. FA chairman Sir Bert Millichip tried for months to bring Venables and Sugar together, and failed. The bottom line was that unless anything was proved, unless something happened that was so big that they had no alternative but to react, then they should let him get on with the football.

The reaction of the fans, I am sure, was to get even closer to Venables than they were in the first place. They are not interested in whether he can be a director or not, or that there is a witchhunt against him. I am not sure whether they are that interested in a Sheringham transfer deal or if it involved a bung, or who took it. What they want is a winner. The players too are right behind Venables. It meant that after another astonishing episode in his career as England coach, Venables emerged from the controversy in a stronger position than when he began the build-up to this Switzerland game.

FIFTEEN

From Wembley to the Witness Box

England v Portugal. Wembley, 12 December 1995.
England 1, Portugal 1. Scorer: Stone. Attendance: 28,592.

England Squad: Seaman, Flowers, Walker, Neville, Jones, Adams,
Howey, Southgate, Pearce, Le Saux, Stone, Lee, Wise, Redknapp,
Gascoigne, Platt, McManaman, Sinclair, Beardsley, Barmby,
Sheringham, Ferdinand, Shearer. Lee and Platt dropped out.
England Team: Seaman, Neville, Adams, Howey, Pearce (Le Saux),
Wise (McManaman), Gascoigne, Stone, Barmby, Ferdinand
(Beardsley), Shearer (Southgate).

Court Three at London's Central County Court is small and intimate.
It is about the size of an average living-room with two rows of chairs
at the back. There is one door in the corner which opens and shuts
regularly, even when evidence is being given. On this particular day
Court Three was full, and you could have cut the atmosphere with a
knife. Every one of the chairs was taken by media, witnesses and
friends. For this was a case which triggered special attention. It was
Wednesday, 13 December 1995, and the English coach Terry Venables
was giving evidence in a case involving his London club, Scribes
West.

What was he doing here? God knows. Did he really need this? The
England coach was standing in the witness box being cross-examined
by some unknown barrister who probably could not believe his luck.
It meant publicity. It was just the kind of case the Football
Association did not want. Just the kind of case they feared when they
gave him the job.

But Terence Frederick Venables is a proud Cockney, from the kind
of family who do not give up until right is proved right. For that we
have to give him great credit, but I could not help feeling as I sat
there watching and listening, that English football, Venables himself,
and certainly the image of the game did not need this court case.

The irony was that this one came just hours after his latest game,
a 1–1 draw with Portugal. At Wembley the night before he had
appeared as the public figure, good old Tel, friend of the players and

the people's choice. Here in court was a more vulnerable Venables, one I had not seen before. You are not usually allowed into the inner sanctum, but in Court Three on this particular day, he had no choice.

A few seats along from me sat Venables's business associate Eddie Ashby, his close friend and England scout, Ted Buxton and a surprise visitor, Jane Notage. She first appeared on the England circuit in Italy 1990 when she acted as interpreter for the England players at their headquarters and hotels around Italy. What was she doing in court? Was it just another Tel mystery? He has been criticised for the company he keeps and Notage was another surprise member of the Venables 'family'. It later materialised that Notage was writing a book with the England coach, a diary-type book which, strangely, came out long before the European Championships. Venables is also writing the history of English football with *Sunday Telegraph* football correspondent Colin Malam. Where does he get the time to do all these things?

When Venables entered the witness box two workmen outside the window behind Mr Recorder Williams's chair started doing something to the brickwork. They were completely oblivious to what was going on inside but their chatter, clattering of tools and moving ladders only added to the unreal atmosphere.

Venables had forgotten his glasses, made fun of the mistake and even borrowed a pair handed to him by Recorder Williams. 'Oh, good,' Mr Williams said, 'I will be able to auction them as the glasses worn by Terry Venables.' It was not the first time that Recorder Williams made light of the fact that the England coach was standing before him. There were other jokes, glances and smiles in Venables's direction and it was not difficult during the two hours of his evidence to believe that Recorder Williams was on the side of the England coach. I am not an experienced court reporter but I would have had a few bob on Venables winning when I left that night.

I even thought Venables would win despite the fact that he did not give a convincing performance when in the witness box. There were many times when he stumbled, others when he snapped at his interrogator. He tried to act as if he was still faced by football reporters, sitting behind his little desk at Bisham with press executive David Davies alongside him and holding his hand. But this was different, this was for real. You cannot make a mistake in court, every word is evidence, and I am not sure if Terry had done enough homework.

He tried to use the case to emphasise the alleged conspiracy against him and the lies he had to put up with. Under oath he attacked Harry Harris of the *Daily Mirror*, a journalist who has continually revealed the so-called shadier side of Venables's business dealings. Venables shouted in court: 'I am fed up with the lies that appear by Harry Harris in the *Daily Mirror* every day.' Harry, sitting next to me, did not flinch a muscle when he was mentioned. He was later to quip: 'If he had said that out of court I would have sued.'

Then came a huge mistake by Venables. When asked about the controversial Teddy Sheringham transfer he said that he did not know that Frank McLintock, the agent acting for Sheringham, had received a cash payment. He had signed a written statement saying that he did not know. He was asked three times and each time he said that he did not know. Venables was then asked to turn to his recent autobiography, a copy of which was in front of him, and examine what he said about the transfer. 'You will see, Mr Venables, that you talk about a cash payment made to McLintock at the time of the Sheringham transfer,' came the damning statement. You knew then that Venables had dug himself a big hole. His book said one thing, his statement another and all Terry could do was stumble, try to wriggle his way out. He admitted, as he looked over the top of his borrowed glasses: 'That part of my book is incorrect, my statement is correct.'

But there were no TV lights this time, no friendly journalists to giggle and laugh just to prove they were on his side. No David Davies. He was on his own and he had scored a horrible own goal. Perhaps it was this mistake that cost him the case.

In a funny way I felt sorry for him. I am a football man. I love the game and I protect it when I can. Sure, I will criticise and I have given Terry more stick than most, but I did not like to see him under this kind of pressure. The game did not need it, nor did he.

Before he stepped down and left the court, almost without turning back, Venables had his say. He told the court that he firmly believed that his enemies were trying to get him out of his job as England coach before the European Championships. He said that he had been turned, unjustly, into a shady character. Here, in my opinion, was another mistake. The phrase shady gave every headline writer a field day. Those who were anti-Venables just splashed the shady headline across their back pages. You could not criticise them and Venables this time only had himself to blame.

In court he said: 'My family and I have had to live with all this for two years. It is all innuendo. People will say that you cannot take his word for it because he is a shady character. That is so unfair.

'I defy anyone, from the Fraud Squad, DTI, Inland Revenue, to the Premier League, to prove anything against me. I have to live with the day-by-day lies. It just goes on and on and nothing comes out of it.

'People say I am paranoid but it is all done to make sure I am not around for the European Championships.'

Venables then linked Jeffrey Fugler and his old club Tottenham in the case. Scribes West were sued for £20,000 by Fugler for work he claimed his company did on the club's recruitment campaign. Scribes denied it and counter-claimed a similar amount, saying the recruitment flopped. Venables clearly believed that Fugler and Spurs were linked in some way. He added: 'I am suggesting that there is a link between Fugler and Tottenham because of the amount of information coming out of Tottenham.

'Unless he found it in the street, I do not know where he is getting it. He is not directly trying to stop us winning the Championships but he is trying to damage me and in turn that would damage England. There is a conspiracy. Mr Fugler is a strange little cameo. He wants money from me but he spends twice the amount pursuing the amount he says he is owed. I find that a very strange scenario.'

Venables also then revealed that his bosses at the FA examined the contents of the offices of his rival Alan Sugar. He said in court that there was never any chance of him and Sugar getting on but never in the two years that they worked together was there any complaint from Sugar about how Venables conducted transfer dealings. 'There was nothing said about the deals with Darren Anderton, Neil Ruddock, Dean Austin or Teddy Sheringham,' he said. 'Then afterwards we get all these allegations. I find it strange.'

It was even more strange for Terry the next day when his sworn evidence was condemned by the judge as 'rather wanton' and 'not entirely reliable, to put it at its most charitable'.

This was the most damning verdict yet on Venables. We had all read and seen the allegations against him made in newspapers and on television, but this was a judge questioning his reliability as a witness. Recorder Williams even said in his summing up: 'I reject the conspiracy allegation that has been put forward at this late stage.' There was also a condemning reference to Ashby, who had given evidence earlier in the case. Recorder Williams said that because of Ashby's evasiveness in giving answers he was going to treat a lot of what he said with 'more than a pinch of salt, more like a handful'.

The judge ordered that Fugler should receive half of what he asked for, £11,292.95, plus interest. Fugler was also told that he would only get half of the legal costs he asked for but the losing bill for Scribes West was still around £100,000.

The FA made their usual noises of being behind the England coach and asserting that court cases like this did not interfere with his job with the FA. It was a prepared statement that was beginning to sound hollow and even if 'cases like this' did not worry Sir Bert Millichip and Graham Kelly inside Lancaster Gate, they were worrying other members of the International Committee. Those members, led by Ian Stott of Oldham and Noel White of Liverpool – there were other faceless men who put the knife in but who refused to have blood on their hands – were soon to emerge.

Who would have thought that all this, followed by the draw for the European Championships to be made in Birmingham on the Sunday, should fall in international week? But that is life with Terry. It is never dull, often controversial and never, never predictable.

It had been business as usual before, during and after the Portugal game. Venables, at the selection press conference, admitted that he was coming down on the players he wanted to take with him into the European finals. 'The door is not closed, it is ajar,' he said. 'But players on the outside, like Paul Ince, will have to put pressure on the ones who are currently there.'

How the mighty fall. Ince, a few matches ago, looked certain to be a cornerstone in the England side and now, at this stage, was not even certain of his place in the final European Championship squad. Ince's reaction to his latest omission was to say from Milan that he did not think he would play for Venables again. It was a strong thing to say, and far too premature, for I could not see England starting in June without the former Manchester United midfield star. But along with Le Tissier, Ince became the second star name to announce that his days were over under Venables. The coach quite rightly refused to rule anyone out. I never expected Le Tissier to get in, but Ince was different. For two years before he went to Italy he was the outstanding midfield player in England. Venables has his own way of dealing with situations and I hoped that he was not carrying to its extreme his disappointment with Ince for missing the Umbro tournament in the summer. But he was adamant: 'I will do this job my way, with my players and how I want it. I will not be influenced by anyone.'

What the game did for us was to prove just how difficult it is going to be for England to win the European Championships. Portugal were a class act and you got the impression that, had this been a competitive match, they would have stepped on the gas and won. England, to their credit, are getting better and showing signs of improvement. It is not there yet but at last there are signals that Venables's way is beginning to rub off. It was the first time I had been slightly impressed, though it was important not to go overboard for these are only friendlies.

It was a critical match for Les Ferdinand, the big Newcastle striker who had been pushing for a spot all season with his goals at his new club. Venables chose Ferdinand alongside Alan Shearer in the twin spearhead that everyone wanted to see. Les made the usual pre-match noises about scoring and being full of confidence. International football is the gauge for all players at this level, however, and after watching him closely I am not sure whether Ferdinand is top quality. You would certainly not put him in front of Shearer. With it likely that Venables will only play one man up front, Ferdinand could find himself an odd man out. Right out of the squad even!

The key to Venables's eventual selection will be versatility, players who can cope with two or three positions. Gareth Southgate came on for the last few minutes against Portugal and looked very impressive.

He has grown in stature since moving from Crystal Palace to Aston Villa and is just as happy in defence or midfield. He can also play at full back. He looks certain to make the squad.

There was an interesting role for Paul Gascoigne. For the first time Venables gave him a new position, holding just in front of the back four. The coach said: 'He showed me he has the responsibility to hold a new position. I was pleased with Gazza.' There was praise too for Steve Stone, the Forest midfield player who has come crashing into the squad in the last two matches. Stone not only scored England's equaliser, he also produced a performance of hard work, support and a stream of crosses. 'He has got everything you are looking for,' said Venables. 'He worked his socks off for the team, and, believe me, international football is bloody hard work.

'It is hard work against teams like these because Portugal are top quality, right up there with Russia, Spain, Italy and Germany. I go out of 1995 pleased. Pleased with so many things. I feel the atmosphere inside the camp is just right, the players are responding. I believe we have won a great deal of respect back from the rest of the world. There are not many teams who will want to play us, and we have not been able to say that for some time. We are getting there.'

So to court. And so to defeat. Embarrassment. Humiliation. Plus the usual backing from the FA. After hearing the verdict from the judge, Venables said: 'I am disappointed at today's result. However, I feel significantly vindicated in that the claim was almost halved. I wish this to be an example that I will not yield to such disgraceful tactics. Never.' And he meant it.

That determination, that feeling against the people he believed to be his enemies, was to follow him out of the England job. Venables in court had told us of hate, victimisation and a conspiracy against him. He would clearly not allow anyone to get away with it without a fight.

The next day he resigned as England coach.

He told Graham Kelly, the FA's chief executive, at a secret meeting in Birmingham where they were for the Euro draw, that he would not be continuing after the European Championships. Kelly asked him to think again and managed to put the final decision on hold until after Christmas and a short holiday that Venables was taking.

But his mind was made up. This proud Cockney was determined to clear his name. He was determined to go back to court and hunt out the enemy. I just wonder if his two-hour experience in that small Court Three had finally persuaded him to go on with his battle for the truth, even if it meant leaving behind his dream of leading England to the World Cup.

I have started . . . so I will finish.

106

SIXTEEN

Tel Resigns

It had just gone midnight when Charles Woodhouse, top lawyer with the Queen's solicitors, Farer and Farer, gave up the fight. He was tired and getting nowhere. The clock told him that it was now Tuesday, 9 January, and time had run out. Arch rivals Terry Venables and Alan Sugar would not reach a compromise. It was an impossible situation. Woodhouse, the Football Association's paid mediator, had failed. He had tried but he had found that Venables and Sugar were two headstrong, determined characters and neither was prepared to give in if the other one wouldn't.

This night had been his last attempt at bringing peace. The FA had employed him to prevent the war between Venables and Sugar raging on and ending in the courtroom. Both rivals had just returned home from their Christmas holiday. They were refreshed, tanned and in relaxed mood. They were not relaxed enough, however, to give Woodhouse what he wanted.

The three men, who had met, spoken and exchanged letters, faxes and memos many times, went their separate ways. Sugar got on with his life as chairman and owner of Amstrad and Spurs, Woodhouse went home and Venables, a few hours later, officially resigned as England coach.

Here lies one of the many mysteries that followed Venables through the quite incredible story that was his England career. After quitting he blamed the lack of support from within the FA's International Committee. He said that if they were wobbling now what would they be like when it became hotter in the autumn when a series of court cases began? The FA's chief executive Graham Kelly blamed the dispute with Sugar for England losing their coach. He made that clear in a conversation I had with him the day after Venables resigned.

But what would have happened if Woodhouse had succeeded in his eleventh-hour attempt to bring peace? And what did peace mean? A hand shake, no court case, what? Did Venables take part in those late discussions believing that they would change his mind about going? He later made it clear that he had confirmed his feelings on his holiday. And, if there had been no Sugar court case, there were certainly others.

Once again we were left with so many twists and turns and not knowing which door to enter. Did Venables know something else?

The bottom line is that he had made up his mind to go. The hard facts are that he did have an ongoing dispute with Sugar and there were a series of court cases pending. But, with Kelly and retiring FA chairman Sir Bert Millichip firmly on his side, were they really big enough reasons to quit as England coach?

It seems incredible to me that the nation can lose the people's choice, and the man the top brass liked and wanted, over a row. The Sugar dispute was unfortunate, embarrassing and a pain in the backside to the FA, but the people who mattered stood firm and the professionals out 'there' in the Premiership, and the fans, were still behind Venables.

The dispute, clearly, is all about money and pride. Venables is suing Sugar for wrongful dismissal and told Woodhouse many times that unless he got paid for being sacked there was no deal. Sugar refused to pay him, especially after Venables had turned down his initial money offer to go, and there was never any compromise. Sugar is also suing Venables for libel following stories in his autobiography.

But if Venables had said to Kelly that he wanted to continue and said that it was possible despite his court cases, there is no doubt in my mind that the FA would have told him to carry on and offered him a new two-year deal. It was Venables who decided that the court cases were going to be too much, not the FA. The FA, I believe, would even have allowed their coach time off to try and clear his name, even if it had meant Venables's staff taking training, or even matches in the early build-up to the World Cup, in the autumn of 1996 while Venables was in court. I certainly cannot take Venables's claim seriously that lack of support within the 15-man International Committee forced him out. That does not wash. There were men, notably Liverpool director Noel White and Oldham chairman Ian Stott, who made it known publicly that they were worried about Venables's off-pitch profile, but do you really resign if you have the boss's support but not that of the man in the background? I do not think so.

Anyway, who are these 'old farts' – as Gary Lineker called them – to force an England coach out? When Venables resigned these were the International Committee members: Noel White, 66, director of Liverpool; Ray Beveridge, 63, property developer and FA vice-president; Arthur Clark, 75, Northern League chairman and retired civil engineer; John Davey, 71, Sussex FA president and haulage contractor; David Dein, 50, Arsenal vice-chairman; Doug Ellis, 72, Aston Villa chairman; Frank Hannah, 71, retired engineer and Manchester FA chairman; Ray Kiddell, 59, Norfolk FA president and retired insurance manager; Gordon McKeag, 68, Football League representative and solicitor; Ian Stott, 61, Oldham chairman; Peter Swales, 62, FA vice-president and former Manchester City chairman; Charlie Thomas, 87, Durham FA chairman and retired labour relations; Chris Wilcox, 78, vice-chairman and retired administrator; Jack Wiseman, 78, Football League representative and Birmingham vice-president; Keith Wiseman, 50, solicitor and Southampton vice-chairman.

Every one of these men would have discussed Venables at some stage. They either liked him and wanted him or could not stand him. Some of these men thought he was an embarrassment, others thought to hell with that, he is the best man for the job. Yet only two came clean. Stott and White. Why?

I have always felt that if you believe something, say it. I thought that the FA took a massive gamble on Venables in the first place and for months and months I could not understand what on earth he was trying to achieve. The best coach in football? You had to be joking. Then came an improvement, signs that he knew where we were heading. Venables and I will never be close friends but you can still admire someone who is good at their job. I work with people I would not invite around my dinner table, but that does not mean I do not appreciate what they do as journalists. The same goes for football. It is just crazy, and so typical of English football, that we lose a coach over a committee who are not sure what they want, plus a row with an enemy that has been going on for years.

But Venables was adamant. If the committee were not behind him he was off. He first told Graham Kelly that he was to quit after the European Championships on the very weekend that the English FA staged the draw for the finals in Birmingham. Venables told Kelly on Saturday, 16 December, after Kelly had been to watch Aston Villa against Coventry and got back to his hotel late because he was unable to get a cab and had to hitch a lift with some local supporters. Venables was waiting and the two men went to the England coach's room. Venables had been concerned for some time that all was not well behind him in the FA and his thoughts were not helped by comments from Noel White in the morning papers.

Kelly was stunned. He was so determined to keep his man that he called for a meeting the following morning and the meeting would include Noel White. Kelly was ready to get the truth out into the open once and for all. Sunday, 17 December, therefore, will go down as one of the most significant days in the history of English football,.

As football dignitaries from all over Europe began waking for breakfast, Venables strode confidently and purposefully into Birmingham's Hyatt Regency Hotel. He smiled, signed a couple of autographs and then took the lift to the 18th floor. It was a ride that was to change the direction of English football yet again. Waiting inside the Jackson suite were Kelly and Sir Bert Millichip. Kelly, tall and slimmer than he had been for years after a strict diet, and Millichip, the retiring chairman who had changed his mind about the man entering the room. Millichip had once said that Venables would get the job 'over my dead body' but now he was determined to retire with Venables still in control. He once said to me: 'I made a mistake with Venables. At the start I did not really understand him. But he has won me over with his wit, charm and football knowledge. I am so impressed how popular he is with supporters.'

There was one more man in the room. A grey-haired man, with glasses and rather shabbily dressed. Kelly stood straight, Millichip welcomed Venables while the third man was edgy and uncomfortable. He knew what was coming and he was plucking up all his courage to say what he wanted to say. This was Noel White, the Liverpool director, and the man who, it is claimed, pushed Venables over the edge.

There were no niceties from Venables. He strode straight over to White and demanded to know to his face whether the International Committee wanted him to continue as England coach after the European Championships, with long time-consuming legal battles with Alan Sugar looming. White knew that this was the moment – one of the worst in his career. He stood his ground and told Venables that, no, he could not give him that guarantee. That was all Venables wanted to hear. He had feared what was coming and minutes later confirmed to Kelly that he was quitting. Kelly asked him to reconsider and think about it over the Christmas holiday. Venables said that he would but he had made up his mind and would not be turning back.

Venables, Kelly, Millichip and White then had to keep a secret. A big secret. With hundreds of journalists from all over Europe gathered for the draw it was an explosive situation for them. Had it come out on that Sunday that Venables was quitting it would have completely wrecked the draw, which they had been stage-managing for months.

Venables was interviewed live on TV by David Davies, passing comments on the draw against Scotland, Switzerland and Holland. He then gave an official press conference before slipping upstairs into a tiny room at Birmingham's Conference Centre to meet the English media. There were about ten of us in the room, with Venables at the head of the table. We sipped coffee and tea and chatted away for about 20 minutes. All the time Kelly stood at the back of the room, listening to every word. At the time I thought it was strange. Kelly never attends Venables's football press conferences yet here he was glued to every word. Now we know why.

What a story we were sitting on top of. And no one knew. If only, if only . . . how many times have we asked ourselves that question over the years?

The secret was held until the day after the final meeting between Woodhouse, Sugar and Venables. Whether the outcome of that meeting would have changed Venables's mind we will never know. On the morning of Wednesday, 10 January, three newspapers, the *Sun*, *Daily Mail* and *Daily Star*, had broken the story that Venables was ready to quit. Martin Samuel, Rob Shepherd and Lee Clayton had met Venables at his Scribes West club following his return from holiday early on the Tuesday evening. They had chatted briefly and it emerged that Venables was thinking of quitting. They wanted to write the story and had to persuade Venables that the timing was right. He was unhappy and took a lot of persuading. Eventually it was agreed and the four of them went off to Highbury for the Coca-Cola Cup quarter-final between Arsenal and Newcastle.

Shepherd of the *Mail* had finished filing before the others and Samuel and Clayton told him to go with Venables in the car provided by ITV, for whom Venables was doing expert commentary at the game. The next morning the *Mail* carried a picture of Shepherd and Venables together in the car as if the *Mail* was the only one close to the story. A good try, fellas, but a bit of an old trick.

Kelly and David Davies broke the official news that Venables was to quit after the European Championships at a news briefing at London's Royal Lancaster Hotel at 4 p.m. on the Wednesday. Davies read out a statement and then Kelly answered questions. It was a 20-minute briefing that was to trigger days, weeks and months of debate.

Kelly is quite clear in his mind that the Sugar row is to blame. He told me: 'At the start the chairman, Sir Bert Millichip, and I spoke to both parties and tried to bring them together. Then the FA called in a mediator and he spent many meetings and phone calls attempting to bring peace. But he was trying to perform a miracle. The gap was too wide. Terry told me that there was a lot of mileage in the Sugar thing yet and that he had to go to concentrate on clearing his name. It is sad but there it is.'

Venables himself puts the blame elsewhere. He says: 'Certain committee members got wobbly. I know it is going to get a lot hotter. If certain people got nervous over innocuous cases I could see problems when it got hotter. So with the wobbly element, plus the court cases, I decided to go.

'They are big court cases, two with Mr Sugar, a big case against the *Daily Mirror* and two against the BBC and *Panorama*. It is going to be heavy work. I will defend them vigorously and I will not be doing anything except seeing them through.

'I am not going to answer the question about what would have happened had I got one hundred per cent backing from the International Committee. Because I did not get it and so it is not worth considering.

'Funnily enough I found dealing with the problems easy. I always have been able to put football aside and cope with other pressures. And all this had happened over three days in court and two small cases. But an allusion of problems was built up by certain people and one newspaper in particular. They had world exclusives every day and yet not one other paper followed them up. Strange, that.

'It is a sad day for me because I loved being England manager. I loved it and it was something that I always wanted. But I had no option. I must clear my name and it was a decision, given all the circumstances, I had to make.

'There are no ifs or buts and no turning back. I am going after the European Championships. I certainly do not have another job lined up. It is probably an embarrassment to the FA but by announcing this now it gives them time to find a new man. The reality is that when England are playing important qualifying games for the World Cup in the autumn I will be in court with Sugar.

'I know Graham Kelly was disappointed. I have not given him the answers he wanted but I told him how I felt and he understands my point of view. He has been very good throughout, just as Bert Millichip has. I have been impressed with their attitude but obviously I was aware that not everyone at the FA felt the same way about me and what the future should be.

'I was made aware of that because of some of the things I was reading in the papers. Some people may question my loyalty but I do not see that as an issue. I am contracted to do a job and will do it to the best of my ability. If anything, the future is clearer. I am in even better shape mentally to get on with the European Championships. All my energies are for that now. I just want to be left to get on with it. Me, the staff and my players.'

One man who refuses to take any blame for Venables's decision is Ian Stott, the Oldham chairman. He had voiced his concern, even ordering the FA not to hand Venables a new contract when the coach was talking over his future with Kelly. 'What is the rush and what is the procedure of deciding that we need to give him a new contract?' Stott said. Then when the decision to quit was out he added: 'Do not blame me, or the International Committee. I just cannot believe that Venables has gone because he did not have the full one hundred per cent support of the committee. Who gets one hundred per cent support from a group of men?

'Tony Blair will go into the next election confident of winning but not with one hundred per cent support of the Labour Party. John Major certainly does not have the full support of the Conservatives. So that argument just does not wash. I said before that Terry Venables was the best coach for the job, and still do. The only reservations I had were the wisdom of giving him a new contract so soon. It was an opinion, that is all. I see no grounds in that for the England coach to resign.'

But resign he did. His announcement came almost two years to the day after he stood at Wembley when he was appointed, his arms opened wide in a 'here I am' gesture. There were some of us who did not think it would last a season and the sad reality is that, under Terry, the end could have come at any stage. The drip, drip, drip of controversy had seen to that.

If his reasons to go were really just to clear his name then you have to say that he did the honourable thing. But I still cannot believe that he would walk out of a job he loved doing because of a few old farts on the International Committee and a row with Alan Sugar, which the FA were well aware of when they appointed him. Indeed, Sir Bert Millichip had managed to reschedule the first court case with Sugar, the libel against Venables's autobiography, from the spring of 1996 to the autumn, so what was the difference? I cannot help feeling that there is or was or will be something else. Kelly and Millichip wanted him and yet he walked.

He quit having weathered the storm. The court cases were still on the horizon but the public were bored with the sleaze – they wanted a successful England team and they wanted Venables. Even Alan Sugar admitted that he had a gut feeling that Venables would still remain in control once the dust had settled. Did he know something? 'No,' he insisted. 'I just have this feeling that Venables will not quit after all.'

Whichever way you looked at it, it was another fine mess the English FA found themselves in. It happens so many times it cannot be a coincidence. They sacked Sir Alf Ramsey, unashamedly and without feeling, after he had won the World Cup, and not once did they ask him to return and use his experience. They had no idea that Don Revie was negotiating with the Arabs midway through a tour, they allowed Bobby Robson to announce that he was quitting 'because I no longer have a job' two days before the squad left for the 1990 World Cup in Italy, and they got it wrong with Graham Taylor. Then they failed to sack him when it was clear he was not up to it.

So we must not be surprised that Venables told them that he was going on the very day that we staged the European Championship draw. Deep down it was what Sir Bert Millichip feared. I caught up with him at his Birmingham home and he was in a terrible state. 'It is always problems, problems,' he said. 'I just cannot concentrate on anything at the moment. We have to appoint a new coach, a director of coaching and we are a few months away from staging a major championship.'

Poor old Sir Bert. He so desperately wanted to bow out with harmony and happiness reigning at Lancaster Gate. Deep down he too blamed the row with Sugar. He had been trying desperately to end the war and wrote to both men, spoke with them on the phone many times and almost pleaded with them to stop fighting. Here are extracts from a letter he sent to them both in August 1995.

'Over the past two years I have observed with increasing sadness and frustration your continuing feud. Its origins are well documented. The depth of its bitterness is all too apparent. The publicity it continues to generate must be an irritation and often an embarrassment to both of you.

'It is of course a private matter but because of the high profile of the game we serve it is a public matter too. Those who thrive on denigrating football have unquestionably found a source of energy in your problems. The game itself can be the only definite loser if this continues.

'And so, for football's sake, the time has come to say enough is enough.

'You are likely to be aware of some of the efforts that have been made to find outside agencies that might help. Those efforts can continue, but they need your encouragement. And they need at very least a joint declaration that both of you want a solution and will seek to end the public sniping, whatever its source, forthwith.

'I urge you as well to meet together as soon as possible to make a sincere effort to resolve your differences for the sake of football. Ultimately only you can find a solution. It cannot be one-sided though. Both of you surely must be prepared to make concessions bearing in mind each other's circumstances.

'I will certainly play my part in any reasonable initiative that either of you believe will further the chances of achieving the solution. The alternative in the High Court is all too obvious and painful.'

The response was a lot of talk and no action. The only public concession we were made aware of was Alan Sugar relaxing the ban he had imposed on Venables at White Hart Lane. But the England coach, certainly right up until the day he resigned, had never taken up the new invitation.

Was Venables being headstrong? I think so. He could certainly look back and see things that would have kept him in the England job, probably for many years. If he had taken the pay-off offered by Sugar there would have been no aggro. But that would have meant swallowing his pride and we are talking here about a proud man who fights his corner. And had he not written that autobiography he would not be facing Sugar in a libel case.

I appreciate that these are more 'if onlys', but they are certainly questions that Kelly and Millichip asked themselves a million times. Millichip certainly was frustrated, annoyed and a little bitter at losing Venables after months of being persuaded that he was the right man for the job.

It left the country even more behind Venables, the FA looking for a successor yet again and Venables himself homing in on the

European finals. There is no doubt in my mind that, in a macabre way, his shock exit would help England. We like nothing better than a man beaten into submission. We pick them up, knock them about a bit and then feel sorry for them. With people like Venables, we eventually get right behind him.

What happens to Venables if he loses every court case, two with Sugar, two with the BBC and two with the *Daily Mirror*? They are big expensive cases. He would be bankrupt, his reputation in tatters after weeks of dirty mud-slinging across the courtrooms of London. I really hope he knows what he is doing.

So who takes over? Bryan Robson was the obvious candidate. Venables had said straightaway that he wanted to groom his successor and he had pencilled Robson in as the obvious man. The FA insisted that this time there would be continuity and the new coach would come from the hard work that Venables and his team had done over the two years. But the Middlesbrough manager soon admitted that the job had probably come too soon for him and he made it clear that he did not want it. So too did Kevin Keegan at Newcastle, Gerry Francis of Spurs and Ray Wilkins of QPR. Significantly, Glenn Hoddle of Chelsea, when asked, refused to comment.

Alan Ball, still as passionate and patriotic today as he was in 1966 as a World Cup winner, said that it was a job that scared off too many people. 'It should be a job that is treasured, the best job in the world, but it has been turned into a pot of aggro that no one wants. People are scared of it.' I cannot go along with that. Anyone asked to manage England should snatch Graham Kelly's hand off. Turn down your country? Are you sure? Those who said they did not want it were either kidding, or they had no bottle. Don't blame the media. If you cannot stand the heat, get out of the game. The higher you go the bigger and tougher it comes. But do not cry over the treatment you might receive before you have been given the job.

Kelly said that he did not believe any of the names who had said they did not want it. He thought the first man they approached would say 'yes, please'. I agreed with him. What is the point of being in management if you do not want to lead your country? Bobby Robson got more stick than anyone in the history of the job but listen to him: 'It is the greatest job in the world. Manager of your country. You do not turn down your country, do you? If they came to me now, at my age, and after all I went through, I would say yes. Why? Because I loved every minute of it, every minute. The excitement, the smell, the passion of the job and everything that went with it. The red, white and blue of England, the full house at Wembley . . . I could go on and on. When I die I will go with those memories, great memories, the memories of playing for and managing England.

'There are only a handful of us who can say we have done it, you know. Manager of England. You cannot get any higher than that.'

SEVENTEEN

How Does He Do It?

The ground-floor bar inside Wembley's banqueting hall was doing good business. A few yards away, behind the barriers, the officials from the Football Association and their Croatian colleagues were sitting down for a meal, while upstairs the players and their guests were winding down after England's goalless draw. The 'third' bar was scattered with old footballers, journalists, other officials from the FA and anyone else who could get their hands on one of the bits of cardboard you now need to enter the banqueting area.

Most people were sipping beer, others drank wine or water. One man stood out, however. Not because he was well known or had anything about him that made you want to look. But he had ordered champagne and stood sipping from his flute. It was a strange drink to have amid the after-match beers and conversations that follow any major sporting occasion. This man was Paul Kirby, an FA councillor, football lover, our representative for New Zealand and a Spurs supporter. Nothing wrong with that. No. But there he was sipping expensive champagne (no drinks at Wembley are cheap) and yet, at the time, he owed Terry Venables £50,000.

I found that strange; not that he owed Venables money, but that he could stand as bold as brass a few yards away from Venables and his followers and order champagne. It would have been almost acceptable had England played superbly and won well but they had not and yet here was Kirby almost gloating.

It was just another twist in the amazing double life of the England coach. Most men would find the strain of being coach to the national side enough to turn them grey. Venables also had a business to run, court cases to win, enemies to cope with and money to collect from men like Kirby. And that is the life he led throughout his two-and-a-half-year reign as England coach. I tried to find out some answers and how he did it from his solicitor, Nick Trainer, of John Bowden Trainer and Co, whose offices are in Tooks Court, just off Chancery Lane in London.

Trainer first met Venables in July 1993 after Terry had been sacked by Alan Sugar at Spurs. Venables had had a certain amount

116

of conflict with solicitors firm Fugler, who also had represented Spurs, and he approached Trainer after getting advice from friends and colleagues. Trainer was soon to realise that he was dealing with a man who had an enormous capacity to take things on board and deal with them without fuss – not one thing, but many, many problems. Trainer says: 'Terry is amazing at isolating problems. I have no idea how he manages to do it. Normally there is one client and one legal problem. Terry had and has various libel actions going on plus other cases. He also had to cope with the enormous publicity generated by the fact that he is who he is.

'What happened in the early days was that everyone jumped on the bandwagon. Other potential creditors looked, read and listened and thought to themselves, "I am not going to miss out on this." So they fired off their own writ. Everyone in the country knew of Terry Venables and knew what had happened to him at Spurs. Everyone had an opinion and there were a lot of people who thought it was too good an opportunity to miss in an attempt to make quick, easy money.

'I have to say that I have never been involved in a case, or cases, with so much publicity surrounding it. It is a big situation, a very big situation, and I cannot think of anyone other than Terry who would have had the capacity to deal with it. But deal with it he did and I give him so much credit.'

There was one big question, one huge issue, to discuss when the two men got together for the first time. What did Venables want to do? Fight the enemy? Trainer adds: 'Terry's option was to say to himself that he did not need all the aggravation and make a commercial decision. The cases against him were not true and out of order, but they were there. Or did he make a stand and take on everyone who came out of the woodwork? That is exactly what he did. And he is still fighting. Hard.'

Trainer says that the decision Venables made in the first weeks after they met, to fight and take on all-comers, was the biggest and bravest of all. Venables was out of work and vulnerable. But he chose to roll up his sleeves and not let people walk all over him. He refused to be beaten and that fight still exists.

'We believe that the decision he made at that time was vindicated by getting the England job,' explains Trainer. 'The FA examined everything, looked into all the corners and found nothing. They found nothing that prevented them giving the job to Terry.' Venables had made the right decision to fight, he was sure of that, although there was still something that nagged away at him. He believed that the public's attitude towards him was one of respect and that they liked him as England coach. But he felt that they also looked upon him as a wide boy and someone who pulled strokes. Trainer says: 'Terry's attitude was "Why should they feel like that?" and it upset him. He knew they were not the facts and that he should not have that kind of reputation. He also felt that people only thought other things about him because of what was claimed on the *Panorama* programmes and the business with Spurs.

'It upset him that he was welcomed as the right man for the England job but that it was coupled with a bitter frustration that the fans thought he was also a jack the lad. He was so convinced that this was wrong and so committed to proving it wrong, that he elected to invest so much of his time and money in going after the truth and clearing his name. You can only admire him for that.'

Here then is the core of this story, the heart of the book. A man happy with the respect he has as football coach, but not prepared to accept the other side of the public image. That image of 'Good old Tel, he has pulled a few strokes in his time' ate away at him and he went in search of what he believed to be right. It is the story of one man's crusade with the law of the land, one man's crusade in combining football with facts and the truth.

He had the world of football in his palms and yet threw it away to continue that campaign. It is a sad story. Will Terry live to regret the decision? I sincerely hope not. It is a brave thing to do and I am not sure how many other managers in football would have made the same choice to turn their lives upside down.

Trainer adds: 'Terry weighed up everything in his mind and obtaining the truth has carried him along. I have had to say to him, "You may be one hundred per cent confident but unless the cases settle out of court you are going to put yourself in the hands of a jury. It is their impression and, like everyone in similar circumstances, you are taking a risk."

'He knew from the outset that the cost of a libel case could be huge. Going to court costs money. Even if you win you usually only recover two-thirds of your costs.' Venables chose to take the risk, no – the gamble with his private and professional life. He put clearing his name before everything else. It was his driving force.

Trainer worked hard over the two years that Venables coached England against the backdrop of legal wrangling and controversial claims. He and Venables were convinced that by the time he went into the European Championships they already had enough evidence to win at least two of the libel cases, against the BBC and *Panorama* and the *Daily Mirror*. Venables's case against *Panorama* was helped dramatically by a front-page story in the *Mail on Sunday* newspaper on 7 April 1996. In their story the newspaper reported that Martin Bashir, the *Panorama* reporter who interviewed Princess Diana, faked private bank documents just weeks before the broadcast. In what looked like an amazing breach of BBC journalistic ethics, it was claimed that Bashir ordered a graphic designer working for a flagship current affairs programme to create two bank statements. One of the sheets, which were made to look like photocopies, purported to show that Alan Waller, former head of security for Diana's brother Earl Spencer, had received £4,000 from the News

International newspaper group. Waller has since claimed that both were faked. This was confirmed by his former business partner, Robert Harper, whose name was also on the statements purportedly from a Brighton Nat West branch.

There was another entry on the fake documents. The *Mail on Sunday* discovered that it referred to a firm called Penfolds Consultants, which had featured in an earlier *Panorama* programme by Bashir on the business dealings of Terry Venables. That programme referred on-screen to Penfolds. The company was the name of a business partnership run by the wife of former Spurs general manager Eddie Ashby, who worked at the club when Venables was manager and chief executive, and who is a close friend of the England coach. Ashby told the *Mail on Sunday*: 'I have no idea how my wife's business came to be on this bank statement. We have never heard of the people involved.'

Trainer was delighted with the *Mail on Sunday* story. It simply gave him more evidence, this time conclusive evidence, that would enable Venables to win his cases against the BBC and *Panorama*. He said: 'It amazes me that a programme of *Panorama*'s prominence should lend itself to the practice of fabricating documents. In the first programme they produced a document on screen claiming that Terry had sold assets belonging to Trans Atlantic Inns to Land Hurst Leasing to get the money he needed to buy Spurs shares. There was much more to it than *Panorama* knew or had evidence of.

'The only evidence they had was the document shown on screen. The *Mail on Sunday* have now proved that evidence to be fabrication, and that there was no such document. The BBC broke the law. All I ever wanted to do was prove that what they showed was not fact. We have asked to see the document many times and the BBC have always failed to do that.

'I do not believe that when, or if, the case ever goes to court they will be able to produce that document. I do not see how they can go to court because they are too discredited about what has happened. They do not have the evidence to back up their claim. I believe we have enough evidence on the other side to defeat their case. If it does go to court, however, then a jury will have to decide who is telling the truth.'

One case that Venables did win was against Kirby. Even then there was bitter frustration for the England coach. Trainer says: 'Before suing anyone you have to make a valid judgement about what they are going to be worth at the end of the case. We thought Kirby had the money but we also discovered that he had a history of county court judgements and the experience of dealing with cases like ours.'

When the first deadline passed after Venables's victory and Kirby had not paid the £50,000 owed to Venables, Trainer discovered two controversial and worrying developments. Kirby's wife told Trainer that her husband no longer lived at the address Trainer had for him, nor did he own the company he was said to have owned at the time of the case. These stories, true or false, left Venables furious and frustrated with the law of the land. He told Trainer: 'What is the point in taking someone to court, winning and proving your case, and then not getting what has been awarded to you? It does not make sense.'

Venables was delighted, of course, with the initial outcome. That in a way was more than half the battle for him, proving people were wrong and clearing his name, but he was damned if he was going to let anyone get away with not paying. Trainer and Venables had no option but to press to declare Kirby bankrupt.

Venables had one hundred per cent confidence and faith in Trainer. He left his solicitor to get on with handling the cases against him, and the ones he was bringing, and sometimes the two men did not talk for days. Trainer explains: 'It was another decision he had to make. How much could he delegate so he could shut things out of his mind while he got on with his football? I do a lot without him and then when decisions have to be made we talk or meet. He makes the decisions, does what he wants, and I go away and organise it. There is no question that he became more and more confident in what he did and how he handled things.

'The decision he made at the start was incredibly difficult. But I soon realised that it was the right one. He is a fighter and does not let go when he feels something is right. People are surprised by just how much he took on. They are also surprised at how much is thrown at him.

'There are not many men who have had all this thrown at them, and the publicity to go with it. Other people of course go through a lot but they do not read about themselves every day. There surely has never been a football story like it. I think it is so sad that he has had to resign as England coach.'

There was more good news for Venables just prior to the European Championships when Brian Fugler, the brother of Jeff, dropped a case against the England coach. It had been brought by Venables for negligence against Fugler, but on Friday, 10 May the two men issued a joint statement saying that there had been an amicable settlement. The costs to Venables were undisclosed, but it was another victory that helped clear his desk before the Championships. The decision was an enormous relief to Venables because the court hearing had been scheduled for 8 July, just a few days after the final at Wembley. It would have meant Venables combining coaching the England players and talking to Trainer about the forthcoming case. Venables no doubt would have coped, just as he has with so much in two incredible years, but it would not have been ideal.

It was just another twist in the tangled lifestyle of the England coach. One thing is certain: you are never surprised about developments when dealing with him. They will go on until Venables has finished with every case, until he has taken on every enemy, until he has left his last courtroom, until . . . until . . . until . . .

Until he can concentrate again only on football . . . will that day ever come? Not even he knows that.

EIGHTEEN

Countdown to Euro 96

England v Bulgaria. Wembley, 27 March 1996.
England 1, Bulgaria 0. Scorer: Ferdinand. Attendance:
29,708.

England Squad: Seaman, Walker, Flowers, Jones, Howey, Pearce, P.
Neville, Wright, Southgate, Ehiogu, G. Neville, Stone, Sinclair,
Redknapp, Gascoigne, Platt, Ince, Wise, Beardsley, Fowler, Shearer,
Ferdinand, Sheringham, Lee, McManaman, Barmby.
England Team: Seaman, G. Neville, Howey, Southgate, Pearce, Ince,
Stone, Gascoigne (Lee), McManaman, Sheringham (Platt), Ferdinand
(Fowler).

The European Championships are in sight now. This was the first
international of 1996 and you could immediately tell that Venables
was in the mood. As always it is hard to gauge exactly what is
happening behind the surface of the England coach but there were
tell-tale signs that the pressure button had been pressed inside him.
At his squad announcement, held this time at the Waldorf Hotel in
London's Aldwych, he spoke of the countdown beginning. Phrases like
'this is it' were used and he admitted that he was forming heartbreak
decisions in his mind. 'There are going to be some disappointed
players when I name my final squad,' he admitted. Venables, after
all, was closing in on the biggest examination of his career. Forget
court cases and vendettas, millions of eyes were about to be turned
on him. He knew that the European Championships represented the
biggest trial of his life, not legal wrangles with Alan Sugar, the *Daily
Mirror* and the BBC. If he got it wrong he would lose money, big
money. If he got it wrong at Wembley in three matches he would lose
his reputation as a football genius. I wonder which meant more to
him.

Could he do it? Could he pull off the greatest victory of all? 'I am
confident we can win the European Championships,' he said as he
prepared his players for Bulgaria.

Injuries forced him to introduce new faces. It was not ideal for his
planning but injuries have always been the bane of an England

coach's career and Venables has continually stressed that he is open to be surprised by late-comers. No one was more surprised to get in than Liverpool centre half Mark Wright, a reject at Anfield until this particular season but a player who had gained confidence and was now playing the best football of his career. 'Yes, I am surprised to be back with England,' he said. 'You never give up hope but you believe your chance has long gone.' It would have done had Tony Adams and Gary Pallister not been sidelined with worrying injuries. Wright last played for his country against Spain in 1992. Two years earlier he had been part of the defence which took us to the World Cup semi-finals in Italy. 'That game against Germany is my greatest memory of playing for my country,' he added. 'Perhaps there will be a new one. That is the glory of football: you never know what is going to happen.'

If Wright was the 'old' new face, Philip Neville, younger brother of Gary, was the fresh-faced arrival. He had only just broken into Manchester United's first team but had proved that he could handle the pressure and, like Gary, was a fine prospect. He also provided Venables with the cover he was looking for at left back now that Stuart Pearce was established to play in place of the injured Graeme Le Saux. Philip Neville was preferred to Julian Dicks, much to the frustration of everyone from East London. The West Ham defender had been tipped for a shock call-up because of his new impressive disciplinary record and the best form of his career. Venables knew that it would have been a controversial decision and a huge distraction for him so close to Euro 96. The media attention around one of football's so-called hard men would have been massive. Venables would never admit it but probably he let his head overrule his heart, just this once.

Robbie Fowler, the prolific Liverpool striker, was called up. There is no question that Fowler is good enough to force his way right through to the starting line-up and make the manager rethink, just like Geoff Hurst did in the 1966 World Cup. Fowler has instinct. He is a predator, a natural goalscorer, just like Jimmy Greaves, Gary Lineker and those men who sniffed out chances before a defender knew what was happening. He was born a goalscorer.

The loss of Adams meant one question had to be answered. Who would skipper the side? David Platt, who had lost the captaincy because of injury, was the obvious choice. But it was clear at the meeting in the Waldorf that Platt was struggling to figure too highly in Venables's thinking. For this particular match or beyond? My guess is that Platt will be lucky to be in the first European Championship match. A year ago that would have been unthinkable because of his goals and his all-action displays from midfield. His two cartilage operations have taken their toll, however. Platt has admitted that Arsenal have not seen the best of him and he has definitely lost the 'spark' that all great players need.

Venables also has a massive headache in selecting his midfield. The competition is strongest in this department. Paul Ince, back in favour and a must after his impressive performance in this game, is a certainty. Paul Gascoigne is another sure starter, then come Steve McManaman, Steve Stone, Dennis Wise, Robert Lee, Jamie Redknapp, Platt and Darren Anderton, if he is fit. Something and someone has to give. One or two of these will be in Venables's 'heartbroken' group.

When asked about Platt being skipper Venables said: 'Do you mean for this match? If he plays against Bulgaria he will be skipper.' I thought that was a giveaway. Platt had no chance of playing against Bulgaria and his place in the Euro side was in doubt. In the end, Stuart Pearce skippered against Bulgaria.

McManaman has grown in stature during the season. At Liverpool he has a free role, is the player that makes Roy Evans's side tick and clearly loves the responsibility. With England, however, he is pushed out wider on the left with a licence to come inside. It restricts him somewhat although Venables insists that McManaman has the freedom to do what he likes. There is an interesting theory here that McManaman and Gascoigne should not be in the same side, that they cannot function to their strengths. It was also interesting to see Gascoigne given a deeper, more holding midfield role against the Bulgarians. Was this a new role to allow McManaman more expression? Or was it a role that allowed Gazza to cope better with the pace of international football as he sought complete match fit recovery from his injuries?

Everyone wanted Fowler. But Venables decided no. He went again for his tried and trusted Teddy Sheringham although there was a surprise in that Les Ferdinand was given the chance to stake a claim because of a mystery injury to Alan Shearer. Venables said that Shearer was troubled by a niggling groin strain and when he announced his team said that it was best not to risk him.

So all eyes were on Ferdinand. They certainly were on the morning of the game when three newspapers, the *Sun*, the *Daily Star* and *Daily Mirror*, carried back-page stories quoting Ferdinand that Kevin Keegan had made a mistake in buying Faustino Asprilla and that Newcastle could have blown the championship race with Manchester United. This brought into play the whole situation of player interviews before and after the England matches. Ferdinand swore blind he did not say that Keegan had made a mistake. The Newcastle manager believed him and complained to the FA that they had to do more to protect players.

There is no question that Ferdinand gave the interview because it was taped and delivered by experienced journalists. The interpretation is what Ferdinand complained about and I have never seen him so angry as he was after the game, despite his winning goal. He turned on Martin Samuel of the *Sun* and Lee Clayton of the *Star* and hissed: 'Of course I am upset, what did you expect? Just don't talk to me, don't talk to me.' David Davies was involved and Ferdinand was consoled by his business advisers Jon and Phil Smith. The bottom line is that players must know what they feel, mean and want to say. Ferdinand is a smashing bloke, helpful, co-operative, but he should not get involved in questions if he does not want to give answers.

The match was not a classic but a win was important for Venables as he trod further along the path to June. Ferdinand's early goal, from Teddy Sheringham's magnificent pass, was the highlight. England threatened to run away with the game but could not convert their chances, particularly in the first half. Venables talked of killing teams off and for the first time was critical of his players. It was not heavy stuff but enough to make them know that when it matters they have to be more ruthless.

There is no question that in this game things emerged and a pattern took shape. He always said it would, and you have to agree that this man does know what he is talking about. That is not meant to sound disrespectful but there were times when I wondered if the job was too much for him. He still, of course, had to play a competitive match but that is no fault of his own.

So, at this stage, who are the players who can be pencilled in for the first European Championship game against Switzerland? Seaman, definitely, Adams, if fit, Pearce, now that Le Saux is out, Gary Neville, probably, definitely Paul Ince and Paul Gascoigne, McManaman, Anderton, if fit, Shearer and Sheringham. That does not leave much room for others and Venables says: 'I am not going to leave players out of the squad or my team because I do not rate them, it is simply because I do not have the numbers. There is going to be some top quality which will be disappointed.'

The progress made under Venables and the respect he has from his players makes his decision to quit all the more astonishing. In another book written by him, this time called *Venables' England* (why it was published before the Championships only he and his publishing company know), he criticises the FA for not doing enough to keep him.

'Money was not a factor, it was all about principle. Nothing else. I have no job lined up. I took over as coach because I wanted the job and I am leaving because nothing was done to make me stay. I could not understand it when it happened and I cannot understand it now.

'I had talked the future over with my wife and we had come to the conclusion that if you are the England coach you should see the job through to the World Cup. I am happy with the way the team is coming together and that, in another two years, we would be once again a great side.'

Once again Venables points the finger at Noel White, the Liverpool director who knifed him in public by saying that he did not deserve a new contract until after June 1996, and so carries the can for England losing their coach. Venables added: 'I felt strongly the FA should speak with one voice, though that seemed impossible to co-ordinate. When I eventually confronted White (in the hotel suite before the European Championship draw) I told him that I understood he had comments to make but why not make them to me in private.

'He then denied he had made the comments. I replied that it was then simple. I said that could he not issue a statement saying he had been misquoted and confirming that he had not said anything about me. Sir Bert Millichip agreed that a statement would be helpful but then White admitted he had said that "I will support Terry until 1996".

'This, of course, was different from saying nothing. What he meant was, he could not give me a new contract until after Euro 96. I said, "But that is what was quoted in the papers, so you did say it?"

'He replied, "But you have not had any competitive matches." I pointed out that I had been playing competitive matches all my life. I do not know any chairman who, if he valued his manager, would let him come to the end of his contract before renewing it. I added that he obviously had his doubts about me and the thing was to leave it.'

All this is very intriguing. When Venables quit in January 1996 the FA told us that the reason he was going was to clear his name in court later in the year, when the World Cup matches were under way. As I have said, Graham Kelly even gave me an interview saying that he blamed the situation with Alan Sugar for England losing their coach. Yet here was Venables clearly blaming Noel White and the lack of support for him. Had Noel White stood up firmly behind Terry and not gone public, would it have made a difference? We can only assume that it would have done. Had the FA offered him a new contract at Christmas time then, I presume, he would have signed it. But what about the court cases? They are still there. How would he have coped with coaching England and being in the dock at the same time? As I have said before . . . there are always more questions than answers.

At least it was clearer on the pitch. The team was winning although Bulgaria were nothing like what we will face in the Championships. A pattern was emerging and the players were confident. So was the coach. So where was the next twist in the saga coming from? There definitely would be one.

We did not have to wait long. The next game in fact.

NINETEEN

It Can Only Happen In England —
Football's Coming Home

As parties go it was small beer – a couple of bottles of champagne, some handshakes, slaps on the back and a few people feeling pleased with themselves. But it was a significant party. The group were gathered at 16 Lancaster Gate, London. They were in the smaller offices of the Football Association, just across the road from the main HQ of English football. The neat and tidy rooms became the nerve tank of Euro 96. On that particular night in November 1992 the English FA had just been told by UEFA that they had clinched the staging of the next European Championships, and the champagne had been popped.

Glen Kirton, the man who was to mastermind the whole operation, recalls: 'That night was like winning an election. There was relief, elation and people feeling pleased with themselves. We knew there was hard work to come but we were going to enjoy the moment. In fact, for the first two years we wondered what all the fuss was about. Then the closer the finals got the bigger the workload became.'

Staging the European Championships, the first major football tournament England had played hosts to since the triumphant World Cup in 1966, was significant for the future of our game. This was about prestige, nothing else, and certainly not money – the profit margin at the end of the finals was only around £2 million for the FA, nothing like the huge amounts the Americans made from the 1994 World Cup. It was not money the FA wanted. The men who run our football knew that England's credibility was on the line. Our recent past had been littered with on-field failure and off-field problems, such as hooliganism and our club ban from Europe following the Heysel disaster in 1985 when 39 people died. Here was the opportunity to get it right in a big way.

So how do you get to stage a major tournament? Simple. You apply. Just like you would for a job. Your application goes in and it is assessed, this time by UEFA. The country which, in their opinion, is best equipped, is chosen. Kirton, once the FA's press officer and then head of external affairs, explains: 'Every member country of UEFA is invited to apply. We made a decision early in 1991 to go for it. The English clubs had been reinstated to play in Europe and we felt that the time was right for England to stage another major tournament.

'We were ambitious. It was pre-Premier League days and we reached an agreement with the Football League to apply. In fact, after a series of meetings with them we decided to apply for both the European Championships in 1996 and the 1998 World Cup. We knew we would not get both but we wanted to prove that we were ready. This was discussed at the top level, the League's management committee and our executive committee. Trevor Phillips, the FA's commercial director (before he resigned) but then working for the League, and I were given the responsibility of making the application.'

Kirton and Phillips went to America to study their methods in applying for the World Cup in 1992. Kirton recalls: 'We milked their ideas and methods and brought home a lot of details.' There was a hiccup a few months later when the Premier League was formed and the FA broke away from the League. Because of that conflict it was agreed that the League should withdraw from the application. 'We at the FA still went ahead,' added Kirton. 'I produced a bid in conjunction with the clubs.'

At that stage the FA were still ambitiously bidding for both tournaments. Then in the autumn of 1991 Sir Bert Millichip discovered through his vast UEFA connections that it would be in our interest to pull out of the bidding for the World Cup. England were told that they would not get the World Cup and would even dilute France's chance if they continued. England made the decision to withdraw and another flying trip by Kirton, this time to France, ended with an agreement that both countries would support each other in their respective bids.

England's first application, delivered to UEFA in document form in November 1991, was made on the understanding that it was to be an eight-nation tournament. Portugal, Holland, Greece and Austria were the rivals. Then UEFA suddenly moved the goalposts and decided to upgrade the Championships to 16 nations. Kirton had to go back to the drawing board and add a supplement to the original document.

The UEFA executive decided at a meeting in Lisbon that it should be England and the news was broken to FA officials. The hard work and big expense – the FA had splashed out £770,000 on the presentation and a world-wide advertising campaign – had been worth while.

The countdown campaign had started at the Sweden Championships with a poster slogan of 'It Can Only Happen In England' delivered at all the major cities used. There was a full-page advertisement in *The European* newspaper and a complimentary copy of that newspaper sent to the members of the UEFA committee who would be making one of the biggest decisions in England's history. Kirton adds: 'By advertising out of our own country we felt it would hit people between the eyes.' There was also advertising done in England. A coupon, asking the public if they would like the European finals staged here, was placed

127

in football programmes and local newspapers and got 10,000 positive answers.

So, the slogan was right. It Can Only Happen In England. And it did. Kirton, who had been to four World Cups – two as press officer, one as an administrative officer for England and one as a FIFA press officer – was given a contract to mastermind the European Championships. 'It was my baby, down to me,' he said. 'It was my biggest project, my first real project and I looked forward to it so much.'

UEFA's executive committee had discussed their worry of hooliganism and giving the Championships to a nation with a history of crowd trouble. It was a concern for Kirton. There had been Heysel in 1985, the Hillsborough disaster in '89, and also the European Championships in Germany. Kirton believes that it was a match against Sweden in the autumn of 1988 that was the turning-point. He recalls: 'We had just come through a very tricky European Championships in Germany when there was a lot of hooliganism and it had been reported extensively, mainly on the news pages and on the news programmes back home. At the Sweden match there were again reports of violence but this time, when we got home, no one could find the proof. There were no pictures to back up what had been written.

'The TV news back home had gone over the top and Mrs Thatcher and the Sports Minister, Colin Moynihan, started to talk about ID cards for fans. But there was a big overreaction. No one liked ID cards but the government insisted. Then came Hillsborough and, sadly, it proved to people that ID cards, as football knew, would not work.

'For the European finals we, the FA, guaranteed security inside the stadiums and the government guaranteed it outside. They guaranteed the security of the country. That was part of our application. Hooliganism has been part of our football but times, things, moods have changed. We at the FA were relaxed and confident about going into the tournament.

'There is no question that there is a nasty element who will want to cause trouble. We and the police know who they are and precautions were taken. There was a police intelligence who worked closely with us right up to and through the Championships. The small element hell-bent on spoiling it for others like publicity and they saw the European Championships as the ideal vehicle for their plans. We had to make sure they were foiled.'

Next, for Kirton and the FA, came the choosing of the eight stadiums. Wembley was the obvious choice and England would play all of their opening games at the famous old stadium. The criteria laid down by UEFA was that all the stadiums had to have a minimum of 30,000 seats and that they were in eight different cities.

Wembley, effectively, ruled out Arsenal's Highbury home. The pitch at Highbury, in fact, is not big enough for the standards laid down by UEFA. The playing area for the European Championship has to be 115 x 75 yards and Arsenal's does not reach that requirement.

So the FA went to Manchester for Old Trafford, Birmingham and Villa Park, Liverpool and Anfield, Leeds's home at Elland Road, Newcastle's St James's Park and to Nottingham with the City Ground. The FA were initially worried about Forest. Their concern was that relegation, the arrival of a new manager after the exit of Brian Clough and money invested on new players would not leave enough cash to finish their stadium and bring it up to UEFA regulations. Forest, however, responded and took their place with the elite.

On Kirton's first day under contract he drew up a battle plan, a master project. He identified the areas which needed attention and decided that there were 15 main projects and 75 smaller situations. He started employing people, including four centre directors to look after the regions. He negotiated with outside agencies, dealt with media services, transport, hotels, design, travel, training grounds . . . this list grew and grew. At the FA there is a staff of 100 and at one stage they were all chipping in with work. 'It was definitely hands on,' said Kirton.

Only he and his secretary were full-time Euro 96 at the start. Then Adrian Titcombe, the FA's head of security, was employed as Kirton's assistant, and by the time the tournament started there were 100 full-time staff and 1,500 volunteers. No detail was left by Kirton. Brochures on 100 hotels, training grounds and travel were supplied for the 16 competing nations. Supporters — there were 250,000 of them from all over the world here in June — were advised that they could stay in five-star hotels, to hostels, to camping sites. They could come for one game or the whole tournament. Everything was catered for.

Such was Kirton's efficient organisation that by the end of February 1996 all competing nations had chosen their hotels and training grounds and a majority of the games were sold out, including all of England's group matches, and the other games in our section.

Kirton was determined not just to make the Championships a money-spinning venture. He adds: 'In 1994 the Americans made a huge amount of money from their World Cup. They set themselves up by taking a big financial risk. It was like a gamble for them. They approached it commercially, we did not. What was at stake for us was the prestige and the effects it would have on our football for many years. The Americans wanted profit. That did not enter our heads. Had we just gone for profit it would have sent back the wrong signals to UEFA. I believe we had to prove that we could stage a successful major tournament and that would benefit the game here for years to come.'

The biggest expense for the FA was the organisation of the

management team and the games themselves, the policing, staffing etc. Kirton and his team had to work hard at getting money back through commercial gains. England received 20 per cent of the ticket revenue, 10 per cent of commercial revenue and 10 per cent of the television revenue. Kirton banked on a 60 per cent income back from ticket sales and that would have broken even for the FA. A 70 per cent return guaranteed a £2 million profit. 'Four years' hard work for a lot of people, that is not a good business return,' says Kirton. 'The Americans would certainly poo-poo it. They, however, were in it for the money. We entered into this for different reasons. We wanted to do it properly and get the right reaction across the world.

'The World Cup made a lot of money for the Americans, but did the country as a whole get a lot of money? Go and ask Pasadena if they made a profit from staging the World Cup. Here, our country will do well. With tourism the country will exceed over £100 million in revenue and the government will take £8 million in VAT alone. We worked and collaborated with the government all the time.'

Despite the small profit margin for the FA, the European Championships represented huge financial packages for some. For instance, Swiss company ISL paid £27 million to UEFA for the commercial rights of the tournament. ISL then negotiated with 11 major sponsors: Canon, Carlsberg, Coca-Cola, Fuji, JVC, Mastercard, McDonalds, Opel, Phillips, Snickers and Umbro. Kirton says: 'We had to tread on eggs to make sure we, as the organisers, did not upset them.' The FA were allowed to negotiate their own sponsors, just as long as they did not conflict with the main sponsors and that they provided a service for the tournament and operated in the UK. In came Sema, Microsoft, Digital, BT, Castrol and Midland Bank, and they alone paid ten million pounds for the right to have their name linked with England and the European Championships.

There was an interesting twist in the revenue from the club shops at the eight stadiums used. ISL wanted to have sole rights to the shops for the month of the Championships. Some clubs wanted to sell their own gear all the time. There was conflict and the FA had to resolve it. Kirton did not believe that ISL should dominate and won a compromise. The shops eventually were taken by ISL on match days and sold club gear on other days. An extra compromise engineered by Kirton was that on match days clubs could sell merchandise just as long as it did not clash with tournament sponsors.

How much bigger than and different from 1996 this all has been, when England staged and won the World Cup. Ah, the memories. There is still, of course, a World Cup Association which meets regularly. It is made up of people who worked at the World Cup; fans, players, anyone can join and they meet and talk over what happened 30 years ago. There is just one person still at the FA who was involved in '66. Pat Smith, now deputy chief executive, was a 17-year-old secretary then. Kirton says: 'The biggest difference I can find, and I have spoken to a number of people who were involved in '66, is the demands of the media and the commercial side of the game. The organisation was tiny in comparison to today.'

My own memories of '66, apart from that Geoff Hurst goal (and I have still to see a picture or film to prove that the ball crossed the line), was the public. As a teenager it was thrilling to see so many people on that Saturday night happy and celebrating as one. I recall groups standing in the street and just being proud to be English. And that is what a major tournament like this does for people. The organisation is one thing, winning is what really matters. Kirton adds: 'Winning leaves a legacy. People only recall the organisation if something goes wrong.'

A successful England team under Terry Venables would lift our national sport on to a different level. God, it has leapt upwards and onwards since the arrival of the Premier League. Standards have risen, so has the money, but a winning national team means more than anything else.

The official draw, which pitched us against Switzerland, Scotland and Holland, was another piece of master planning by Kirton and his team. Staged at the Birmingham International Conference Centre, it went smoothly, watched by 400 million people around the world. The small children introducing the competing nations did not forget their lines, Simply Red sang their own song for Europe, and Terry Venables was in good-humoured form. No one would have realised that he had just resigned as he talked with great knowledge about the prospect of playing Scotland again. 'It is a fixture the whole country has missed and both nations deserve to meet again,' he said. We kept our fingers crossed for no trouble at Wembley on 15 June.

Later we knew about Venables and what would happen to him after the European finals. Kirton's future was not so certain. His contract expires in December 1996 and by that time he hoped to have been offered something bigger and better, perhaps at UEFA's HQ in Nyon, Switzerland. 'I have worked for the FA for 24 years but this has given me a taste of the big league,' said Kirton, who speaks French, Spanish, German and Italian. 'It makes you want to do it again. While I was organising the Championships, I heard and read that I was definitely going. My contract expires at the end of the year and I am sure I will be in discussion with people before then.'

Kirton was rightly proud of his achievements. He added: 'When England walked out for the first game against Switzerland I thought to myself, "Oh, this is what all the planning, preparation, blood, sweat and tears has been about. Men kicking a football." It is what mattered.'

As the posters and the song said . . . It Can Only Happen In England . . . Football's Coming Home.

TWENTY

More Confusion

England v Croatia. Wembley, 24 April 1996.
England 0, Croatia 0. Attendance: 33,650.

England Squad: Seaman, Flowers, Walker, G. Neville, Jones, Campbell, Wright, Ehiogu, Pearce, P. Neville, Lee, Ince, Gascoigne, Platt, Wise, Redknapp, McManaman, Wilcox, Stone, Sinclair, Collymore, Sheringham, Fowler, Barmby, Ferdinand, Beardsley. Beardsley, Ferdinand and P. Neville dropped out. A. Wright called in. England Team: Seaman, G. Neville, M. Wright, Pearce, Ince, Gascoigne, Stone, Platt, McManaman, Fowler, Sheringham.

Will he, won't he? Should he, shouldn't he? Does he want to? Will he be allowed to? Why haven't the FA asked him . . . ?

A thousand questions all aimed at one subject. Will Tel stay? It was the subject that dominated the five-day build-up to this game. On the Saturday before the match, after England's training had finished for the day at Bisham, the FA's press executive David Davies announced that there was definitely no change in the situation although, with a five-day get-together, he knew and accepted that there would be speculation. That triggered a wry smile from Venables. 'Don't mention speculation to Wooly,' he said. 'You started this,' he added as he nodded towards me sitting in the front row of the gathered group of journalists.

I may have started it but it certainly was not speculation. On Monday, 15 April, the *Sun* ran a small story to say that the FA's headhunter, Jimmy Armfield, was going to ask Terry, one more time, to change his mind and stay. Armfield was a strong supporter of Venables and I discovered that he was going to meet Venables for a chat before Armfield reported again to the sub-committee. The next day I spoke with Venables and he said that he could not comment because he had not been asked officially by the FA to change his mind. Venables at that stage, I believe, was still ripe for change. Indeed, I believe he wanted an arm around the shoulder. He needed to feel wanted.

Doug Ellis, the Aston Villa chairman, appeared on Sky TV's

Footballers Football Show, and urged his colleagues at the FA to persuade Venables to stay. Ellis said: 'Terry is like a woman. He says no but he means yes.' So was the England coach for turning?

The FA did not react. Venables had handed out the invitation but they did not respond. So by the time he met up with his players Venables had accepted that there was to be no change and that his initial decision stood firm. We have said before that he is a proud man but even proud men change their minds. To me he looked slightly hurt that the FA had not been more persuasive.

The plot still thickened, however, especially when stirred. On Friday, 19 April, the questioning was strong on why the FA had, at first, not gone back to Venables, or why there had been no meeting to ask him what was best for the future of English football. When resigning back in January he had offered the FA help with the future structure and in recommending his replacement. But for four months the FA had done nothing. After the press conference had broken up Davies was pressed hard by a group of us. Why hadn't the FA reacted? Was it not insulting to Venables that the FA had not shown him the courtesy of a meeting? Davies said things were progressing and to stay in touch.

Two hours later Davies called me on my mobile phone and asked for an off-the-record conversation. He said there was to be a meeting between Venables and Kelly in the near future but please do not assume that England were to ask Venables to stay on. He asked me to pass the information on to Bob Driscoll of the *Daily Star* and Kevin Moseley of the *Daily Express*, as they were sitting with me having lunch. He would ring Nigel Clarke of the *Daily Mirror*, who had been hardest in the questioning of Davies. I rang Neil Harman of the *Daily Mail* later that day to inform him of the meeting between Kelly and Venables. It was a twist in the story although there was not yet enough evidence that things were moving along quickly inside Lancaster Gate. Davies passed on other information which, he said, had to stay between the two of us for the time being. I was still not convinced that the FA would have called a meeting with Venables had it not been for the mood of the press conference. The Davies tip certainly headed off 'Venables snubbed'-type headlines planned for the next morning's papers.

So where did all this leave the England coach in the middle of a build-up to a match that he had said was going to be one of his toughest in control? It left him slightly bewildered and insisting that he was definitely going to quit. 'There is nothing the FA can do to change the situation,' he said.

I was still not convinced. Although Glenn Hoddle of Chelsea was emerging as the firm favourite, there was a definite feeling inside Lancaster Gate, especially from Davies and Armfield, that it would be worth one last try to keep him. There were interesting pointers.

Venables said that he had to clear his name in court and could not guarantee the time to be with England. But what if he had fallen ill throughout the autumn? What would England have done then had Venables still been in charge? They would have left control of the team in the hands of Don Howe and Bryan Robson, who had already made it clear that they were willing to run the show in the absence of Venables. Also, Venables has an amazing capacity to do more than one thing at a time. If any man can organise three major court cases, run the England football team, and front a top London club it is Venables. The other significant factor, of course, was his bitterness towards Liverpool director Noel White. There was always a little voice inside his head that told him never to change his mind because of White's public behaviour and the lack of complete support for him inside the FA.

The match arrived, at last, with the speculation pushed to the background. But for how long? The FA still insisted that the new England coach would be in control before the start of the European Championships. As they say, the clock is ticking . . .

Venables was interesting in the build-up. He said that had it been possible, at some stage in his career as England coach, to have had all his players together, every day for two months, he would have been able to have everything in place. His team, tactics, everything. Instead, he had to rely on a few days before each match. 'And then injuries dictate who I can coach,' he said. This time he was without Tony Adams and Gary Pallister, again, Steve Howey and Gareth Southgate – his first-choice and second-choice centre halves – Alan Shearer and, after the squad had been announced, Peter Beardsley, Les Ferdinand and Philip Neville. Venables said: 'It is no good crying, just get on with it. I have to. What all this has created is competition. Players are now looking over their shoulder. Established players now realise that someone can come into their slot and do the job. What I have achieved is that everyone is saying about someone else: "He is a good player."'

There has been no questioning the spirit in the camp, whatever the players Venables has ended up with. He says: 'I do not have to insist on pride and certainly do not have to work on it. The players accept what you want and I have that respect. Everyone is proud to play for their country. To me that goes without saying. It is how you go about it.

'Everyone wants to win. But at this level it is tough. Some give in, some don't. All of my players want to be in that final squad of 22 and choosing that, especially only 19 outfield players, is going to be so hard for me. But it is what I am paid to do. Pick the best players, in my opinion, for the job of winning the European Championships.'

Paul Gascoigne was certainly one of those. Gazza and Venables go hand in hand and there was praise for the midfield star. Venables said: 'You have to accept Gascoigne for what he is. And one thing he is, as a person, is a giver. It is not a show when he takes time out for kids, it is because he likes to do it. Things he does for charities and other projects are not often reported. The mistakes he makes, of course, are.

'Players like him. A lot of the time the star of the team is not always liked by the rest. Not so with Gazza. You could not get away with the things he does if the other players did not like or respect you. Gazza is a team man. Listen, we have all come here into an England squad from different directions. Me, the players, the coaching staff. You are thrown together with one love, football. I am the coach and am trying to create something successful and exciting. The players have responded. It is a partnership and one that I enjoy.

'I love this job. I have said that before. I do not want to leave but I have to for the reasons everyone knows. I did not have the full support of the International Committee and that helped me make my decision. I wanted a new contract, they did not want to give me one. I understand that. So it is best I go.

'That does not stop me giving everything for the country, these players and the job. I want England to win the European Championships. I believe we can.

'My philosophy on life is simple. Today is OK, tomorrow may be a disaster. Whatever happens the job has been a high of my career. The lows have been, and will be, the court cases. I do not enjoy them, they are an embarrassment to the FA, but have to be dealt with. They are not going to go away.

'What has pleased me so much are the unexpected people who have turned up trumps and been supportive. There have not been too many rotters against me.'

Venables opened himself up for criticism by deciding to change the system against Croatia. Always a progressive thinker, this time he decided to go for a more European system and approach, with only three defenders and a framework that had a ring of Dutch football about it. It was a brave move by the coach, especially as we were only six weeks away from the start of a major tournament.

But why should we not go continental? For years our up-and-under attitude, the blood and guts football, had proved not good enough. We would still need the determination of the English but the subtlety of the continentals, coupled with the imagination of Venables. It was worth a try. Venables rightly pointed out that this way of playing was not a huge change from things he had been trying out during the course of build-up matches. Venables said: 'People talk of me suddenly doing something but I have been looking to change this over a long period of time. Look closely, it should not be a shock. Before going against top foreign opposition we had players at the back not doing anything. Then in midfield we had men outnumbered and running their socks off all the game. This is a case of getting extra help to midfield.

'We have all got our likes and dislikes. I do not think that three centre halves and two full backs will get us playing the right way. It is my opinion but I am the coach and this is how I want to see England play. I want to test it and see how it goes. It is also a system that allows you to adapt. We have got a lot of experience in the side, coupled with some youngsters. The balance is right and good. It would have been foolish of me suddenly to go from one way of playing to another. I haven't. I have had to be patient but this has been coming together for some time now. Don't people see that?

'We are seeing how far we can go. The front of the team stays the same, the midfield is slightly different and the defence is slightly different. It also depends on what the opposition do.

'I spoke about this earlier in the season in a meeting I had with other managers. There were two big questions I had for them. When we discussed the problems our clubs faced in Europe this season I asked: "Do you want to do anything about it? Do you intend to?" They were terrific. They wanted to change and catch up. I wish we could meet more often. It is difficult for them because of everyday club commitments. I have time to travel, to look and talk to other coaches across the world. But more meetings between the managers in this country could only benefit the game. I could throw something into the pot, to provoke and stimulate ideas.

'What I have tried to do since taking charge is bring fresh ideas to English football. I have tried to catch up with what is going on around the world. The players have responded and shown a willingness to learn and change. There is a long way to go but I am pleased with this contribution. I have been delighted to have had the best players in England to work with and carry on what I believe is the right way for us to be heading.'

Venables decided that his two 'full backs' would be Stuart Pearce and Gary Neville and his one centre half Mark Wright. It was Wright's 44th cap but his first for two years. In his finest moment for England, the 1990 World Cup semi-final, Wright played in a five-man defence. Now it was three.

Venables recalled David Platt as captain and the only other significant change was a full debut for Robbie Fowler, the little Liverpool forward who had scored 36 goals for his club. Fowler's selection was greeted with enthusiasm across the board by all the papers, tabloid and broadsheet. Here was the player, we said, to answer our goalscoring prayers. After only five goals in our previous five matches Fowler's call-up was significant. There was talk of him breaking right the way through to first choice, just like Geoff Hurst's late arrival in the 1966 World Cup-winning side. Venables rightly refused to join the wild predictions being made. 'He is in, let us see how he goes,' said the coach.

The match was cat and mouse. For those who like their football spilling over with sweat and cheers, then it was not for them. But considering what Venables had asked his players to do they adapted well. They had only practised the new system, as a team, twice behind locked doors at Bisham Abbey.

It was a slower build-up but England created chances – six of them. Steve Stone blazed over in the first half with an opportunity that either hits the net or, as in this case, spears towards the crowd. David Platt should have done better with a header from Gary Neville's cross and there was also a header for Fowler. In the second half Steve McManaman hit a post and saw a shot saved when clean through. The last chance, and possibly the easiest, fell to Fowler. It was the type of opening he had been gobbling up all season yet this time, pouncing with his favoured left foot, he sent it over the bar.

It was a miss that saw Fowler criticised next morning with headlines of 'Fowler Howler'. That was unfair. Here was a player we had built up to a crescendo on the morning of the game. 'I want to become the greatest striker in English football,' said Fowler and we encouraged him to say it. Yet here we were knocking him down. It was a newspaper trick that was not lost on Teddy Sheringham, the one player who had refused all interviews in the build-up to the game. The message had come back from the FA that Sheringham was not interested in talking after what had happened with Les Ferdinand in the previous match. This time I agreed with him. Fowler did not deserve his treatment and some of the headlines after a performance that was interesting, full of chances and encouraging, was not justified. I do believe that all players should be bigger than just refusing to give interviews but Sheringham had a point.

It certainly did not reflect the mood of the country. There is a tradition in England for fans to get behind the nation, the team and the coach when we near a major football championship. I thought the newspapers lost sight of that. The *Daily Mirror* dismissed England's performance with an extraordinary back-page attack. They printed the name of Croatia down the left-hand side and spelt out alongside each letter: Clueless, Rubbish, Orrible, Awful, Turgid, Inept, Aimless. It was a massive overreaction. I understand that the sports editor was to ask his staff the next morning, 'Did I go too far?' He did. Venables was rightly bemused by the criticism. He had carefully explained the changes and the fact that it was not such a huge turn of direction. We, as a group, and there are always exceptions, chose to ignore him.

I felt at this stage that it was time for all media people to get behind Venables and the England team. Whatever you felt about the coach and his court cases and public problems, it must not rule your opinions. England winning the European Championships would benefit us all.

What would have happened had Fowler been the goal hero? We

would have heaped praise on them, said that we had a chance of winning the European Championship and forgotten all about boring England and the changes that Venables had made. You must never lose the right to criticise but let it be constructive rather than heavy-handed. Moving towards the finals the fans want an up press rather than a down one.

There were impressive performances. Paul Ince was again outstanding. Whatever the system he adapts so well. He looks in the mood to be one of the players of the Championships. Paul Gascoigne clearly enjoys playing alongside Ince. The two dovetail together and Gazza's fitness is improving. Gary Neville is maturing into an established England international and there are plus signs popping up all over the team. Venables always said, 'Judge me in June 1996', and he was confident. There were signs that he was getting it right despite the criticism.

The Croatian coach said that we were still too predictable but then tipped us to reach the final. So you can dismiss any criticism he threw up. Once again the question was asked, 'How much did a friendly mean to the opposition?', but Venables was having none of that. He knew how vital this match was to both sides. He also saw the criticism coming of no goals. He said: 'There are nil-nils and nil-nils. This was not the same as a year ago because we created so many chances. Had we taken two of them there would be no criticism. We have created more chances against Croatia than any side in the four previous matches I watched them play in.

'The players showed that they can adapt, and want to. We can adapt with the opposition. We changed the pace of the game and I could not ask for any more than what they did. We were the better side and deserved to win. I feel very positive.'

There was one last word for his critics: 'This is what we are going towards. This is it. The facts in the past suggested that we were not doing it right, so we are trying to do it better. The public will understand it when we win games. Surely that makes sense. I was pleased with it all, a good all-round performance.'

Venables eventually got back to his West Kensington home in the early hours. He poured himself a glass of champagne and watched a video re-run of the game. It looked just as good the second time around. He was a satisfied man when he slumped into bed at 3.45 a.m. He was therefore surprised when he got up a few hours later to read the back-page headlines. He could not believe the criticism. This time I agreed with him.

It was, however, just another match in the life of El Tel. So much had happened to him over a period of five days it was incredible. Two things had been established, however. He was sticking to the system that had brought him so much stick. And he was definitely quitting.

TWENTY-ONE

Hell in Hong Kong

England Squad: Seaman, Flowers, Walker, G. Neville, Howey, Jones, Adams, Wright, Southgate, Campbell, Pearce, P. Neville, Ince, Platt, Lee, Redknapp, Wise, McManaman, Wilcox, Anderton, Stone, Beardsley, Barmby, Shearer, Sheringham, Ferdinand, Fowler. Standby: James, A. Wright, Ehiogu, Sinclair, Collymore.

England v Hungary. Wembley, 18 May 1996.
England 3, Hungary 0. Scorers: Anderton (2), Platt. Attendance: 34,184.

England Team: Seaman (Walker), G. Neville, Wright (Southgate), Pearce, Ince (Campbell), Anderton, Lee, Platt (Wise), Wilcox, Sheringham, Ferdinand (Shearer).

England v China. Beijing, 23 May 1996.
England 3, China 0. Scorers: Barmby (2), Gascoigne. Attendance: 65,000.

England Team: Flowers (Walker), G. Neville, Adams (Ehiogu), Southgate, P. Neville, Anderton, Redknapp, Gascoigne, McManaman, Barmby (Beardsley), Shearer (Fowler).

England v Hong Kong Select. Hong Kong, 26 May 1996.
England 1, Hong Kong Select 0. Scorer: Ferdinand. Attendance: 26,000.

England Team: Seaman, P. Neville, Howey (Campbell), Adams, Pearce, Stone (Anderton), Ince, Platt, McManaman (Wilcox), Sheringham (Fowler), Ferdinand (Shearer).

What a change in the mood of the England coach. Terry Venables looked and acted demob happy as he entered the final furlong before the competition he had planned for over more than two years. There were jokes, a relaxed atmosphere and a 'not a care in the world' attitude in the countdown to the last three friendlies against Hungary and then China and Hong Kong on the heavily criticised tour.

He certainly did not look like someone who was nearing the end of employment. Nor someone who was soon to be out of work again. But he was definitely going and Venables had the air of a man who was going to milk every moment until it was all over. Anyway, what more could happen to him? If England did well in the European Championships he would go out as a hero, if they failed he would slip away quietly. No one could point the finger and say, 'Go now.' Nothing could go wrong any more. Oh yes it could, and did.

By the time Venables returned from Hong Kong he was faced with the biggest football crisis of his two-and-a-half-year reign. His England players had caused £5,000 worth of damage to the Cathay Pacific aeroplane carrying them home from the Far East. The first finger was pointed at Paul Gascoigne. It had been his birthday – no, not his fifth, his 29th – and the party in the Marco Polo section ran out of control. It was men behaving badly, according to Cathay Pacific officials.

It was the worst possible preparation for the biggest and most important tournament in the lives of Venables and most of his players. The one thing that Euro 96 officials feared about the competition was the return of hooliganism and yet here were England players allegedly behaving like yobs. The complaint from Cathay Pacific and a police investigation led to ferocious media coverage. The players returned on Tuesday morning, 28 May, and the next morning the national papers were full of the controversial story. It was front- and back-page news.

The next morning, Wednesday, 29 May, there was a full-blown crisis for English football. MPs demanded that the guilty players be kicked out of the Championships and declared that, as ambassadors for the country, they were a disgrace. Cathay Pacific officials said that it was the worst incident in 25 years of carrying Britons and the police said that they wanted to interview eight of the England players.

What would the FA's reaction be? You guessed it: nothing. Not a word. Oh, yes, plenty of waffle and the news that Venables was to hold an investigation when he returned from a trip to Switzerland to spy on our first Euro opponents. The FA's performance on that Wednesday was nothing short of pathetic. I have to blame chief executive Graham Kelly and press executive David Davies, and to a certain degree Venables. All three should have made statements. Instead they let press officer Steve Double hang out to dry. Double is a likeable, helpful man but new to this press office game. This needed experienced, senior handling and the other two went missing. So we had contradictions, no comments and ridiculous statements that Gascoigne's behaviour on board the plane was normal. 'He was the life and soul of the party,' said Double.

At 6.30 a.m. on that Wednesday I was outside the FA's Lancaster Gate offices doing an interview for TVAM. I was very impressed to see Graham Kelly walking through the front door just as I arrived. I thought he was there to start the investigation into the scandal. No chance. When I spoke with the chief executive he simply said: 'I have no comment to make. The press office are handling this. If they tell me I have something to say, I will.' Thanks, Graham.

By mid-afternoon on that day the investigation should have been over, the guilty man or men named, an apology broadcast and the damage paid for. End of story. Instead, the dear old FA let it drag on into the final week of England's build-up. Pathetic, stupid, wrong . . . call it what you like. It could only happen in England. Imagine the Germans dealing with it like this. Mind you, top German and Italian players know how to behave when they are representing their country.

Venables too must shoulder some of the responsibility for that Wednesday of no comment. They were his players. It would have taken him a couple of phone calls to one or two senior players to discover the truth. But he did not seem to want to get involved. He later bitterly criticised the media for not attempting to talk to him before he flew to Switzerland but it was a hollow point. I wonder how the late Bill Shankly, Brian Clough or Kevin Keegan would have handled it? Would they have vanished into the background? I don't think so.

As for Gascoigne, when it was first established that he was alleged to have been involved, the reaction of everyone in football was the same. We are not surprised. That, sadly, is how far we have come with Gazza in six years. Still a great player, but a pest, an embarrassment and beyond a joke.

Are the demands on these players too great? They are built up as gods, when they are not. They are talked of as world-class, when they are not. They are paid huge amounts of money to play football, often averagely, and the spin-offs are enormous. In the approach to the European Championships sponsors, advertising men and business advisers swarmed around them like flies. The players' every move was plotted, they could not go to the loo without someone knowing, or trying to sponsor the occasion. The demands are greater but so are the rewards.

Maybe I am old-fashioned but I thought pride came before anything else when you represented your country. There are players that still apply that principle. The FA only allowed all the players to be tarnished with the same brush by not acting immediately and naming the guilty men.

It was not as though the players were celebrating a great performance over in Hong Kong. Against opponents made up of former Football League players like Mike Duxberry of Manchester United and Carlton Fairweather of Wimbledon, England struggled to produce any inspiration in their last friendly under Venables. We had to be satisfied with a second-half header from Les Ferdinand. Venables blamed the long grass of the pitch and that was suitably laughed at. Then came the flight home, and later the news that some of the players had been in the famous China Jump bar in Hong Kong until 2.30 getting absolutely legless. Venables kept his quiet until the first media day of the final build-up to the opening game of Euro 96. Then for the first time he really laid into the press. He got it off his chest.

My own attitude about last games before Championships is not to be too critical. I recall in 1990 when we went to Tunisia and only drew 1–1 with a late goal from Steve Bull. It bares no reflection on the real stuff. Venables had seen enough, made up his mind and a scramble against Hong Kong was not that important to him, apart from more much-needed match fitness practice for Tony Adams, Darren Anderton, Steve Howey and Alan Shearer.

The only concern for the England coach was the form of Shearer. The Blackburn striker, who scored goals at will in the Premiership, could simply not do it for England any more. He flopped against China and that made it 939 minutes without a goal. We had to go back to September 1994 for his last one, against the USA at Wembley. Another blank 45 minutes against Hong Kong only added to the embarrassment. It meant that Venables had to go into the Europeans with his number one striker out of form.

The match against China was the one that he used for his final decision-making on who should be in the Euro squad of 22. Nick Barmby of Middlesbrough made the significant contribution. He scored twice in the 3–0 victory and edged out Peter Beardsley of Newcastle. It was a controversial decision and one that brought criticism from Beardsley's own manager, Kevin Keegan, and from Gary Lineker, who always rated Beardsley as his favourite strike partner.

England played well against China. Venables had said that the match would be as tough as any we faced in the Championships. By the time Gascoigne had got a third goal England were strolling and Venables was happy. He had been happy, in fact, since the day he sat alongside Glenn Hoddle when the new England coach was introduced. It was as if the baton had been passed and there would be no more speculation. He said: 'There were regrets about going and I did agonise for hours that I was doing the right thing. I would be lying if I did not admit to feeling some sadness and envy when I sat beside Glenn on the day of his appointment. Because it is a great job. There was envy because of the young people coming through and not being able to see the end of it. It is only natural. But once I have made a decision I stick to it.

'I did take gambles with my life but the financial side of things is good now and there is a lot of money coming in. The decisions have gone now and all I am interested in is the Championships. They mean everything to me. It is a big thing for the country and, hey, a very big thing for me. Afterwards I can concentrate on what I have to do in my life.'

That composure, that relaxed atmosphere, was not even dented by an injury crisis to his defence that surrounded the game against Hungary. Adams had not played since January, Gary Pallister was struggling with a bad back, Steve Howey had been out for six weeks at Newcastle and then, in the opening minutes of the game against Hungary, Mark Wright was injured. It was desperately unlucky for the Liverpool defender as history repeated itself and robbed him of a third major tournament. In 1986 a broken leg stopped him going to Mexico for the World Cup and on the eve of the 1992 European Championships in Sweden he dropped out with a leg injury. There was anguish on Wright's face as he went down clutching his knee against Hungary.

It led to a dramatic, heartbreaking scene in the second half with Wright, now showered and back in his England blazer, talking to Venables behind the English bench at pitch level. Venables shook his head and Wright, gesticulating with his arms, talked for about five minutes. The body language told the story. It was the end of the European Championships for the tall central defender. Two days later Wright was told by a specialist that he had damaged knee ligaments and there was no chance of a recovery.

Wright's nightmare was Gareth Southgate's joy. Southgate had been included for a few games without establishing himself as a certain starter. He had looked convincing in everything he had done and off the pitch was an impressive figure, a mature head on young shoulders. He talked sensibly and there was a lot of the Gary Lineker and David Platt about him as he conducted interviews with polish and sense.

When he came on for Wright his performance probably sealed his place in the final squad of 22. Southgate is a modern-day footballer, quick, comfortable, a good passer, strong in the tackle, reads the game well and has the flexibility to play in different defensive and midfield positions. He can also only improve with age. His attitude to the injury to Wright and others that let him in was one of regret for the individual but a sense of determination that it was suddenly his chance. 'You have to be selfish,' he said. 'You have to have an attitude of feeling sorry for your colleague but the fact is that it could have been you instead. When I was injured in the FA Cup semi-final against Liverpool I felt for a few minutes that my season was over. The relief was tremendous when I was told that I should be able to play again before the end of the season. It allowed me to clear my head and plan.'

It is incredible to look back at the centre half position under Venables and realise how late Southgate made it through. The England coach, in fact, picked an entire team of central defenders: Tony Adams, Gary Pallister, Steve Howey, Neil Ruddock, Steve Bould, John Scales, David Unsworth, Colin Cooper, Mark Wright, Sol Campbell, Ugo Ehiogu and Southgate. Adams and Pallister were his first choice. Adams just made it although he could not have been completely match fit going into the Championships, Pally could not play two games a week because of his back and had to be left out,

Howey scraped in despite injury and the others were dropped by the wayside. Southgate timed his arrival to perfection.

Hungary proved to be poor opposition. That did not matter – a win did in the last Wembley match before the finals. Darren Anderton scored twice to take his tally to five goals in ten matches, much better than his scoring record for Spurs, and David Platt got his first for some time to lift his own record to 27 in 58 matches. The disappointment for me was the size of the crowd. It could and should have been so many more. Why do the FA and Wembley not slash prices when they know that they are not selling enough tickets?

Nothing, however, worried Venables. He was all smiles, relaxed and in the kind of mood that gave no indication of the forthcoming finals or the fact that he was nearing his swan-song. Down in the dressing-room area the FA and UEFA had a trial run of the dreaded mixed zone interview. It is hated by all journalists and in my opinion simply does not work. It was chaos during the World Cup in America and will be chaos in the European Championships. This is how it works, or does not work. Around the area of the dressing-room a section is roped off to allow the players, coaches and officials to walk through without being pushed and shoved by media people. There is a stage where official interviews are carried out, through an interpreter. Simple? Don't you believe it. Some players do not want to go on stage, as Darren Anderton did not want to after his two goals against Hungary. Instead, he was interviewed standing on his side of the rope with the media men on the other. I hope you get the picture because I am trying to make it sound as simple as possible. The trouble is that not one person wants to speak to Anderton, or whoever the goalscoring hero is, from whatever country. There are hundreds of reporters from TV, radio, newspapers, agencies, as well as onlookers, all desperate to hear. It leads to rows, pushing, shoving, cameras broken, tempers frayed, tape recorders trodden on, complete chaos.

Venables seemed to find it all very amusing when he went up on stage to talk about the Hungary match. There were three microphones, one for him, one occupied by Graham Turner, the UEFA official and interpreter, and another UEFA man. 'You hum and I'll play,' said Venables, strumming an imaginary guitar. As Ugo walked by the England coach joked: 'There goes a fit centre half, take a picture, it is a rare one. I have told Ugo and Gareth not to travel home in the same car because something will happen.' It was all slapstick stuff from a relaxed England coach. He could not have known it was the calm before the storm of his players' behaviour in Hong Kong and on the flight home.

144

The New England Era

On the evening of Monday, 29 April, I had a five-minute telephone conversation with a top official of the Football Association. We discussed Glenn Hoddle. I told him that I had no idea whether the FA were considering Hoddle for the job as England coach but asked him if he realised what was going on at Chelsea. I explained that Hoddle was closing in on a new deal.

Hoddle's business adviser, Dennis Roach, had met Chelsea chairman Ken Bates the previous day, Sunday, 28 May, and talks were progressing. There was another meeting planned for Wednesday, 1 May, when I felt sure that Hoddle's new four-year contract, worth an estimated £350,000 a year, would be finalised and signed. The FA man asked me if I was running that story in the morning. I said I was, he thanked me for the chat and the conversation was ended.

Three hours later FA chief executive Graham Kelly rang Hoddle at his Ascot, Berkshire, home and offered him the job as England coach. I have no idea whether the two situations are linked. The FA man has never mentioned our conversation again, never thanked me for the information or never spoken to me about how Hoddle was chosen. It was simply a conversation between a journalist and a contact. It goes on all the time.

Hoddle eventually accepted the job after waiting 48 hours to make up his mind. Jammed into that time were two days of intrigue, cloak and dagger meetings and a frantic effort by Hoddle's friend and Chelsea director Matthew Harding to keep him at Stamford Bridge. In fact, the build-up to Hoddle saying yes had started on the previous Saturday following Chelsea's 1–1 draw with Spurs at White Hart Lane. Hoddle had been in relaxed, confident mood when he gave his after-match press conference. The Sunday newspaper journalists had not pressed him on his future and it was left to the Monday papers to ask him what he intended to do. He said that he could not comment on England or make a decision because he had never been asked, informally or officially. That proved to be a white lie because at the official press conference to name Hoddle chief executive Kelly revealed that FA headhunter Jimmy Armfield had spoken to him about the possibility of becoming England coach. At that secret meetings weeks earlier Hoddle had told Armfield that he would be interested and would take the job if offered. Hoddle was secretly and genuinely excited. He began planning in his mind what he would do if he got the job, and he also decided then that his assistant manager would be John Gorman, a Scot who had been Hoddle's number two at Swindon. Chelsea, of course, knew nothing of that informal approach. They would only become aware if and when Hoddle was the choice of the International Committee choosing Venables's replacement.

You can understand now why Hoddle told his white lie after the Spurs game. He realised the prospect of becoming England coach was getting closer. It was a job he always wanted and one that he felt he was destined for, even if at 38 years old it was perhaps premature for him. He had also been only one of three managers who had not turned it down flat to Armfield. The others were Howard Wilkinson of Leeds and Nottingham Forest's Frank Clark.

On that Saturday after the Spurs game I sensed that he was a man expecting something to happen, with club and country. He said that talks with Chelsea were progressing and that if he got the right answers about the club's future in the next few days he would sign a new contract. Twenty-four hours later, on the Sunday, Roach met Bates at the Chelsea chairman's farm in Beaconsfield and Roach was given more answers and more assurances about the direction in which the club was heading. Significantly, Hoddle was promised that there would be no interference on playing matters from the chairman. Roach reported back to Hoddle and another meeting was arranged with Bates for the Wednesday. It would have been the last meeting. Enter the FA.

Hoddle was relaxing at home with his wife Ann and children, Zoe, Zara and Jamie, when the phone rang. Hoddle was not totally surprised that it was Kelly. In a way he had been expecting it. After a 15-minute conversation Hoddle asked for 48 hours to make up his mind. He wanted to speak to his wife, parents and Roach, someone whom he trusted one hundred per cent and who had looked after his business interests since he was a player with Tottenham.

D-day for Hoddle would be Wednesday, although his final decision was not communicated to the FA until Thursday morning. Wednesday, however, was the day for meetings and make-your-mind-up time.

The first meeting of an extraordinary day was between Bates and Roach. Chelsea's offer plus the job details and more assurances about the future was then presented to Roach. It was a superb offer, making Hoddle one of the top earners in the country. It pushed him right up there alongside Alex Ferguson at Manchester United and Kevin Keegan at Newcastle. It also proved Chelsea's fierce ambition. But would it be too late? It also begged the question why had Chelsea left it to the last minute to give Hoddle the answers he had been looking for since before Christmas? He had said: 'This was never about money and my contract. Had that been the case I would have signed on the dotted line long ago. No, this was about getting it right for the club and the wonderful fans.' Had Chelsea got their act together and chairman Bates and his rival Harding not been at loggerheads, Hoddle would definitely have been under contract when the FA made their approach. Chelsea would not have released him and Hoddle would not have walked out.

By the time Roach had completed his Wednesday meeting with Bates, Hoddle had left his home, confirming to reporters waiting outside that he had been offered the job, and set off for a secret meeting with Harding. The meeting had been called by Hoddle, who on Tuesday morning had rung his friend and requested a chat to help him make the biggest decision of his life. Hoddle and Harding met at around 11.30. Harding went into the meeting resigned that he was about to lose a manager he affectionately called 'Saint Glenn'. Four hours later he emerged more confident. 'I have done all I can to persuade Glenn to stay. I believe at the moment it is 50:50,' he said.

While Hoddle and Harding were talking Roach had left Beaconsfield and driven into London for a meeting with Graham Kelly at Lancaster Gate. At that meeting Roach was presented with the FA offer to Hoddle and the job description.

So now Roach had two contracts and two superb offers in his briefcase. One from Chelsea, worth £1.2 million over four years, plus bonuses. The other from England, worth slightly less in contract money but a lot more in spin-offs and, of course, prestige. Hoddle was lucky. The man who was never really appreciated as a player in this country was now the most wanted manager in England.

Hoddle left his meeting with Harding to drive home to Ascot. Roach left Lancaster Gate to do the same. The two men met at Hoddle's home and thrashed out what Hoddle should do. Roach got back to his Bournemouth home at around eight o'clock but there followed a series of phone calls from Hoddle with questions and assurances. It was not until one o'clock in the morning that Hoddle finally made up his mind and said yes to himself and his wife Ann. He fell asleep happy that he had made the right decision.

The biggest deciding factor for Hoddle was his ambition. Since he was seven years old he had savoured a dream to become England manager, or coach, as the FA like to call it now. That dream had hardened inside him as he played for Spurs and Monaco and managed Swindon and Chelsea. When all the discussion was over he realised that it was not a job he could say no to. His country had called and Hoddle was proud to say yes. He also worried, after his talks with Harding, that he would be used as a pawn in the power game between Harding and Bates. He did not want to be played off by one against the other.

One man who welcomed the appointment was Bobby Robson, the former England manager who had just won his second successive championship in Portugal with Porto. Robson said: 'Glenn wanted it and, significantly, he was not scared of it. That is the right attitude. Anyone not sure is not wanted as far as I am concerned. Good luck to Hoddle. He is young and it is going to be a severe test. But half the battle is feeling proud and wanting to do the job. He is not afraid of it, as so many others seem to be. It is not a job to be scared of. It is a fantastic job.'

It was Robson who ended Hoddle's playing career with England and he remains someone who never really appreciated how to tune the skills of one of England's most talented footballers into the framework of a side. He adds: 'It will be interesting to see how he plays. My message to him is this: "Go on then, Glenn. Show us all the things you have been preaching over the years. Show us how the game should be played when the chips are down in a tough World Cup qualifying match. Show us the beautiful game."

'Will he have a digger in midfield, or will he have the silky skill players? Now he has the chance to prove what he has preached. There will be a lot of people watching his every move.'

So England got their man. Hoddle was paraded before the media at a press conference at four o'clock in the afternoon on Thursday, 2 May, at London's Royal Lancaster Hotel. Venables was there, so was Kelly, with David Davies orchestrating the goings-on. It was the first time the FA had actually admitted that Hoddle had been offered the job, let alone accepted it. Even when Hoddle and Harding were confirming the offer on Wednesday morning the FA, bless them, still refused to say it was Hoddle. Hoddle himself told reporters: 'I have been offered the job,' but the FA simply said: 'This is all speculation as far as we are concerned.'

Hoddle emerged for his press conference from a side entrance and was hit with hundreds of flashing light bulbs and pleas from cameramen of 'This way, Glenn' and 'Glenn, over here' or 'Smile, Glenn, please'. His life would never be the same again. At the press conference he looked slightly bemused and confused. Hoddle has never been a man with a big personality and he keeps his cards firmly to his chest. After Bobby Robson, Graham Taylor and Venables, here was a 'different' man. Dealing with the media would be his toughest test. It would not bother him, for Glenn has always been his own man. But as I watched him answering questions and playing a straight bat I sincerely hoped that he would enjoy the job. Perhaps he would loosen up when Venables had finished with the European Championships and he was in sole control.

He certainly gave all the right answers without stopping to take breath. After praise from Kelly, who emphasised how important it was to continue the sophistication of the Venables way, Hoddle said:

'It has happened so quickly for me. When you get asked to do this job it is a privilege and an honour. That is why I am here, I wanted it. I wanted it badly.

'The main issue was that it was my country. This was the only job I would have left Chelsea for. And that includes my job home and abroad. It has been a burning ambition of mine and the time is right for me. It is the pinnacle of my career and I had to take it.

'My contract starts on June 1st and until Terry goes I will be homing in on the teams we are going to have to beat in qualifying for the World Cup. Terry and I are close on how the game should be played. It is a smooth handover.

'I will be positive, the talent is here and I am excited. There is a crop of exciting youngsters coming through and I looked at these when making the decision. The thought of those young players made it exciting and the decision in the end was easy.

'If I had felt I was not right for it I would not have taken it. People will say the England coach needs more experience but experience should not always be gauged by grey hair. I have played abroad and been a manager here for six years. I believe I am ready for this.'

Venables praised the FA for their choice: 'I remember Glenn when he was with me with the Under-21 squad. He was keen to learn and was always intelligent in his beliefs. I am sure that he has the right credentials. I have enjoyed the job, Glenn will, it is well worth it. Do you know, if the time ever came again for me than I would definitely consider doing it again.

'The media side of the job is tough but not impossible. Glenn has got his own ways of working. I do not need to give him any advice. He will cope well. I am now used to the idea of going, especially now that Glenn has been given the job. There has been a lot of speculation but it is on with the next now. Glenn can have all the information from me he wants. Good luck to him.'

Hoddle is determined to play the game the right way and with a system that is close to his heart and one that the public will enjoy. He says: 'Terry has been brave in doing what he wants and the players like what he has done with them. My job is to qualify for the World Cup and I believe we can. I would love to play my first match on 1 September with England being European Champions. Success breeds success. I have always felt that.

'It is interesting that we as a country often look abroad and like the way the continentals play. But then when someone tries to do it here he gets raised eyebrows. I know the correct way. As for the public taking it on board, they will if we win matches doing it.'

Hoddle had to field a lot of questions about the media. TV pundit Greg Dyke actually quoted Hoddle from an interview he did from 1994 when he said that if he ever became England manager he would be worried about Graham Taylor-type treatment and the effect it would have on his family. It was a cheap trick. Hoddle answered: 'The media was not an issue to turn the job down. My wife Ann has never had any hang-ups about anything I have done in football. My wife and parents have always been supportive.'

The thing about the 'rotten old media' really started to annoy me by the time the press conference was over, and in the next few days I must have been asked the same question 50 times. How will Hoddle handle the media? The question was even asked by people in my own industry. What they were really saying was, 'We are not going to dig Hoddle up, but you will and how will he deal with it?' Ian Payne from BBC Radio Five Live actually approached me at the press conference and asked if there was any newspaperman who was against Hoddle getting the job. When I said no, he added that we are no good to him. Why didn't he, or others who felt that Hoddle was not the right man for the job, go to him face to face and ask the question? There are not enough brave people in journalism, I have always said that. Not enough journalists to sit on the front line and ask THAT question. Not enough people to say what they really feel.

I have known Hoddle for 15 years, have seen all his matches for England and have appreciated his skills and ability. He is a tough character, far tougher than people realise. He is his own man who knows what he wants. No one should worry about Hoddle. He can look after himself and will. He will expect criticism if things go wrong and will certainly enjoy the praise when England win important World Cup matches.

As expected Hoddle went back to Gorman, who had decided not to go to Chelsea with him and stayed at Swindon instead. He was eventually sacked by Swindon and was working as assistant manager at Bristol City when Hoddle rang him. 'I was expecting the call,' said Gorman. 'I was surprised no one guessed it would be me because Glenn and I are very close. From the day we first met in 1976 there has been a special bond between us.'

There are a lot of similarities between Hoddle and Venables although Kelly said with a wry smile: 'We did ask Glenn before he signed the contract whether there were any skeletons in his cupboard, other than that dreadful record he once made with Chris Waddle!'

No skeletons. No controversy. No worries other than on the pitch. It must have been a huge relief to the FA that they had found a coach who could concentrate only on football. Chairman Sir Bert Millichip even said that he hoped Hoddle would stay for at least ten years. 'We need a long period of stability,' he said.

I believe English football is in safe hands.

The Venables era is over. And what an era it was. An incredible ride, often bumpy, never dull. A remarkable story.

What does Glenn Hoddle have in store for us? . . . The nation waits.

150

TWENTY-THREE

The European Championships 1996

It was around Christmas 1995 when Terry Venables started to realise that England were going to have a good European Championships.

The players were responding to his ideas, his planning and tactics. He began to ask them to do different things and pieces of the jigsaw fitted into place. He says: 'The openness of their minds was terrific. Whatever I asked of them they responded to. They wanted to listen and learn. I would say educating those players to what I wanted, and them carrying it on to the pitch, was my greatest achievement as England coach. Together we proved that the rest of the world do have to stand up and take notice of England. We have given the nation back a football team.

'I will not say a word against them, or criticise any of them. I am proud and throughout my management career not one player, not one, has ever been critical of me. I hand chose the group and by the time we went into the Championships they knew exactly what I wanted. And I knew exactly what they were capable of.

'There were tough decisions to be made, like telling David Platt that I was keeping Tony Adams as captain. But anything I did was done with England in mind. Nothing else.'

So after two and a half years of friendly internationals Venables was ready for the greatest challenge of his career. It was amazing that he had been through so much, on and off the pitch, and yet England's first game in Euro 96 was his first competitive match. His first real test. That was not his fault. He was ready, so were the players. So, too, was the country. We had been waiting for this moment.

England v Switzerland. Wembley, 8 May 1996.
England 1, Switzerland 1. Scorer: Shearer. Attendance: 76,567.

England Team: Seaman, Neville, Adams, Southgate, Pearce, Anderton, Gascoigne (Platt), Ince, McManaman (Stone), Shearer, Sheringham (Barmby). Booked: G. Neville, Adams.

It began with a row and ended with a row. That was the build-up and the follow-up to our first Euro 96 match against the Swiss. It was the worse possible PR exercise by Terry Venables and the FA, on and off the pitch. Not for the first time in England's history the coach and the players got themselves in a twist over media coverage, criticism and comment. When will they learn that they have to cope with round-the-clock media attention in major tournaments?

It is not a secret. Players are public property. Everything they do, say and how they play is analysed down to the smallest detail. If they play well and behave properly then there is no problem, it is plain sailing right the way through the tournament. That is exactly how every journalist I know wants it to be. I would much rather write and comment about England playing superbly and taking on the best in Europe with the flag flying high, than negative, controversial reporting. Venables will not believe it. But it is a fact.

Going into the Europeans I was excited by our chances. Venables had convinced a lot of people that he knew exactly what he was doing and that the players were in great shape. I feel very passionately about my country when it comes to sport. When I was a kid I used to get up in the middle of the night to listen to the radio cricket commentary from Australia when England were playing for the Ashes. I got a buzz when Brian Johnston's voice finally came crackling down the airwaves.

Today is no different. The goose-pimples stand on the back of the neck when England walk out at Wembley and the national anthem is played. I feel proud when Linford Christie wins the Olympic gold and still get up in the middle of the night to watch Frank Bruno take on Mike Tyson or watch the now live Sky cricket coverage from Australia. So don't accuse me of not being patriotic. No way. But I cannot turn a blind eye to bad behaviour.

It was Tuesday, 4 June, five days before the Euro kick-off, when Venables held his first press conference since returning from Hong Kong. Why on earth the FA had let him wait that long before discussing the Cathay Pacific flight home when property was vandalised, or the huge booze-up in Hong Kong, I will never know. It meant that Venables had to start the Euro countdown by looking back instead of forward. He was in buoyant mood and ready and waiting for the first question about his players. When I asked him if we could discuss last week he said: 'Yes, sure. What would you like to know? I am sure I will tell you everything although it sounds as if you know everything already, so you do not need my help.'

It was the first shot in a press conference that saw Venables attack the media, the principles of reporting and our relationship with him. It got personal, bitter, although thankfully ended with Venables shaking hands and leaving us with the message: 'Let's get on with the football.'

What he was most upset about was the fact that the previous Tuesday, when the Cathay story had broken, none of us had attempted to contact him. He said: 'What disappointed me most was that I did not get a call from a newspaper. For two and a half years I have always returned calls, apart from to Harry, that is (glaring at Harry Harris of the *Mirror*), and I was entitled to a call. You had a big story. Well, it has gone on for a long time, and you did not give me the chance to give my side.

'Not one paper rang me to ask me if it was true and what did I know about it. No one asked me for my opinion. That is inconsiderate, to say the least. On the Tuesday, before I went to Scotland (to watch Switzerland in action) I was at my club Scribes and on the end of a phone until six. When I got to Switzerland I rang Michelle (Michelle Rogers, the FA's international secretary) and still no one had tried to contact me.

'It was not until later in the week that I started to get messages. I did not feel like answering them. You did not show me any decency, why should I return it?' He then added bitterly: 'You will still get co-operation during the European Championships. That is my job.'

Venables missed a big point here – the FA's handling of the situation. On the Tuesday there was no statement from them. On the Wednesday neither press executive David Davies nor FA chief executive Graham Kelly made an official comment. Press officer Steve Double did and what we got was a lot of contradiction and waffle. Incredibly, it took the FA a week to clear up the matter. It was not until the following Monday, 24 hours before Venables's press conference, that they made a statement. Why, oh why, did they not react quicker? All they had to do, right at the start, was admit the incident, say the damage had been paid for and cleared up and it would have been killed off. They have only themselves to blame.

A week of non-action – they said they had to wait for Venables to return and meet the players before anything could be done – allowed the speculation, the accusations and the reporting to intensify. The first culprit was said to be Paul Gascoigne, then Steve McManaman and Robbie Fowler were mentioned by the *News of the World* as being the guilty men.

Of course, it was painted by Venables as the tabloids' fault. Wrong. It was first the players' and then the FA's.

During the heated press conference Venables suddenly pointed at Gary Newbon of ITV and said: 'Ask my good friend over there from ITV what happened. He was on the plane.' Newbon told me later that he thought everything had been exaggerated and that as far as he was concerned nothing had gone on during the flight home. Nothing that he knew of, anyway.

Venables was by now in full flow. He added: 'There was a little something that went on which has been blown up way beyond what it deserves. I have not had any problem from these boys in two and a half years. Last night we had a meeting and talked about it for hours. We tried to get to the bottom of it. We ended up by dealing with it the best way we could and that is everyone, and I mean everyone, takes joint responsibility. That is our solution. I am not going to explain, make your own observations. Now get behind us in the Europeans. If you feel otherwise, fine.'

But explain he did. When I said that we did not make the stories up he almost burst out laughing. 'Don't be daft, all the stories I have read over the last week have been true, haven't they? What happened was that there was a little problem upstairs on the plane and you have made it sound like a party. They (the players) were playing cards all night. He was there (pointing at Newbon again). Ask him.'

OK, Terry, but what about Cathay Pacific? 'Oh, you believe them, do you, and not us? I think they got it wrong. Ask one of their pilots if there was any problem.'

Why should we make it up, Terry? 'You tell me. Did you ask me? Did you ask me on the day? Did you ring me? No one had the decency to ring me. All the papers knew by four o'clock in the afternoon. What time can you get anything in your papers, eleven, twelve? Come on, come on.'

OK, Terry, if it was exaggerated why did the FA pay the bill? He snapped: 'I have not paid it, I do not know why it has.'

David Davies, sitting alongside Venables throughout, finally spoke. He said: 'We have talked to Cathay Pacific and the matter is now closed.' Thanks, David.

Venables was quickly back in the firing line. 'The reason the FA have paid for the damage (£5,000) is because we want the situation behind us. They came to a quick decision.' Quick? It took them more than a week to clear it up.

Venables then fiercely defended his players: 'They are very angry. They are high profile and accept criticism. But they do not accept what has gone on here. They have even been called spineless. I will tell you something. These guys are going to be at the sharp end, heroes or villains by what they do out there on the pitch. They are not just writing about it, they are out there doing it. I am sorry if that upsets any of you but you should not be so sensitive. We have to take criticism, you do too.

'I was not going to say all this but feel I should stand up on behalf of the players. The public have been given a lopsided view.' I asked him what was the right view. 'Well, you should know, you have been writing about it with great authority all week.' So, you are saying that it is not true? 'I am saying that it is exaggerated beyond reason.'

OK, what about the booze-up in Hong Kong? 'That was different. We had been preparing for two and a half weeks and they were given a night out. They had a few drinks and were in on time. I know the pictures did not look good and attractive. Hey, I have seen some of you guys out at night, right . . . right . . . right . . . come on, do me a favour,

I have known you for years. Don't worry, I am not writing this.'

Of course journalists like a night out. The pressure is great on us as well. To produce hard back-page stories for big newspapers is a pressure I have lived with for more than 20 years. But I do not remember being strapped to a dentist's chair and having bottles of liquor poured down my throat. And, of course, we were not two weeks away from representing our country in the biggest tournament England had staged for 30 years.

Venables added: 'That is not the issue. The other one is, the one you have made so much of. I am satisfied I know now what happened. It has taken a long while but I am satisfied.' So who did the damage? 'Let us put it this way, it is going to be dealt with in-house.

'Listen, I know you are under pressure. There are about six sports editors who tell you what to do and you do as you are told.' He then mentioned one reporter who he claimed writes what he is told. It was a cheap shot. 'We all have jobs to do,' Venables added. 'I am making a point because you all have had enough to say.'

By now Venables was enjoying himself. He had got his grievance off his chest and it was almost slapstick stuff. The expert of the one-liners was in full flow. When Harry Harris asked a question Venables turned on him and said: 'Is that you, Harry? I did not know you had a voice. For two and a half years I thought you were worked by a ventriloquist.'

When I asked him if we could switch the subject forward he reacted: 'It is not football, is it?' Has the criticism helped the bonding and spirit of the players? 'I was going to congratulate you,' he said laughing. 'Congratulate you all on your help. You can't be more than one hundred per cent but there does seem to be an extra edge in there.'

It was explosive, interesting, great copy – a coach determined to have his say. It was too late but at least it represented a strong, positive response from the FA. Venables had at least cleared it up. While the PR machine inside Lancaster Gate reacted with the positive mobility of a pregnant cow on a hot summer's afternoon, Venables had met the players, thrashed out some sort of end to the saga and brought it out into the open.

Now it was down to the serious stuff of the European Championships. There surely could not be any more off-pitch distractions. Well, not for a few days, anyway. I have to say, however, that the public did not seem to mind about the players' behaviour, just as long as they performed on the pitch. My mailbag, when I returned to my office after Euro 96, was full of demands to get off the players' backs. Only a few agreed with my criticism of the boozers and the television breakers. Maybe standards are falling.

The football build-up to the Swiss game was positive, despite a scare for Gary Neville, the Manchester United full back who was certain to start if he could shake off a leg injury. There was speculation about the team and it seemed that David Platt, the captain, would have to sit out the first match with Venables playing a flat back four and Darren Anderton and Steve McManaman wide. Venables told the players the team on Wednesday and by the Friday morning it was in the papers.

The players, despite the controversial publicity, acted professionally and like adults. Platt and Gareth Southgate were the first to be interviewed and then Stuart Pearce talked passionately about his dreams of winning the European Championships. I like Pearce. When you talk to the Nottingham Forest full back he gives it to you as it is, straight and no frills. He knew that he was second choice at left back and was realistic to admit it and say that this was probably his last chance of winning something with England. 'We have got as good a chance as anyone,' he said. 'I think it is the most open Euro tournament there has been. We have got the ability and in someone like Paul Gascoigne an individual who can win a match on his own. We are going to need that bit of luck and a rub of the green. In 1992 against the French I hit the underside of the bar with a free kick. Had that gone in we would probably have qualified for the quarter-finals.'

Then there was Gazza. The clown prince. The genius. The match-winner. The most controversial player in our history. Could he produce? Could he cope? Venables revealed that Gascoigne had been trying to do too much in training and he had been forced to pull out of the last 15 minutes. That is Gazza's problem. His will to win, his desire, is so great that he gets himself hyped up until he cannot control himself. During the World Cup in 1990 he played squash in a searing 100-degree heat 24 hours before a match and then, on a day off, jumped on a pedal bike and rode off for hours, causing a huge security risk.

Former England manager Bobby Robson called him 'daft as a brush' and his Glasgow Rangers manager Walter Smith agrees. Smith often bumps into Gascoigne at seven o'clock on the morning of a big match. 'I ask him what he is doing up and he just says he cannot sleep. It is not uncommon for him to go for a walk down to a nearby village and chat to the locals. That is him. You have to give him leeway,' says Smith.

The build-up at last swayed away from the controversies. There was a growing feeling in the country that it was time to get behind our boys. All reporters were happy with that although the bottom line is that you cannot ignore bad behaviour. And heading for the opening day of Euro 96 there remained an awful lot of questions unanswered. They were: why were the players allowed out until 2.30 a.m. in Hong Kong on an amazing bender with the manager's permission and assistant Bryan Robson with them in the bar? Why was damage caused on the plane? Why didn't the FA clear it up quickly? Why did they wait for Venables to return from Switzerland? Men like Sir Bert Millichip and Graham Kelly have the power to do anything they want, overrule anything. They chose not to. What was David Davies doing in the seven days between the party returning and the announcement that the players had accepted collective responsibility? If there was no damage why did the FA pay up? Millichip shot down all 'collective' arguments when he said after the announcement: 'There had to be joint responsibility because no one owned up.' So he admitted that someone did do it. They were unsavoury and unnecessary incidents and the full answers, I suggest, will never be provided.

Robbie Fowler and Steve McManaman made noises about it not being them and the fact that they were going to sue. Paul Gascogine, according to FA spokesman Steve Double, was the life and soul of the party upstairs on the flight home, then it was reported that Gazza had been asleep all the way home. It would not have happened to the Italians or the Germans, would it? You could not see Jurgen Klinsmann strapped to a dentist's chair having spirits poured down his throat.

Another question. At the first camera flash inside the Hong Kong bar why did Robson not gather up his troops and take them somewhere else or back to the hotel? He must have known that England footballers getting drunk and flashing camera bulbs was not a cocktail mix that tasted satisfactory. You can get drunk in private, not with your shirt ripped off your back, spitting beer at each other and in full view of the public. Whether they like it or not, they are English footballers abroad representing their country.

Terry would not have it. 'I have no problem with their drinking on that night. They did not break a curfew and had a few beers,' he said. He was wrong. Does the behaviour of the players reflect the coach? Is he too lenient with them? Does his image of 'Good Old Tel, he is one of the lads' rub off on them? I also thought he was taking a terrific gamble in allowing the players home after the Switzerland game. That is another story.

Boredom is always a big problem with footballers when they are away on tour or playing in a competition like this with a lot of time to kill. Venables treated them like adults and expected them to act responsibly and sensibly. Most people thought they let him down – and we have to say that because they have accepted joint responsibility – but the players and the coach would have nothing to do with it.

To avoid that boredom during the Championships, the team's hotel had facilities to watch videos, play tennis, head tennis, badminton, snooker, cards and all the usual things that entertain footballers.

On the Wednesday night Venables did a live TV link with ITV when he was interviewed by Bob Wilson and a panel of Jack Charlton, John Barnes and Kevin Keegan. While Tel was on camera a group of England footballers danced crazily behind him, running across the camera and in full view of the public watching at home. Venables made light of it but, again, it was silly behaviour. Childish, immature behaviour. Especially in the light of what happened in the build-up. Was Gazza there, Fowler? No names ever came out. I wonder if they were reprimanded? Somehow I doubt it.

I suspect there will be a stricter code of conduct under Glenn Hoddle. Let us not forget how he handled the Dennis Wise situation, when he stripped Wise of the captaincy after his infamous fight with a taxi-driver, and how he argued face to face with Craig Burley pitchside after the Scottish international had complained about being substituted.

As the Swiss game approached, Gascoigne was charging around training in the searing heat, boiling over in fact, and had to be pulled out of training to relax him. If Gazza was on fire, Alan Shearer was staying ice cool as the game approached. All eyes were on him because he went into Euro 96 without a goal for longer than anyone connected with England liked to remember. Shearer was not bothered – so he said on the outside – and nor was the coach. That meant that the Blackburn star would definitely start. 'I am not relying on one person for goals,' said Venables. 'If anyone can handle the pressure of not scoring going into a tournament like this then Alan can.'

On the eve of the game Venables talked about his pride in walking out at Wembley. He said: 'It would mean a great deal to me to win this tournament, more than anything else I have done in my life. It would be my greatest achievement. It is so big.

'Normally you are fighting for your club. I feel I am fighting for every club, every fan, every person in England. When I walk out it will be a goose-bump-on-the-back-of-the-neck situation. I will feel it, I want to feel it. It is going to be a great occasion. We are well prepared and confident.'

So it arrived. Saturday, 8 June 1996. The day Venables had waited two and a half years for. When he was given the job by the FA he looked into the future and saw this year, this month, this day, this game. The waiting was over. He had told his critics, his friends, the country, to judge him in June. We were behind him, but there was a curious edge to the occasion because it was his first competitive game as England coach. Incredibly, after two and a half years, he named a side that had never played together. Not once. Partly because of injuries, partly because of form and mainly because with Terry Venables you can never tell.

The players went for a walk after breakfast at their Burnham Beeches Hotel. Then Venables chatted with them briefly before they boarded the coach to arrive at Wembley at 1.45 p.m., right in the middle of the opening ceremony. The cheers of the crowd as the players walked on to the pitch in their suits drowned what was taking place in the official goings-on out in the middle. It could only happen in England but no one seemed to mind.

The last player to leave the pitch and get ready for the game was, inevitably, Gascoigne. He stood, hands on hips, occasionally looking at his watch, while Mick Hucknell and Simply Red sang their song for Europe, 'We're in this Together'. Gazza is certainly the people's champion. They love him because he is our best player. They identify with him because he is a cheeky rebel. But he knew he had to produce. This time. Would it be his day? His tournament?

After the first game the question was still unanswered.

England for an hour were good, encouraging and full of signs that we could be a success. But it was not enough. Gazza and the team ran out of stamina. We ran out of Gaz. Was it the booze? No, don't be stupid, said Venables and the players. Was it the heat? Maybe, but the Swiss seemed to cope. Was it the tension? Yes, the tension, the expectancy. Poor excuse that. Was it that already we do not look good enough? Well, it is a bit early but that could be right.

Or was it that the coach, the greatest coach we have, had been conning us all these years? Again too early. But the jury was definitely still out on Venables and England after game one of Euro 96.

For the first hour we were impressive. Gazza floated like a butterfly without stinging like a bee. The movement was good, the crowd encouraged and in the 23rd minute Alan Shearer ended his long international run without a goal. It was a superb strike, the ball moving from Gascoigne to Paul Ince and on to Shearer. There was a hint of offside but the flag stayed down and Shearer was on to the chance in a flash to drive it in off a post. His relief, our relief, was obvious as he reeled away to sprint down the side of the pitch and celebrate in front of the England fans.

It was a grand moment for him and us. Switzerland had hit the bar just before half-time after the dangerous Kubilay Turkyilmaz had outwitted and outpaced Stuart Pearce. But everything was relaxed at half-time. It looked good and encouraging and a second goal would kill off the Swiss and send England towards the quarter-finals.

The second goal never came. The Swiss proved to be stronger and England by the end were hanging on. The equaliser was deserved, although Terry Venables insisted that it was never a penalty as the ball hit Stuart Pearce's hands rather than him trying to control the ball. It looked like a penalty to me and Turkyilmaz wrong-footed David Seaman. The Arsenal goalkeeper made a superb save in the last seconds and a goal then would have been disastrous.

Disappointment, frustration and worry. They all came to mind at the final whistle. Switzerland celebrated and England trooped off dejected. Venables put on a brave face after the match and the players talked of definitely beating Scotland in a week's time to make sure of going through. It was going to be a long wait.

There were many questions still to answer. Seaman had done all that was asked of him an d Gary Neville produced an impressive

159

performance on his first competitive match for England. But the form of Tony Adams was worrying. He was caught for pace and pulled out of position too much. Was his knee still concerning him? It looked as if the fact that this was his first competitive match since January might catch up with him. Alongside Adams, Gareth Southgate was outstanding. A cool head under pressure, he produced a performance that suggested that here was an England international for many seasons to come.

Stuart Pearce, who sang the national anthem at the top of his voice, gave everything for his country. But the legs do not get him forward like they used to. Venables may have to think about a change at left back before the competition is over.

Across midfield Darren Anderton was bitterly disappointing. He did not look match fit and never accelerated past defenders like he once did for England. Coming into the side after so long out with a hernia injury was clearly a lot to ask. Gazza was Gazza. All eyes were on him and he did not disappoint until the team fell away so badly in the second half. But do we expect, no, demand too much from Gascoigne? If he is not producing magic moments all the time do we mistake that for an ordinary performance? The pressure on him to have a great European Championships is enormous. Bigger than any other player.

Ince, allowed to get forward more, was not the swashbuckling player we had seen and come to expect, and Steve McManaman failed to deliver. He had begun well and then faded badly with the rest. It was still a surprise when Venables took off Gazza and McManaman and the crowd showed their dislike for the double decision.

Shearer's goal excuses him from all criticism while alongside him Teddy Sheringham only gave freedom to those critics who say that he is only in the side because of his friendship with the coach. Against Switzerland Sheringham failed to ignite any England attacks. He looked lacklustre.

Venables broke with tradition and gave the England players 48 hours off after the game. They dispersed at Wembley and were told to return to the Burnham Beeches Hotel on Monday night. I thought it was a strange decision. I believe it is best that the players stay together for the duration of a major tournament. Time off, away from the coach and the pattern of build-up and preparation, means the players are vulnerable to outside pressures and goings-on.

Sure enough, Venables had another crisis on his hands by the Monday morning. It materialised that three players, Spurs pair Sheringham and Sol Campbell and Liverpool's Jamie Redknapp, had been spotted in a nightclub until 2.30 a.m. on Sunday morning. They had not broken any rules but staying out that late after the controversies of Hong Kong and off the back of a poor performance was naive and unprofessional. They should also have known that we are in an era of kiss and tell. The public

Venables at Heathrow Airport returning from the infamous tour to Hong Kong and China. Televisions were broken but Venables defended his players.

ABOVE:
Paul Gascoigne's magnificent goal against Scotland. One of the European Championship highlights.

LEFT:
Gazza and Teddy Sheringham celebrate the goal against Scotland.

The picture of the year. Six years of emotion is released after Pearce's penalty against Spain.

Seaman has just saved another penalty and he tells Europe that England are in the semi-final.

One of the saves that made Seaman the World's Number One: this time in the penalty shoot-out against Spain.

England are in the semi-final. David Seaman is congratulated by Steve Stone (left) and Nick Barmby after his penalty save.

RIGHT:
The misery of a missed penalty. Southgate is consoled by Paul Gascoigne while David Platt looks dejected.

Venables puts over a point to Bryan Robson, his assistant, whom he wanted to groom as the next England coach.

Out with the old, bring in the new. Venables hands over to new England coach Glen Hoddle. He admitted later that he was envious.

will pick up a phone to a newspaper if they do not like something, or believe that someone in the public eye is out of order. Sure enough the players' nightclub visit was splashed all over the front page of the *Sun* on Monday morning and it produced another stinging Venables press conference the following Tuesday.

On the Monday afternoon at Villa Park Scotland drew with Holland, a result that only put pressure on Venables. By the time he walked into the tented press facilities at the team's Bisham Abbey training camp he was ready for the cross-examination, on and off the pitch. It ended with Venables accusing the English press of being traitors to the national team. It was a word that was to haunt him all the way up to the match against Scotland.

The one thing I have noticed about Terry is that you cannot take him by surprise. As far as the media are concerned he is streetwise, cute, clever and ready for most things. If he wants to say something he will, if he does not then there is no way you are going to prise it out of him. On this Tuesday morning he was ultra-defensive of his players, particularly the trio in question. He snapped: 'The three players came to me last night upset and amazed by the publicity. They had done nothing wrong. They were three young lads out together having a few beers. I had given them permission.'

Until 2.30 a.m., only hours after letting the nation down with a disappointing performance? 'Whatever time it was I have no problem with them,' added Venables. 'There is no alcohol ban when they are not in the camp. The other players went home to their families and probably had the same amount to drink but no one knows about that. The German and Italian players have wine with their meal. What would we make of that? We would call it progressive thinking.

'Jack Charlton and his Irish players always drank Guinness in public. Jack, in fact, made a big issue of it. I know for a fact that the German and Dutch players have been out in bars or clubs. It is part of relaxing. Why will you not accept that?

'The criticism we get is awful. We are becoming hardened to it but do not understand it. Why is it necessary to do what you are doing? There are some people who appear like traitors to us. We feel that you are trying to turn the public against us. In turn that reflects the mood in the stadium. It is negative. I thought we would all be pulling together. The players feel they are on their own. It is certainly building up a strong resolve in the camp.

'I have received many letters offering support. It is not, however, coming from the media. We are the host nation but at the moment I feel we are throwing away the advantage of being at home. Steve Howard of the *Sun* was here last week and told me that if there was not anything to write about, you would all find something. At least he was honest even though it was strong to say it. Then everyone backs him up.

'I have known a lot of you a long time and I do feel that traitors is the right word. Every time a major tournament comes round there seems to be an insatiable appetite to criticise. What is the aim of trying to turn the public against us? I am the one under pressure. If I was unhappy with the players I would say to them, "What are you doing?" or "What are you doing to me?", but I have no complaints.'

Venables was particularly upset by criticism of Gascoigne from Jeff Powell in the *Daily Mail*. Powell is a close friend of Venables. But he christened Gazza 'The Guzzler' and said that Venables had to drop him against Scotland. The coach replied: 'It is ridiculous to suggest that Gascoigne should be dropped. What was wrong with his performance? I took him off but this is a squad situation. Replacing players is part and parcel of my job in the next few weeks.

'Yes, we did go off the boil after an hour. We started playing long and it came straight back to us. But I am not particularly unhappy. Had this been in a foreign country we would not be too unhappy. But different emotions are involved. My message to you all is do not panic, don't lose your nerve.'

The traitors issue triggered a fierce reaction. TV stations, at home and abroad, and radio wanted the media to answer. Did we feel like traitors? I took great exception to the suggestion and said so many times. I was insulted by the term 'traitor'. I have been covering England for many years and there is no one more patriotic than me. I desperately want England to win the European Championships but you simply cannot ignore players behaving badly and poor performances.

Fact: A ridiculous booze-up in Hong Kong. Fact: Property damaged on the way home from the Far East. Fact: A disappointing and frustrating first game in Euro 96. Fact: Three players out until the early hours, drinking and surrounded by punters, directly after the Swiss match.

If Venables had to give the players time off with their families why not invite wives, children and girlfriends to a huge family get-together at Bisham? There they could booze, bonk and do what they liked behind closed doors.

I also thought it was ridiculous that the FA waited until Tuesday morning for Venables to have his inquest into the Switzerland game. It should have been done on Sunday. Bang. Out of the way and on to Scotland. Instead it meant that we had got to the middle of the week and we were still trying to explain why we faded away in the second half at Wembley five days earlier.

There was more bad news when Newcastle centre half Steve Howey twisted his ankle on a training jog back home in Newcastle on the Monday. Howey was advised to keep his fitness up and turned his ankle over in a pot-hole while running around Newcastle's training camp. 'It is the curse of the central defenders,' moaned Venables. 'Tell me about it.' Howey was on crutches and almost certainly out of the European Championships.

TWENTY-FOUR

Gazza the Great

England v Scotland. Wembley, 15 June 1996.
England 3, Scotland 0. Scorers: Shearer, Gascoigne. Attendance: 76,864.

England Team: Seaman, G. Neville, Adams, Pearce (Redknapp) (Campbell), Southgate, Anderton, Ince (Stone), Gascoigne, McManaman, Sheringham, Shearer. Booked: Ince, Shearer.

Football came home on this day. So did Paul Gascoigne.

There was something wonderfully refreshing about Wembley on 15 June 1996. It was a match that had been built up as the confrontation with the auld enemy. Yet when I walked up to the stadium there was not a sniff of intimidation or rivalry. That atmosphere was transferred inside where the England fans celebrated a great England victory with a show of sheer delight and unity.

It was a happy occasion. A great occasion. The song, written by *Fantasy Football League* pair Frank Skinner and David Baddiel, and sung by the Lightning Seeds pop group, has been adopted as the anthem for Euro 96. Football's coming home, three lions on the shirt, 30 years ago . . . and Skinner and Baddiel were there to wave the baton from their seats in the stand for the wildly celebrating fans.

What a transformation from the mood after the first game, and the mood within the press centre. For a ten-minute period after the game, with Paul Gascoigne, Alan Shearer and David Seaman, the three main heroes, dancing around the pitch, it was the happiest atmosphere I have known in the famous old stadium for years. It brought home just how much the English public want us to succeed.

It also brought home to me that perhaps we are too hard on the players. We, the critics, may not be reflecting true public opinion. Do the fans care that Gascoigne goes on a bender in Hong Kong, or that some of the players are up half the night only hours after a disappointing performance? It seems they don't. What they want is success and here was evidence that all was forgiven.

When I returned to my car shortly after seven o'clock, a group of people from Manchester were having a drink before driving home. They were keen to talk about the game with me and quickly made me realise that they thought we were too harsh on the players. 'Get behind Gazza, get behind the team,' was the message. I thought about that a lot over the weekend. As a newspaperman you know what a story is and are also disappointed if the players drop below standards. As a fan, and we all are, there is clearly a balance to reach. Those supporters inside Wembley on this day only cared about one thing. It certainly was not late-night boozing, or the people who wrote about it. Their sympathy and magnificent vocal support was with Terry Venables and the players.

It was an impressive England performance. This time they did not fade. In fact we finished stronger. The plan was to pace ourselves for the first half and then hit Scotland hard during the second. It worked perfectly, even if it did take a David Seaman penalty save to turn the game.

Venables selected the same team and the build-up involved a lot of tub-thumping from his assistant Bryan Robson. The Middlesbrough manager, a veteran of controversial England tours and tournaments, urged everyone to get behind the team. 'Young lads like Robbie Fowler and Steve McManaman are going to be out of order now and again. But to knock them is far too easy. Let's get together and start working for the same things.'

Robson said that England were better than Scotland. That we had more skill, ability and were stronger. He also thought that it was the perfect game for Paul Gascoigne, the current Footballer of the Year in Scotland. Venables talked of the passion and commitment of his players. There was concern over it developing into a war with a series of inter-club battles in prospect, Tottenham's Teddy Sheringham v Colin Calderwood, Blackburn's Alan Shearer v Colin Hendry and Gascoigne and Stuart McCall in a Rangers head-to-head.

We over-worried. It was not a war. It was a great occasion, with England this time producing all the aces in the second half. After a game of cat and mouse in the first half, England suddenly rose to the occasion. Jamie Redknapp replaced Stuart Pearce with Gareth Southgate switching to left back and we were a different side. For 20 minutes at the start of the second half Scotland were overrun. Steve McManaman produced his best spell for his country, running at defenders, going past them and causing havoc. Gascoigne was alive and kicking. Shearer began to look dangerous and the movement of the England team was inspirational.

The breakthrough goal came after 53 minutes. Gary Neville, impressive, confident and developing into a true international, produced the best cross of the game and there was Shearer again, bending low to power a header beyond Andy Goram. Shearer stood in front of the England fans, arms spread wide to engulf the flames of joy, drinking in the atmosphere. What a heady moment that must be for any sportsman. You and the fans, locked in emotion.

England went for the kill and it almost came. Another goal in that onslaught would have seen Scotland cave in. Scotland somehow survived and regained their organisation, control and composure. They were awarded a penalty when Tony Adams was judged to have tripped Gordon Durie and English hearts fell. The next 60 seconds, however, were to prove not only the turning-point for the team but the moment that Paul Gascoigne had been waiting for. It might, just might, have been the minute that transformed England's European Championship. There is nothing like confidence.

The penalty, taken by Scotland captain Gary McAllister, was saved by David Seaman. The Arsenal goalkeeper always guesses one way to go and this time his body was in the way of McAllister's fiercely struck kick. The ball crashed into his elbow and soared away for a corner. 'I can't explain how I felt. It was the best feeling I have known,' said Seaman. 'To save a penalty at Wembley in a game that mattered so much has to be the best. It does not matter how you save a penalty. Get anything on it, even it means water coming to your eyes.' Seaman revealed that the ball had rolled off the spot just as McAllister was running up to take the penalty. 'He was entitled to stop and retake it,' added Seaman. 'I was surprised he carried on but delighted that he did.' If Seaman felt elated, it was nothing to how Gazza would feel a few seconds later.

In the 79th minute the ball fell to Darren Anderton, who switched it inside to Gascoigne. In a trice Gazza had knocked the ball over Colin Hendry, chested it down and hit a stunning volley past Andy Goram before the ball hit the turf. Brilliant, superb, a goal in a million, the goal of the championship. Gazza went berserk. As he threw himself down on to the ground he signalled for his team-mates to squirt juice into his mouth in a rerun of the dentist's chair routine in Hong Kong. It showed what he thought of the publicity surrounding that.

Love him or hate him, admire him or ignore him, you can't stop talking about him. This was suddenly Gascoigne's match. This was his answer to all the doubts, the anti-headlines, the media machine that has written millions and millions of words about him. It was one of the greatest goals England had seen. Delivered by a player who has more talent than any other. Venables admitted: 'I could never have scored it. To score a goal like that at pace was incredible.'

Gazza, of course, would not talk after the match. Hurt by the criticism, he and Steve McManaman were out of the dressing-room and up the tunnel 15 minutes after the end of the game. Head down and no comment.

Right or wrong to act like that? It has to be wrong, doesn't it? You have to be bigger than that. Yes, he has been criticised but he has also been praised more than any other player. What Gascoigne must come to terms with is the media. If he does not, if he reacts to everything, then it will haunt him for the rest of his career. If you are a superstar you have to accept publicity, good or bad. And it cannot always be good. What he has to realise is that a lot of anti-press that comes his way is self-inflicted.

The players, on both sides, talked long and hard about the pressure Gascoigne is under. His Rangers team-mate Ally McCoist said: 'I have never known a player in my life under so much pressure. It is incredible and I have no idea how he handles it. But he does. This goal was probably his answer to a lot of people.'

The goal excited young Gary Neville so much that he 'lost his head' on the pitch. 'I have never been so elated,' he said. 'I was on a high.' That is the effect a good performance and a great goal has on us all.'

It materialised that Gascoigne raced away from Wembley to meet Sheryl, his girlfriend and mother of his son, Regan, to propose. She said yes. Their fiery on-off relationship was definitely back on and the wedding was planned for 1 July, the day after the European Championship final. Gazza was desperate for a double celebration.

Venables now had the problem of keeping Gascoigne fit, calm and in perfect shape for the forthcoming matches. Holland came next, on the Tuesday, and Gazza held the key. One master plan by Venables was to pack Gascoigne off for secret fishing trips with goalkeeper Seaman. Both are fishing mad and the coach felt that two hours sitting quietly by the water's edge would be good for him. On the Thursday and Friday afternoons before the Scotland match the players slipped away to a trout lake close to the team's Burnham Beeches Hotel. There they sat, unnoticed, catching fish, chatting away and completely out of reach of the media. Gazza has always been hyped up, especially in big tournament situations. Steve Double of the FA press office explained: 'Sending him fishing was the only way we could keep him quiet. Sometimes in the morning he is banging on the players' doors wanting to know if they fancy a game of table tennis.'

The victory sent England heading towards the Dutch in super-confident mood. David Seaman was at the top of his game and talking of being regarded as the world's number one. He said that one save in the game, going to his left to clutch back a header from Gordon Durie, was the best save of his career. While the penalty stop got the headlines it was interesting that he rated another save as his most important.

In front of Seaman, Gary Neville is here to stay. Tony Adams was back to his old self, despite feeling the knee injury and Gareth Southgate proved not only his international pedigree but his ability to switch positions mid-match.

Stuart Pearce, taken off at half-time, is a problem. Venables may need to introduce a younger man with Philip Neville, the younger brother of Gary, the obvious candidate. It would make them the first brothers to play together since the Charltons, Bobby and Jack, won the World Cup 30 years earlier.

In midfield McManaman was outstanding, Darren Anderton again disappointing, Gazza wonderful and Paul Ince tough, determined and an important team player. Teddy Sheringham can still give the side more while Alan Shearer looks suddenly full of goals.

There were disappointments. Jamie Redknapp twisted his ankle and left Wembley on crutches. He was quickly ruled out of the Holland game. David Platt's rib injury is causing concern and he was not fit to play any part in the match against Scotland. Also, Shearer collected a booking. One more and he misses the next match. It was a problem Venables wrestled with in his build-up to the match against Holland. He needed Shearer yet did not want him to miss the quarter-final looming on the Saturday. A silly booking by a fussy referee would ruin that.

But worry was not really on the menu and England moved towards yet another important clash with a country which had the Indian sign over us. Holland had beaten England during the 1988 European Championships in Germany, with Marco Van Basten scoring a superb hat-trick. Then under Graham Taylor they drew at Wembley 2–2 after England had led 2–0, and beat us 2–0 in Rotterdam to prevent us qualifying for the World Cup. Dennis Bergkamp scored in both matches. It was time to paint over the orange gloss of the Dutch with some good old English red and white emulsion. It was also the game Venables had been looking forward to most. He loved the Dutch style, and desperately wanted to show his doubters that his England could master them.

TWENTY-FIVE

Football Comes Home

England v Holland. Wembley, 18 June 1996.
England 4, Holland 1. Scorers: Shearer (2), Sheringham (2).
Attendance: 76,798.

England Team: Seaman, G. Neville, Adams, Southgate, Pearce, McManaman, Ince (Platt), Gascoigne, Anderton, Sheringham (Barmby), Shearer (Fowler). Booked: Ince, Southgate, Sheringham.

It does not get any better than this. No way. It can't, can it?

Wembley on this night was alive to the sound of music. Magic music composed by coach Terry Venables and played with passion, skill, excitement and success by his players. It was the greatest night Wembley has seen since England won the World Cup 30 years ago. Fans unashamedly wept tears of joy and emotion as England thrashed the Dutch masters from Holland. It was not expected and that made it all the more satisfying. It was a party inside the famous old stadium and you had to be English to really savour and appreciate the moment. We had waited so long for a night to remember and here it was.

Nights like this do not come around very often and they have to be sucked in and tasted. This one will stay with the fans and everyone else for many, many years. It was one of those where you will say in years to come, 'I was there.' Terry Venables was bursting with pride, desperate to say what he really wanted to about victory over a side he has greatly admired. Venables loves Dutch football and studied it closely during his two-and-a-half-year reign in control. Then, when it mattered, he destroyed it. Holland coach Guus Hiddink admitted: 'Terry Venables made a fool of me. We had a plan but it was destroyed. We could not compete with England, they taught us a lesson in every department of the game.'

Venables called it the greatest, most satisfying night of his life. 'Because of the way we played, because of the opposition and because of the importance of the occasion,' he said as he stood on the stage down in the mixed zone area half an hour after the final whistle.

After two and a half years of pressure, frustration, disappointment, on a roller-coaster ride of ups and downs, Venables had been building and planning away in his mind. This was the culmination. He always said that we must judge him in June 1996. Well, on a lovely, warm, summer's evening he passed the test. The jury were no longer out, they were on their feet applauding with the rest of the jubilant supporters.

Could England get better? Could they raise themselves again for the quarter-final against Spain? You sensed that anything could happen, and would. The players were bonded, they had the utmost respect for Venables and the confidence now was sky-high throughout the side. The passing and the movement of the England team was breathtaking. We outplayed the Dutch, out-thought them, outwitted them, we were quicker in mind and fitness. It was the best I had seen England play in more than 25 years. Our performance in the 1990 semi-final against Germany had been outstanding, this was better. And different. It was the football we had seen so often from the continentals. Football on a different wavelength, sophisticated passing, interchanging, football that made every fan say, 'Bloody hell, I did not know we could play like that.' Holland's Dennis Bergkamp said after the rout: 'No one is laughing at English football now.'

You did not want to leave the stadium because you had witnessed something special. Back at the media centre English journalists walked around with broad smiles on their faces. It was not a look that had followed us around many times. Venables had put it there and what a moment this was for him. How crazy that here he was just a possible three games from quitting. What would happen if England marched on in this form to take the trophy? The FA would end with egg on their faces and Noel White, the Liverpool director who, Venables claims, forced him to resign because of lack of support, would be public enemy number one.

Before, during and after the Dutch game Venables got a standing ovation from the Wembley crowd. He will be a national hero if we are crowned European Champions. So now, after this performance, the FA must realise that here is a coach, whatever they think of him, to master the rest of the world. Why had he been allowed to go? It is a question that is going to be asked all over again. At this stage I wonder what Glenn Hoddle is thinking. Taking over a successful European Championship team, with everyone wanting Venables to stay, is a tough job for such a young man.

Enough of that for the time being. Let us savour the moment. What England's victory over Holland did was to transform a nation. Suddenly football fans from all over the country woke up to realise that, just maybe, we had something special here. The phrase of the day was 'the feel good factor' and the England football team had introduced it to the people. And not just football people.

Isn't it amazing what a couple of victories can do? But it was the way in which we played that led to the change of attitudes. Flags appeared at windows of houses and shops, people celebrated in pubs all day, competitions started to offer tickets for the 'greatest game' and even the England footballers began to relax with the media. Ish.

The *Daily Mirror* newspaper, on the Thursday morning after the Holland victory, dedicated its entire back page to calling its football writing staff traitors for daring to criticise Terry Venables. Nothing like it had been seen before. It is what football does to people and we must never underestimate that.

Venables found himself trapped in the middle. On one side he had more good publicity and support than he had ever dreamt of, on the other he desperately tried to keep his players' heads out of the clouds. He knew that Spain would be tough. He could not go overboard. Not yet.

Before the match he had spoken of an acid test for his players. 'Holland', he said, 'are intelligent, sophisticated, experienced, mature opponents. It is going to be our toughest test so far.' We had not beaten them since 1982 and they, of course, had smashed our dreams too often. Before the game revenge was in the air. Humiliation for the Dutch most certainly was not.

Venables warned that Dennis Bergkamp had not been dealt with well enough in the past, but he stressed that Gazza's goal against Scotland would have fired a warning shot across the bows of every other side in the European Championships. 'We are not getting carried away,' he said, 'there is a lot of work to be done.'

How could he have imagined what would happen? He named an unchanged side and then sat back and watched them play out all his fantasies.

Alan Shearer got the first, a penalty after Paul Ince had been brought down by Holland captain Danny Blind. Shearer and Gascoigne had said before the kick-off that one of them would take it. It was Shearer, full of confidence and in the goal mood again. It was a perfect penalty and the atmosphere began to heat up.

The first 16 minutes of the second half were pure joy. Teddy Sheringham headed in Gascoigne's corner, Shearer got his second after magnificent work by Gascoigne, and Sheringham got his second when Darren Anderton's shot rebounded off the goalkeeper. It was not just the goals, it was the football. At one stage Gascoigne touched the ball eight times in an England attack that involved 14 passes without the Dutch getting near the ball. There were cries of 'Ole!' from England fans. It was carnival time.

Seaman emerged from the game rated as the world's number one after another superb save, this time from Dennis Bergkamp. Gary Neville has not yet put a foot wrong in the Championships, Tony Adams was a towering strength once again, Gareth Southgate grew in stature and Stuart Pearce used all of his experience.

Gazza was magnificent, clearly loving every minute. His passing was pin-point. He toyed with the Dutch. Paul Ince produced his best performance so far, only to blotch it with a booking that ruled him out of the quarter-final with Spain. Steve McManaman, switched to the right, was a revelation, just as he was in the opening 20 minutes of the second half against Scotland. Darren Anderton at last looked like his old self, while up front the S men shared the goals. Sheringham said: 'It was England's greatest performance for years and I was just so proud to be part of it.'

If Venables wanted to keep things calm, Pearce's arrival in the press tent the morning after could not have been better-timed. His answer to the question about England's finest performance was at least honest. 'No, a few years ago we won in Yugoslavia 4–1 when the pressure was on. I watched that match from the subs bench and thought it was better.

'Of course, our football against Holland was magnificent. We always said that once we had the game won the ball-players in the side like Paul Gascoigne and Steve McManaman could express themselves. That is what they did. And the boys up front are doing the business. But I like to be judged on winning things.

'Someone told me that Forest had a good season in Europe. No, they didn't, we got to the quarter-finals and then got thrashed by Bayern Munich. Yes, we have beaten Holland, but have only reached the last eight. Like them, let us wait a bit longer.

'The only thing I will say is that I have never known an atmosphere like it. The national anthem, for instance, is being sung by so many people. That is good. It is a party atmosphere. Winning helps, you know, it is a good feeling.

'Let us not go too berserk. As a player you keep averages and we are doing that within the squad. We must not get too excited or too depressed. The public will be looking for us to beat the Spanish. Our attitude is just to play them and see what happens. In my mind Holland has gone, my mind is focused on Spain. I am sure the manager is doing the same. He will be thinking about Spain and no doubt will be telling us to adjust, as he has all the way through the tournament so far.'

Pearce was right. Venables immediately said: 'You know the ritual, we have got a game coming up. The feet must go back on the floor, Spain will be tough. I have only admiration for their coach and he will be doing his homework on us.' Venables paid tribute to the crowd and the fierce feeling of English pride in the fans. 'The country is desperate for success and when we get a sniff they really go for it.'

The coach praised his players: 'I have said for a long time I don't think they realise how good they can be. It is getting there. It takes time. It is especially good and helpful when I can have the players together for this period of time. What I want is coming. We showed it against Switzerland. We improved against Scotland because we had looked at what went wrong. The confidence of the second half against

Scotland spilled over into the Holland game. It is progress.'

Venables talked about his sadness and envy about handing over to Glenn Hoddle and you could understand his feelings. Here was the team he had built playing magnificently and, deep down, I still believe that he regretted having to go. But go he would. Hopefully it would be in three matches' time, the quarter-final, semi-final and final of the European Championship.

If England got to the final what would the public do then? Venables already had them eating out of the palm of his hand. It would be an extraordinary situation. It must have been running through Venables's mind as he plotted his next move. The master coach. He could not have overlooked the fact that in three matches' time the nation might demand he stayed. Inside he must have been laughing, especially after all he had been through. But first Spain. The country where he managed at Barcelona. The country he loves and visits frequently for a short-break holiday.

There was one big difference now. After Scotland and Holland, especially Holland, the whole nation expected England to win. Venables knew that was dangerous. But whatever happened to him in the future he could wallow in the glory of beating Holland. It was a game to have a video of and watch over and over again.

TWENTY-SIX

Never So Nervous

England v Spain. Wembley, 22 June 1996.
England 0, Spain 0 (England won 4–2 on penalties). Attendance: 75,440.

England Team: Seaman, G. Neville, Adams, Southgate, Pearce, Anderton (Barmby), Gascoigne, Platt, McManaman (Stone), Shearer, Sheringham (Fowler). Booked: Neville

I first went to Wembley to watch England play in 1959. Brian Clough was centre forward, Don Howe played, so did Jimmy Greaves and other famous names at that time like Ronnie Clayton, John Connolly and Eddie Halliday. Sweden beat us 3–2. I stood behind the goal with the father of a friend of mine and took in the excitement, the occasion and the sheer pleasure of being there. I have never lost that feeling about going to Wembley. I don't care much for the approach, apart from the history of the Twin Towers, but once inside the famous old stadium has never lost the feeling of expectancy.

The matches since then, first as a fan and then a journalist, have been many. Some great, some nerve-racking, some disappointing, some bloody awful. All of them, however, stay long in the memory. I stood on the terraces when we beat Germany in 1966. I was in the press box when we tried desperately to beat Poland in 1972, I have marvelled at Bobby Moore, Bobby Charlton and Jimmy Greaves, applauded Gary Lineker's goals. I have never seen us play better than we did against Holland. Away from Wembley there was that night in Turin when we lost in the World Cup semi-final, the fabulous European Championship victory in Belgrade in 1987, the victory over Cameroon in the quarter-final of the World Cup, the memories . . . But I have never been so nervous and excited as I was at Wembley on this June Saturday afternoon. The tensions, the raw feeling of passion from the crowd, the nail-biting climax of the penalty shoot-out got to me.

Extra time was bad enough. For the first time the golden goal was introduced in a major tournament. The first scorer wins. Sudden death. Every time Spain attacked there were screams of 'no' from the press box as journalists, caught up in the feeling of the nation, willed

England to victory. The tension was greater than Turin. Probably because, with the tournament in England, everyone of us was gripped in the feeling that had caught the country. We were not locked away inside the camp, as you are abroad, we were right in the middle of it. And it was great and so exciting.

Every match at Wembley in the European Championships was a happening. It was more than a football match. By now Terry Venables and his players were public heroes and the feel-good factor had spread right the way through England. Wives, girlfriends, people who knew absolutely nothing about football, were caught up in a roller-coaster ride of dreams. By the time David Seaman made his penalty shoot-out save from Nadal millions of people were on the edge of their seats.

The biggest cheer of the Test match, played across London at Lord's, was reserved for Seaman and England going through. Umpire Dickie Bird stopped play so the crowd could see the replay on Lord's giant TV screen. England were the first item on the news broadcasts, people danced in the streets, Trafalgar Square was full of celebrating fans until the early hours of Sunday morning.

It was staggering, the transformation of the public in the space of two weeks. Switzerland had been disappointing, Gascoigne's goal and Seaman's penalty save against Scotland had set the tone, the country went berserk after Holland and by the end of the Spain game everyone, and I mean everyone, was talking about Venables and the England players. Anyone who did not feel elated, or did not get caught up in the sheer English pride of it all, was either a liar or unable to express true feelings.

What an incredible turnaround for Venables. No one was questioning him now. The master coach had proved himself. A controversial two-and-a-half-year reign was ending in a blaze of glory. Not even he could have dreamt that it would climax like this. The further England went the more popular Venables became. The better England played the more embarrassing it became for the Football Association. The bigger the publicity the better Venables liked it.

He was enjoying himself. Deep down he was laughing his head off. He had not been given a vote of confidence by the International Committee, particularly Noel White, and had resigned because of it. I suspect that the International Committee were squirming with embarrassment by the time England reached the semi-final.

I discovered early in the European Championships, after the victory over Scotland, that moves were being made to keep Venables after all. Hoddle was the new coach but there were people inside Lancaster Gate who thought it was crazy that Venables's brain, coaching ability, ideas and world-wide knowledge be lost completely. They had spoken to him on a number of occasions and he was aware of the growing support building up for him inside and outside Lancaster Gate.

I spoke with White, the Liverpool director, on the Sunday night following England's quarter-final win. He did not, he said, feel like a Judas or a traitor. 'Why should I?' he asked. 'I said what I felt and Terry made a decision. He and I have met many times since he resigned and have nothing against each other. I wish him well and want him to win the European Championships. No, I would not feel embarrassed.'

White did reveal, however, that he and Venables had agreed not to say anything in public about each other, or the situation, during the European Championships. That was a giveaway that there was embarrassment and perhaps regret building at the FA. There were certainly some people, men who had become close to the coach, who would have liked him to stay in some capacity.

Venables could not lose now. By the time he went into the match against Spain he had the nation and the players as one. Spain, dark horses for the Championship, made noises about stopping Paul Gascoigne and Alan Shearer and a big, strong defender called Nadal, known as 'The Beast' in Spain, got a lot of publicity. Shearer's response was to say that he was not frightened by any words. 'The time to do the talking is out on the pitch,' he said. 'I have heard it all before.'

Venables, who recalled David Platt for the suspended Paul Ince, was the man of the moment. This was his team, his tactics and it was as if the players and the country knew that we were in safe hands. He asked the nation to roar England on. They did not need any persuading. On the Saturday morning I woke up early with THAT song, 'Three Lions' echoing in my head. I was a combination of excitement and nerves. God knows what it was like for the players.

The atmosphere inside the stadium was electric. The national anthem has never been sung so passionately and loudly as it has during these Championships. Stuart Peace screams it at the top of his voice, such is his fierce pride in his country. Gary Neville is the only England player not to sing the words and it took his brother Phil to reveal that Gary gets too nervous and caught up in the grip of tension to relax and sing. 'I have never known an atmosphere like it,' said Phil. 'When I hear the national anthem being sung I am a little envious of the other players. But just being out there is brilliant. You get goose-bumps on the back of your neck.' Phil revealed that Gary received letters from fans complaining about him not singing and accusing him of not having enough passion. 'That is nonsense,' said Phil. 'You only have to see how he celebrated Gazza's goal against Scotland to know how much he cares.'

The match was tense, with Spain unquestionably the better side for long periods. England had a spell at the start of the second half when they stepped up a gear but you feared every time Spain smoothed their way forward.

Alan Shearer had a left-footed shot saved superbly in the opening minutes, Gary Neville was booked, Seaman made a save from Manjarin as he came hurtling out of his area like a defender, Salinas scored a goal that was ruled offside only for TV replays to prove the referee wrong, Venables made a tactical change at half-time to prevent Spain attacking too dangerously down our right-hand side and the game went into extra time.

Venables said: 'The golden goal was introduced to make the games more positive and exciting but I think it has a different effect on teams. They become cautious and more defensive.'

And so to the penalty shoot-out, just as there had been in Turin six years ago. England won the toss and elected to take the first kick. Venables and his players had huddled in the middle of the pitch. It was interesting that they stayed on their feet while the Spanish lay down, jiggling their legs in the air in case of cramp. Tony Adams went around his players advising, inspiring. 'I told them to keep their legs moving because I had seen players seize up before in the tension of these shoot-outs,' he said.

The five takers before the game had been elected as Alan Shearer, David Platt, Stuart Pearce, Paul Gascoigne and Teddy Sheringham. Sheringham, however, had been substituted and Robbie Fowler was to take the fifth. Pearce, who had missed the vital penalty in Turin, had volunteered. When asked by Venables before the game he had said: 'You bet, number three.' It was Pearce, in fact, who went around the penalty-takers just before the start of the shoot-out, encouraging them and making sure they were in the right frame of mind. That was a big moment for a player under intense pressure not to miss again.

Shearer scored powerfully to goalkeeper Zubizarreta's right. All eyes on Seaman now. Could he make another save after his stop against Gary McAllister in the Scotland game? He did not have to. Hierro hit the bar. Wild scenes from the England fans.

Platt next. Tucked away cool as you like. So did Spain and then up stepped Pearce, just as he had done six years ago. Every eye in the country, inside the stadium and outside, watched him. He confessed afterwards: 'I felt my wife Jill's eyes burning a hole in my back. I could see her standing in the kitchen and asking, "Why is it always you who misses the penalties?"' He placed the ball on the spot, walked back a few paces, turned and smashed the ball into the bottom corner. There was a split second before realisation set in. Then Pearce turned to the crowd, pumped the air with his fists and screamed, 'Come on, come on.' It was a face of pure relief, delight and joy rolled into one. Six years of waiting were in that explosion of tension. It was the face of a hero and, for me, the face of 1996. Take a look at the picture. It is what sport is all about. The joy of winning. The release of tension.

Spain scored again and it was 3–2. Gazza next and we should never have doubted him. Easy. He took the acclaim with his chest puffed out, Chris Eubank-style. So Spain had to score to keep in the competition. Up stepped Miquel Angel Nadal, 'The Beast', who had not put a foot wrong in a super performance at the heart of the Spanish defence. He hit his penalty to the bottom right-hand corner. Seaman guessed the right way to dive and beat out the shot with his fists. The ball spun away to safety.

Chaos. Sheer joy for a nation drawn together in pride. Seaman, usually so unflappable, jumped to his feet, punched the air and wore the smile that said it all. Venables and Bryan Robson hugged each other, the other England players were enveloping Seaman in a mountain of celebration and even press executive David Davies, usually so calm, jumped to his feet in wild response. It was one of the great moments of sport.

You can't write scripts like this.

In the dressing-room area there was a great feeling of achievement. Smiles and hugs too as players, particularly Pearce and Seaman, talked about their great moments. Gazza had a piggy-back ride around the room, screaming and shouting at the top of his voice. There was even a rollicking for me from Seaman. As he emerged from a celebrating England dressing-room he caught my eye and said: 'I want a word with you later.'

I had made the mistake of writing an article a few days before calling Seaman the greatest goalkeeper in the world. Seaman, a reluctant hero, did not like it because it embarrassed him. I have taken a few rollickings for controversial stories in the past but never one for calling someone the best in the world. How funny footballers are that, even in a moment like this, they can find time to have a moan. I did not care. Seaman is the best and he should be proud to say it.

Pearce was happy to talk about his penalty but did not go overboard. 'There was never any question of me not taking one,' he said. 'A week after Turin I would have taken a penalty for England. Bottle? Not really. I think the English have a lot of bottle. They put their necks on the block when it matters. That is all I did. I will only repeat what I have been saying all along. We set out to win the tournament and now we are in the semi-final. Two games to go. Then we can celebrate.'

Pearce was right, of course, but the nation wanted to celebrate. Now. And they did. And how.

Some said that England were lucky. Perhaps. But who cared? You make your luck and ride it in football. Were we meant to win? Was our name on the trophy? Was Terry Venables supposed to go out in a blaze of absolute glory? We would find out soon enough.

Victory, however it was achieved, set up a semi-final showdown with Germany at Wembley. It was 1966 all over again, the chance to get our own back for that Turin semi-final defeat. Revenge was in the air and it was taken to the extreme by some tabloid newspapers. On the Monday morning, 24 June, the *Daily Mirror* carried a front page with pictures of Stuart Pearce and Paul Gascoigne in war helmets, with the headline 'Achtung! Surrender' and a story by their editor declaring *Daily Mirror* football war on Germany. It was to trigger days of abuse for the *Mirror* and other newspapers for using a football match with Germany to drag up the war in a sleazy attempt to win the circulation battle. On that Monday morning, and again in the evening, I did radio phone-ins for the BBC and was shocked by the feeling of anger that the public carried.

I believe that there is a thin dividing line between humour and bad taste and agreed that the *Mirror*, on this occasion, had gone over the top. They had meant it to be a joke, of course. What I did not realise was that the public did not find any of it humorous. They wanted to get behind the team in the right way and I have to say that if there was a lesson to be learned this was it. Public feeling ran high against the tabloids. We think we are sometimes clever in the things we do but on this occasion the *Mirror* were too clever for their own good.

The *Sun* has been guilty of going OTT in the past but I felt on this occasion we got the balance right. But tabloid newspapers will never please everyone all the time. My own pet hate about people who complain are those who say they would never read the *Sun* but do not like what it printed on the front page or page six. My other dislikes are radio or TV interviewers who begin their question, 'Well, the tabloids have been tough on you this week . . .' Where is their own opinion?

Terry Venables too felt strongly. On the Tuesday before the German game he said to a huge gathering of journalists, the biggest turnout so far at a media day at the Bisham training HQ, 'We have all had our battles in this room. That is fine as long as you do not step over the line. It is like anything in life. If you step over the line and make a mistake then you must pay the consequences. This time there has been an area of insults which are not funny. The people in this country are certainly not happy about them.

'The team have been supported wonderfully. Spain, for instance, could not believe the atmosphere that was created. They are envious of it. But you must have respect. For the opposition, another country. Let us get away from wars. We do not want to be reminded.'

I have never known Venables more relaxed than at this moment, going into the semi-final. Over the two and a half years he had always been helpful but a little standoffish. During the European

Championships, after that touchy start, he had clearly enjoyed himself. He was right in the middle of doing what he enjoys best, being with his players day in and day out and pitting his wits against the best coaches and players in Europe.

He had not lost his sense of humour. When I reminded him that tomorrow against Germany could be his last match he quipped: 'That is the third time you have said that.' And when a German reporter asked him if he felt the pressure he answered with a smile, 'Now that you mention it.' Both comments brought the house down and there was not a hint of animosity or ill-feeling towards him in the room. He had won. Whatever happened against Germany, Venables had answered all the question about himself as a football coach. And he knew it.

He had not yet said everything he wanted to say. That would come later, when it was all over. He said that beating Germany and reaching the final would represent the greatest moment of his life. He knew that he had the nation behind him and he said the right things: 'It is rare in your life to be able to forget all selfish feelings. To be able to give someone something else. We are in a position here to give the English people who have not felt too good about different things for different reasons something back. It does not happen very often.

'I have received thousands of letters from the public, wishing me well and it is nice to be wanted. I do not want to say too much because we have come this far. We are close but there is a long 90-minutes to play. If it is down to wanting, we want it. But there is a problem – so do Germany. That is the contest.'

There was a ridiculous fuss over the colour of England's shirts to be worn against Germany. Because both teams play in white UEFA had to toss a coin for the right for one country to wear their national colours. We lost and had to play in our second registered strip of grey. 'Grey?' everyone screamed. 'Why not the 1966 World Cup red?' That was impossible because the FA had a deal with manufacturers Umbro and the shirts were chosen long ago. Venables and the players did not mind. He added: 'It is not the colour, it is who goes in them. As long as they have three lions on the shirt, that is all that matters. Let us have no excuses, especially about the colour of the shirt. Come on, let's play the game.'

And so to the semi-final. The biggest game of Venables's and all the players' lives. Could England do it? Could we take revenge? Could we play as well as we did against Holland? Was our name on the trophy? The country waited with bated breath. Footballmania had swept through the nation. As Venables said: 'We are ready, confident and think we will do it. But in the end it can come down to anything. Anything can happen.'

179

TWENTY-SEVEN

England's Euro 96 Players

After two and a half years, 18 friendlies, nine wins, eight draws, one defeat, 27 goals for and ten against, 54 players called up and 47 used, including 27 new caps, Terry Venables finally named his 22 for the European Championships. He said separating the players he had worked with for so long was the toughest job of his career. He finally made up his mind on a pre-Championships trip to Hong Kong and the full list was released by the Press Association at 11.15 a.m. on Tuesday, 28 May, 24 hours before the official UEFA deadline for submitting squads.

Here are the men Venables entrusted with winning the European Championship:

DAVID SEAMAN (Arsenal). Age 32, caps 24, goals nil. An automatic choice as England's number one. Big and unflappable, his strength is his composure and confidence. Never panics, even under pressure. Is prone to the big-match howler, like against Nayim in the Cup Winners' Cup final, Paul Gascoigne's FA Cup semi-final free kick and Holland's two goals that knocked us out of the World Cup. But usually Mr Reliable. A big tournament for him, Seaman had a lot to prove.

TIM FLOWERS (Blackburn). Age 29, caps eight, goals nil. Venables stayed loyal to him despite a poor season. His form dropped alarmingly and he made too many mistakes for his own liking. He said at one stage that he thought his chance had gone. A great shot-stopper. If it is his day then he is as good as anyone.

IAN WALKER (Spurs). Age 24, caps two, goals nil. Lucky to be in. Was it because of Venables's Tottenham connection? Walker was one of four Tottenham players in the squad. There is no question that he has improved tremendously over the last 12 months after taking over as his club number one from Erik Thorstvedt. Walker is agile, a good shot-stopper and deals confidently with crosses. There was a justifiable lobby, however, to make Liverpool's David James the England number three. Selecting three goalkeepers was a stipulation of UEFA.

GARY NEVILLE (Manchester United). Age 21, caps ten, goals nil. Has come surging through the United academy of youth. For a 21-year-old Gary is confident, intelligent and a versatile player. He is useful to Venables in so far as he can play in two different defensive positions, either as full back or central defender marker. Has grown in confidence at international level and can be England's right back for years.

TONY ADAMS (Arsenal). Age 29, caps 40, goals four. Rated the best centre half in the country. Strong, determined, Mr One Hundred Per Cent, a great leader and invaluable at dead-ball situations. I believe that Adams was Venables's first choice as captain, despite his handing the skipper's job to David Platt. Managers and coaches say that Adams is underrated as a footballing centre half and is not just the old-fashioned stopper. It will be interesting to see what Venables does when he plays just three at the back. Will there still be room for Adams? And, going into the tournament, was he really match fit? His last competitive game was for Arsenal back in January.

STEVE HOWEY (Newcastle). Age 24, caps four, goals nil. Lucky to be in. He did not play for the last six weeks of the season and even his manager Kevin Keegan admitted that he could not be match fit. Howey only got in because Gary Pallister was ruled out with a back problem. Venables likes his ability to switch from defence into midfield. He is comfortable on the ball.

GARETH SOUTHGATE (Aston Villa). Age 25, caps four, goals nil. His ability to play in three positions, full back, central defender or midfield, made him a certainty. With only 22 men in his squad Venables knows that versatility is going to be vital. Southgate came through late to emerge as first choice to play in the defence. Good pace, reads the game well, tackles and intercepts well and his distribution is outstanding. Amazing to think that he was playing for Crystal Palace only a year ago.

SOL CAMPBELL (Spurs). Age 21, caps one, goals nil. Lucky to be in. Again, is it because he plays for Spurs and is known to be a favourite with Venables? Campbell's strength, like Southgate's and Neville's, is his ability to adapt to different positions. He can play at either full back, centre half or the holding player in midfield. But he did nothing really outstanding for Spurs and in my opinion still lacks quality on the ball. A fitness fanatic, he never eats the wrong food or does anything that would lessen his performance.

STUART PEARCE (Nottingham Forest). Age 34, caps 65, goals five. What a fantastic professional this is. He was told by Venables when he took over that he could not guarantee him a place and that Graeme Le Saux was his new first-choice left back. Pearce told the coach that he was prepared to sit in the stand if it meant being picked by his country. When Le Saux was injured Pearce came back stronger than ever and was in top form when the season ended. The fiercest tackler in football, he shows superb commitment and is a man to have on your side when the chips are down. Does not get forward like he used to.

PHIL NEVILLE (Manchester United). Age 19, caps one, goals nil. Younger brother of Gary and another Manchester United kid to break through. Venables could not find an understudy to Pearce until Neville became a United regular halfway through the season. Like Gary, he is mature for his age. The bonus is that he can play at both right and left back.

DARREN ANDERTON (Spurs). Age 24, caps 11, goals five. Terry waited all season for him. Anderton had three operations on a worrying groin injury and at one stage there looked no chance for him. He kept faith, as did the England coach, and Anderton got himself fit to play in Tottenham's last three games of the season. Then he scored twice against Hungary and there was never any doubt after that. Great pace, control and the ability to go past defenders. His goals are a bonus. He is comfortable either wide on the right or in midfield, where he plays for his club.

STEVE STONE (Nottingham Forest). Age 24, caps six, goals two. An outstanding hit as Anderton's understudy, he took to international football as if he had been playing it all his life. Good attitude, he is confident and believes that he is the best in the business at what he does – yes, better than Anderton! Stone is a players' player. He will run and work all day for you. He is quick, brave and scores vital goals. He feels he should be in the team but is likely to have to revert to the role of understudy.

PAUL GASCOIGNE (Glasgow Rangers). Age 29, caps 38, goals seven. What more is there to say about this man? The best British player I have seen since George Best. But a fool to himself. He has abused his body and has never grown up. A genius on the pitch, a controversial figure off it. These Championships represent the turning point of his career that has promised so much but failed to produce. If Gascoigne delivers then the nation will forgive him for his behaviour one more time. If he fails and England struggle then it could be the end of Gazza. That would be a sad, but inevitable, climax to an extraordinary story.

Has he got that pace to take him past the best defenders in Europe? Can he dominate big internationals again? The nation holds its breath.

PAUL INCE (Inter Milan). Age 28, caps 19, goals two. Don't leave home without him. My first choice in any England side. Tough, hard, great tackler, good ball-winner, outstanding commitment, useful distribution and pace, Ince has the lot. It is incredible that going into the Championships he had only 19 caps at the age of 28. There has been some waste somewhere down the years. He is one of my tips to be among the outstanding players in the European Championships. If we are successful one of the main reasons will be this man. He has got a fierce on-pitch temper but that is just part of the never-say-die attitude. He is the one world-class player in the 22.

DAVID PLATT (Arsenal). Age 29, caps 58, goals 27. You had to go for Platt's big tournament experience and his goalscoring record, the best by far in the England squad. He missed a big chunk of the season with two operations on a right-knee cartilage injury and struggled to reach his best form for Arsenal. But he grew in confidence towards the end of the season and his goal against Hungary at Wembley emphasised his importance to the side. He still has the ability to arrive unnoticed into the box. Not, however, guaranteed his place in midfield when the competition begins.

JAMIE REDKNAPP (Liverpool). Age 24, caps four, goals nil. Lucky to be in. One of the new generation and with a big future, but fortunate to ease out Robert Lee of Newcastle United and especially Dennis Wise of Chelsea. A hamstring injury kept him out from before Christmas right the way through to the FA Cup semi-final against Aston Villa, when Michael Thomas was furious to be replaced. Redknapp has pace, is hard-working and can play either a defensive midfield or full attacking role. He scores spectacular goals from long range. Went into the Championships saying he felt like one of the luckiest players in the world.

STEVE McMANAMAN (Liverpool). Age 24, caps ten, goals nil. Has the ability and pace to take on any defender in the world and cause havoc. That is what he does for Liverpool, only in a free role with the licence to do what he likes. With England he is more restricted to a position on the left of midfield, where he is not so effective, and there are those who believe that it is impossible for McManaman and Gascoigne to play in the same side. A big tournament for him – McManaman has to prove that he can cut like a knife through the best defences around.

LES FERDINAND (Newcastle). Age 29, caps ten, goals four. There were question marks against him being in right up until the last moment. He said he was very relieved to get the nod. He has electric pace, is strong, scores great goals and looks a million dollars in the Premiership. But there have always been question marks against his class at the highest level – and his bottle for the big match. His record of four goals from ten caps, however, is better than that of Alan Shearer, Venables's first choice striker.

ROBBIE FOWLER (Liverpool). Age 21, caps three, goals nil. The Tosketh terror, the little striker from Liverpool who was the goalscoring sensation of the season. Can he do it for England? How many times have we asked that question of our best league strikers? Fowler had a disappointing debut against Croatia and a dreadful Cup final but had to be in because of his ability to score goals out of nothing. At Liverpool he struck a wonderful understanding with Stan Collymore and we were still working out his best England pairing when the competition started. The kind of player to have on the bench if things are going badly. Could turn out to be the Geoff Hurst of 1996, getting in late and staying in to become the hero.

NICK BARMBY (Middlesbrough). Age 22, caps six, goals two. Lucky to be in. Again, one of Venables's favourites. He signed him for Spurs and has always been an admirer. Barmby scored twice against China to win the vote over Peter Beardsley and this was the most controversial selection of them all. Venables received heavy criticism for axeing Beardsley, including from Newcastle manager Kevin Keegan and Beardsley's old England strike partner Gary Lineker. They both felt that Beardsley's experience, big-match temperament and ability to change a game would have been ideal. Keegan said he should have been used on the bench as a secret weapon. 'I feel sick for him,' he said. Barmby, however, has the ability to play in the role just behind the strikers that Venables likes and his potential to score more goals probably just won him the vote.

TEDDY SHERINGHAM (Spurs). Age 30, caps 15, goals 2. No-one is more loyal to Sheringham than Venables. There have always been question marks against his pace at the highest level, but the England coach is more interested in his intelligence and ability to link things together. There is no doubt that Sheringham is Venables's on-pitch brains. For me, however, there were still not enough goals from him going into a tournament of this importance.

ALAN SHEARER (Blackburn). Age 25, caps 23, goals five. Desperate for a goal going into Euro 96. Rated the best striker in the country and an automatic choice. Intelligent and hard-working, he leads the line superbly, is unselfish, brave and the scorer of wonderful Premiership goals. But the pressure is on because it has been too long at international level without a goal. Venables would have to drop him if the run continued and England were not winning matches. Shearer says that his confidence has not been dented and that the goals will come. 'Anyway, I am more than just a goalscorer,' he said. But it was goals that England were desperate for and all eyes were on Shearer.

There are ten survivors from the first squad Venables picked two and a half years earlier: Seaman, Flowers, Adams, Pearce, Anderton, Gascoigne Ince, Platt, Sheringham and Shearer. Three more, Pallister, Le Saux and Jones, would have been in had they not suffered injuries. It is a squad with a mixture of youth and experience but a worry over the lack of a left-footed attacking player to give balance down that side. Jason Wilcox, who made an impressive debut against Hungary, is unlucky not to have been selected. I can't understand why Venables introduced Wilcox after a season of injury, played him and then discarded him. Wilcox also makes a lot of club goals for Alan Shearer. Beardsley is the biggest shock exit, although Dennis Wise, a friend of Venables and a regular visitor to his London club, had every reason to expect to be in. His axing shows that the English coach has a ruthless streak behind the smile.

There were three survivors from the 1990 World Cup: Platt, Gascoigne and Pearce. It is the squad Venables has built and kept in his mind ever since he took over. As Bobby Robson said before he played his first international as England manager: 'That's my team, and we are coming to get you.'

The waiting is over. All the controversy, drama and intrigue of Venables's reign is forgotten as he goes into the most important three weeks of his career. The European Championships 1996. Venables and his men are ready. Will they, can they, produce?

TWENTY-EIGHT

German Penalty Heartbreak Again

England v Germany. Wembley, 26 June 1996.
England 1, Germany 1 (Germany won 6–5 on penalties). Scorer:
Shearer. Attendance: 75,862.

England Team: Seaman, Southgate, Adams, Pearce, Platt, Anderton,
Ince, Gascoigne, McManaman, Shearer, Sheringham. Booked:
Gascoigne.

Anything can happen. It did. Alan Shearer scored after just three
minutes.

Anything can happen. It did. Germany soon equalised and these
great, old rivals produced the contest of the Championships. It should
have been the final. No, this was the final.

Anything can happen. It did. Darren Anderton hit a post in extra
time and Gascoigne missed two chances.

Anything can happen. It did. It went to penalties and after five
great strikes by both sides, Gareth Southgate missed.

Terry Venables's 'anything can happen' words haunted him
throughout another magnificent match that once more had a
capacity, emotional, excited Wembley crowd on the edge of their
seats. England had been involved in three superb matches, against
Holland, Spain and Germany. They were out but the memory will
live on. So too, we hope, will the legacy.

There were words of praise all round for Venables and the way
England had performed. We had seen a different England. Confident,
skilful players interchanging, passing, creating chances and offering
up a completely different argument about English football.

Venables would have liked to have won the title – of course he
would – but you could see in his eyes after the game, and in the
morning following the defeat, a sense of achievement. It must have
been nervous for him going into the Championships. His reputation
was on the line. Phoney or great coach? Con man or convincing? For
so long he had told us to judge him when it mattered and, on
Wednesday night, despite defeat, he knew he would go down in
history as one of England's most successful managers.

We had only won two of five matches but it was the level of

186

performance and the new look about the team that was so refreshing. When it was all over Venables gave his speech on the stage at the mixed zone area and as he finished he was given a spontaneous ovation by German and English journalists. As the applause broke out he hugged his old friend Graham Turner, who was acting as an official UEFA interpreter.

These are special moments that are hard to explain. You have to be there to witness it. To appreciate it.

It was also a tournament when so many of England's young players came of age and the established ones added to their reputation. David Seaman grew in stature throughout and in my opinion is the world's number one goalkeeper. Arsenal will benefit from his success in Euro 96. Gary Neville was magnificent and can be England's right back, or wing back, under Glenn Hoddle for years to come. He did not put a foot wrong, apart from two reckless tackles that cost him two bookings and his place in the semi-final. Tony Adams has never played better than his performances against Spain and Germany. He was a magnificent inspiration to the side. When I asked him if he rated his displays as the best of his career he answered: 'You just don't realise where I am coming from, do you? It is not me that matters, it is the team.' A modest lionheart no less.

Gareth Southgate went into the tournament with five caps. If he keeps his form and fitness he can turn that into 55 easily. Despite his missed penalty he was my England defender of the tournament. Here is a mature, talented, skilful player who can adapt to any position he is asked to play. He proved he had bottle by volunteering for the sudden death penalty and I will never forget how he handled himself in the mixed zone interview area after the match. I cannot think of another England player who would have been able to handle that bitter frustration and the tears he spilled, then give first a radio interview and after a ten-minute wait while German manager Bertie Vogts spoke, an interview for the newspapers. Southgate's eyes were red with crying but he answered every question honestly and said that he would have to live with it and he was determined that it would make him a stronger, better person and player. He apologised for letting the country down.

What a transformation of emotions two faces tell. Pearce's explosion of emotion after his penalty against Spain. Southgate's misery. They told the story of England's European Championship.

In his last major tournament Pearce captured what went on in the country during those three weeks. Fierce pride, commitment, a never-say-die attitude and comradeship. No one will ever forget his penalty against Spain and what he went through mentally. To do it all over again against Germany took enormous bottle. When it was all over he announced his retirement from international football. That was another big decision from a big man. Let us also not forget how he spent hours with Southgate after the German defeat, building him up mentally and making sure there would be no long-term hangover.

The European Championship left us with so many talking points. Gazza. His goal against Scotland was his answer to everyone. When he scored his face told the story. Everything was released. Emotion, hate, happiness, all rolled into one. It was the highlight of his European Championships. When England were toying with the Dutch in the second half he produced a cameo display of passing and midfield skill. If he can just hold on to his maturity and marbles, he should be around in 1998 when England, hopefully, go to the World Cup. He says that is his target before he quits Britain to get away from the hassle that comes with being Gazza. Hoddle will be delighted if Gascoigne can maintain his fitness and form through the two years qualifying for France.

Gascoigne did not give one interview during the Championships and was always the first out of the dressing-room, with Steve McManaman. Up the tunnel and away. He has still to come to terms with his critics and how to handle it. He is loved by the nation but something inside him does not let him handle the media attention properly. Will he ever?

Paul Ince. He produced his finest hour for his country against Germany. He was the driving force of the side, along with Adams, throwing himself into tackles, surging forward and simply refusing to lie down. Ince is my favourite England player. The Wembley crowd turned the 'Three Lions' song into their signature tune. I am sure Ince has them tattooed on his chest.

Steve McManaman took on and beat more defenders in the European Championships than we have seen before. Opponents were scared of him and he had the confidence to take games by the scruff of the neck, if only for short periods. Who will forget his opening 20 minutes of the second half against Scotland or the way he tormented Holland? It was his club form. He was more effective when Venables swtiched him to the right side.

David Platt. I suspect that he was burning up inside with frustration after the captaincy was taken away from him. But, like the true pro he is, Platt did his job professionally and adequately. He had to switch positions and rose to the occasion and was there for the penalties when it needed cool heads.

Darren Anderton was a big disappointment for me. He never looked completely match fit although I accept that he had to play for long periods as midfield cover on the right-hand side. I always felt that he was just short of what was needed.

Alan Shearer. Superb. He looked the best centre forward in Europe. Five goals in five matches meant he ended as the European championships' top scorer. His strength, pace, brain, character, finishing all came out in a magnificent three weeks for him. No praise is high enough for Shearer. I felt that he did need more support against Germany. They were terrified of him for an hour, after his early goal, and with a partner up front England could well have gone through. Les Ferdinand or Robbie Fowler for Teddy Sheringham in the last ten mintes of normal time would surely have been worth a gamble. Not once did he have the kind of supply of crosses that he deserves. He went into the Championships with a question mark against his ability to score at this level. We need not have worried. Shearer is as good as, no, better than we thought.

Teddy Sheringham. One of my almost men. Two goals against Holland but he did not hit those heights again. He played deep, often under orders, but that left Shearer stranded. Sheringham looks the finished article in the Premiership but in the company of the best is left wanting.

The tournament provided invaluable experience for youngsters like Robbie Fowler, Philip Neville, Jamie Redknapp, Nick Barmby and Sol Campbell and they will be better for it. Fowler hardly got a chance to show what he can do at this level. I would certainly have sent him on in the last seconds against Germany, if only to have his penalty expertise. He was the fifth taker against Spain and was 'up for it' against Germany. It could have meant that he, and not Southgate, would have been the first in line when it came down to sudden death.

There was an emotional goodbye for Venables and his players at the team's hotel after our exit. In the dressing-room the players had asked, 'What do we do now?', and Venables had told them that they were free to go. But every one of them went back to the hotel to drink, talk and say goodbye to Venables until the early hours of Thursday morning.

Venables explained: 'It is amazing how close you can get. It became like a journey, a film, to the players, staff and me. The spirit in the camp was like the Wembley crowd itself. As one. I said my goodbyes to them when we had a few drinks after the game. Every one of them was there. I eventually crashed out in my hotel room. Emotion. No, not much. That will come later. How long? A day or so probably.'

It was a credit to Venables and his players that we went into the semi-final not expecting to be beaten. That feeling has not been around the England team for a long while. It was confidence spread through the nation by the team's performances. Venables said before kick-off: 'Yes, we are ready for them and confident we will go through. We want it badly. The country needs it.'

The atmosphere inside Wembley was, once again, something to experience. The flags carrying the cross of St George decorated the stands as the crowd burst into what became the side's anthem, 'Three Lions'. The singing was thunderous and in tune, the will to win cascaded down from every fan. I have never known a Wembley crowd like it. It was magic to be there. Even Jurgen Klinsmann, the great German striker who was injured and had to miss the game, admitted: 'I have played in front of some beautiful crowds all over the world, in Meixco, Milan and Barcelona. But nothing like this. It must have been wonderful for the home players to walk out to that, and to have the fans behind them all the time.'

England made the perfect start. Paul Ince's 25-yard shot had been tipped over by Andreas Kopke and from the corner, taken by Gascoigne, Tony Adams headed on and Alan Shearer bent low for his fifth Championships goal. But instead of pushing home the advantage, England went on the back foot and lost their middle stump after 15 minutes. David Platt lost the ball in midfield and it was soon whipped in from the left. There was Stefan Kuntz to hammer it beyond Seaman.

The rest of the game was an agonising tight-rope walk of missed chances, superb football, magnificent defending, especially by Adams, Southgate, Sammer and Eilts. England should have won it in extra time, which was the most exciting 30 minutes of football I have seen for a long time – the missed chances, the drama.

In the second minute McManaman, at last back on the right, crossed for Anderton to make contact only to see the ball come back off the post. Goalkeeper Kopke just got a touch on the shot. Maybe we were not meant to win. The picture of Venables with his head in his hands told millions of watching television viewers that perhaps the gods were not on our side.

The Paul Gascoigne twice went close at the far post, the ball just rushing past his outstretched toe. Another inch . . . if only, if only . . . How many times down the years have we said that about England, especially against Germany?

And so to penalties for the second time in five days. This time the kick-in was at the other end, not in front of the players' tunnel, but at the far end, under the big scoreboard and where the 3,000 German supporters were gathered. Shearer, Platt, Pearce, Gascoigne and Sheringham all scored with superb penalties. So did the Germans, alas. The words of Venables came back to me: 'If it comes down to wanting, we want it badly. There is one big problem: so do they.'

The climax. Southgate walked confidently forward, with every pair of eyes watching him, including those of his parents sitting in the stand. We were all willing the ball in. The country was behind this man. Southgate picked up the ball and placed it 12 yards from the German goalkeeper. Did he realise that more than 26 million English eyes were trained on him? All over the country people at home were ducking behind sofas, rushing out to the kitchen, leaving rooms or covering their eyes. Willing him to score.

He did not. It was a poor penalty, struck too close to Kopke's right.

He dived and got to the ball. England were out. There was not a hope in hell of Germany missing. They did not.

Southgate was already crying, a desperate figure of uncontrollable grief. He had frozen to the spot in a 'What have I done?' moment and then turned to face the misery. Stuart Pearce consoled him, so did Venables and Don Howe and skipper Tony Adams led him by the arm to join in England's parade of thanks to the fans. Southgate was big enough to take it and big enough to face up to it afterwards. No hiding, just sensible comments – my heart went out to him. Here was a big man in every sense, a future England captain for sure.

The crowd sang, Venables smiled and the players collapsed on their dressing-room benches, drained, frustrated, shattered, bitterly disappointed. They knew they had been involved with something special and they had so desperately wanted to go all the way.

Venables stood in the middle of the room and praised his players. 'You have nothing to be ashamed of,' he said. 'You have served your country proud.' Deep down he had believed that England were going to beat Germany and reach the final. Deep down he had felt that these European Championships were meant to be England's.

'I would not have changed anything,' he said. 'The preparation, planning, selections and I would not have swapped my players for any other squad in the Championships. I am satisfied.

'What this England side has done is make the rest of the world sit up and take notice. There is no need for us to fear anyone any more. I have enjoyed the last five weeks more than anything else in my life. Someone once said that this is an impossible job. It isn't. It is hard, but not impossible.

'It is true what previous managers have said. It takes two years to get to know the job. Well, I have had two and a half years and it has been better than I thought it would be. I have had a go and that is something I had always wanted to do.

'There were controversies along the way and controversies at the start of this Championship countdown. But I maintain that you have to give the players relaxation time. You must, of course, keep your house in order. I do not believe that our house was ever out of order.'

The highlight for Venables was beating Holland. That perhaps was the pinnacle of his football career, so far. He had won the Championship in Spain with Barcelona and taken that club to a European Cup final. But to beat the team he admired most, to beat the team the rest of the world could not work out, was special. And England did not just beat them. They thrashed them. Venables said with a grin: 'And no one to this day realised that I used the Christmas tree formation against them.'

Ah, the Christmas tree. Tactics, coaching, the very core of the Venables reputation. He came in as the master coach, the man the professionals wanted. He went out with that reputation intact, perhaps even higher. And he went respected by even more. He was a proud man, proud that he had created the best England side since the 1970 World Cup. Football did come home to English in June 1996. Just as Terence Frederick Venables said it would.

After his last press conference, at noon on Thursday, 27 June, at Bisham, he collected up his final belongings, said goodbye to the people who had become close to him, like press executive David Davies, and drove away from the England job for the final time. A few days later Graham Kelly confirmed that Venables was indeed history. 'I am sorry to see him go but it is finished, over,' Kelly said.

Over, finished. I suspect that Venables, in years to come, will remember his last three weeks more than anything else – the think-tank that became his room at the hotel, room 110, the coaching, the press conferences, the matches, his relationship with the players. Venables is not a sergeant-major-type manager. He is a friend who demands respect. You cannot tell a £20,000-a-week footballer to 'do this' or 'do that' any more and he got the balance right with these England players.

The highlights for me were the performance against Holland, the sheer look of pleasure on Stuart Pearce's face, Gascoigne's goal, David Seaman's saves and Alan Shearer's goals. The greatest memory, however, will be the Wembley crowd. They turned Euro 96 into a happening that will go down in history.

Football did come home. Germany were champions, Gazza got married, Pearce retired, Shearer went to Newcastle for £15 million, Sir Bert retired, England waited for Glenn Hoddle and Terry Venables went off to court and, no doubt, another job in football.

He left behind a remarkable two-and-a-half-year reign as England coach. This remarkable story.